Korea, the Iron Silk Road and the Belt and Road Initiative

Emerging Markets Studies

Edited by Joachim Ahrens, Alexander Ebner, Herman W. Hoen,
Bernhard Seliger and Ralph Michael Wrobel

Vol. 9

PETER LANG

Bernhard Seliger / Ralph M. Wrobel (eds.)

Korea, the Iron Silk Road and the Belt and Road Initiative

Soft Power and Hard Power Approaches

PETER LANG

Bibliographic Information published by the Deutsche Nationalbibliothek
The Deutsche Nationalbibliothek lists this publication in the Deutsche Nationalbibliografie; detailed bibliographic data is available in the internet at http://dnb.d-nb.de.

Library of Congress Cataloging-in-Publication Data
A CIP catalog record for this book has been applied for at the Library of Congress.

This book is supported by the 2020 Korean Studies Grant Programme of the Academy of Korean Studies (AKS-2020-C19).

ISSN 2190-099X
ISBN 978-3-631-86066-3 (Print)
E-ISBN 978-3-631-86800-3 (E-Book)
E-ISBN 978-3-631-86801-0 (E-Pub)
DOI 10.3726/b19100

Peter Lang – Frankfurt am Main · Bern · Bruxelles · New York · Oxford · Warszawa · Wien

This publication has been peer reviewed.

www.peterlang.com

Preface

Korea as a "middle power" in the last decades saw a growing importance, partly through greater economic clout, partly through greater cultural and soft power ("K-pop"), partly through collective action in institutions like G 20. However, recent instability in Northeast Asia, plus growing trade conflicts and political conflicts in the region and worldwide, endanger this position. Moreover, the tremendous rise of China in economic, geo-political and cultural terms overshadowed the Korean development. Seeing the need to come to concerted action with its neighbours on issues of regional stability and exchanges, Korea several times proposed new policies for better relations and economic linkages like the Iron Silk Road, the Northeast Asia Peace and Cooperation Initiative (NAPCI), and recently the "New Northern" and "New Southern" policy. However, also here the Chinese Belt and Road Initiative (BRI) seems to dominate the headlines, as well as the policy fora and practical business decisions.

Therefore, the conference "Korea, the Iron Silk Road and the Belt and Road Initiative - soft power and hard power approaches", held online on 19 to 21 April 2021 at the East Asia Centre of the University of Applied Sciences Zwickau focused on the relation between both Koreas, the Chinese BRI as well as the Iron Silk Road in particular. The conference discussed an urgent, indeed pressing topic: how can middle powers like Korea and Germany benefit from closer economic and political linkages across the Eurasian landmass, in particular the BRI dominated by China. Should they rather jump on the bandwagon or should they follow distinct own initiatives, either in their region or inter-regionally? At the same time, the conference strengthened the newly-established East Asia Centre at University of Applied Sciences Zwickau in Korean studies, in particular for students and academics of social sciences and humanities. It was the first larger academic activity of the centre and therefore gained a lot of attention inside and outside of the university. The outcome of the conference is published in this book.

The book is divided in four parts. In the first part four authors from four nations, Germany, South Korea, Russia and India, are discussing the geopolitical challenges of the BRI for their countries showing overlapping but also diverging points of view. In the second part, three experts are analysing the chances and consequences for both Koreas, starting with some insights into North Korea's abilities in participating in the Trans-Korean Railway to South Korea's possibilities to participate in the BRI, at all. In the third part, several researchers investigate the advantages and disadvantages of BRI for its western destinations in

Europe and Africa. And in the fourth part, soft power approaches of the BRI in Korea, Europe and Asia are analysed.

The editors would like to explicitly thank the Academy of Korean Studies for financing the online conference "Korea, the Iron Silk Road and the Belt and Road Initiative - soft power and hard power approaches" by its generous grant AKS-2020-C19 and the East Asia Centre at the University of Applied Sciences Zwickau for hosting the conference.

Dr. habil. Bernhard Seliger
Seoul (South Korea)

Prof. Dr. Dr. Ralph Michael Wrobel
Zwickau (Germany)

Contents

Part III: Destinations of the Belt and Road Initiative

Part IV: Soft power approaches of the Belt and Road Initiative

Part I: Geopolitics of the Belt and Road Initiative

Hans-Ulrich Seidt

Korea and Germany as endpoints of the New Silk Road: Opportunities for cooperation

1. Introduction

Thirty years after the end of the cold war the world now realizes that it has entered a new era. It is characterized by great power competition, conflicting grand strategies and disruptive events. Three weeks ago, we witnessed such a disruptive moment when the Suez Canal was blocked by a huge container ship. According to the German tabloid "Bild Zeitung" ordinary citizens suddenly realized that they were directly affected. The headline "Our summer is in danger!" Bild (2021) demonstrated that Western consumers will become interested in geopolitics and strategic infrastructure when their supply of garden equipment is under attack.

This conference will look far beyond individual interests. Your objective is to analyze and better understand the political dynamics and strategic risks the world is facing. Together you want to identify the prerequisites for a peaceful and prosperous future – not only for Korea and Germany as endpoints of Eurasian infrastructure, but for the whole international community.

Let me at the start of the conference share with you some thoughts that came to my mind when I read your program and reflected on previous experiences. I remembered observations of transformation and change during my years in Korea. These souvenirs were followed by concerns about competing strategies in Beijing and Washington. But in the end a rather bleak outlook on increasing risks and current threat assessments was balanced by positive perspectives of Korean-German cooperation.

2. Experience of transformation

The decline and fall of the former Soviet Union and the rise of the People's Republic of China fundamentally changed during the last thirty years the equation of power on the Eurasian landmass. At the same time the supremacy of the United States, which enjoyed in the decade before the turn of the century the privilege of nearly uncontested global leadership, was challenged by failed military interventions in Iraq and Afghanistan, the financial crisis of 2008 and increasing domestic tensions (Farrow 2018). And all over the world the rapid development of modern communication technologies has put into question accepted traditions, political routines and ideological concepts.

The impact of transformational trends can be observed in a diverse and fragile international system, in changing patterns of social cohesion and human behavior. I was able to study this phenomenon together with my Korean students when I was teaching as guest professor at Chonnam National University in Gwangju/Korea a couple of years ago. In a situation of reverse mentoring the students, representatives of the generation called "the millennials", taught me how they were perceiving, living and embracing transformational processes.

As bright young people they were confronted with all the consequences of a changing society. They were well aware that their expectations of life were not only determined by individual decisions, but were also linked to historical events and social developments. They talked about their family's experience in Gwangju and Chonnam province, a part of Korea that in the local perception was often neglected and even discriminated by the political center. They welcomed the opportunities of liberal democracy, an open society and modern infrastructure, but at the same time they critically reflected about the consequences of demographic change and technological progress. And they felt that their individual future was inextricably linked to a broadly connected global community and, in particular on the Korean peninsula, to an aggregate of collective desires and disappointments.

As capital of Chonnam province, the south western region of the divided peninsula, Gwangju is hopeful to become one day like the city of Busan one of the end points of the railroad system that will connect the Eurasian landmass from the Atlantic to Korea, a country that exemplifies the dramatic, often tragic events and profound changes that took place in East Asia since the beginning of the 20th century. Standing one cold winter morning at the counter of Pyongyang train station, I thought about the impact of these changes on the Korean nation. From a friendly lady I received my ticket for the train that would bring me to the Chinese city of Dandong and from there to Shenyang with its huge BMW plant. The ticket was printed in Korean, Chinese, Russian and German. From my interpreter I learned that in Pyongyang you can even buy a ticket for a train ride to Berlin. But will it ever be possible to buy a ticket for Gwangju or Busan via Seoul and cross the demarcation line on the 38th parallel by train?

Horizon scanning became extremely difficult during the last years and my crystal ball is not better than yours. Certainly, we all were observing long-term trends during the last decades. We saw the Republic of Korea and the Peoples Republic of China moving forward rapidly. In the 21st century both are now playing lead roles in many fields of science and technology. While South Korea developed an amazing set of soft power tools, China became the strongest country on the Eurasian-African landmass.

But even long-term trends can be disrupted. When the pandemic broke out in Wuhan at the end of 2019, many China watchers asked: What will happen to the Chinese economy, the country's political system and the surrounding region (PricewaterhouseCoopers 2020)? Today we know the answer: More than one year after the outbreak of Covid-19, we recognize that East Asia, at least for the time being, remains the dynamic and driving hub of the world's economy.

3. China's grand strategy

Against this transformational background your conference will address specific questions: How can middle powers and export driven economies like the Republic of Korea and Germany further benefit from ever closer ties across Eurasia? Can they participate in mega-sized infrastructure projects like the Belt and Road Initiative or the Nord Stream 2 gas pipeline without becoming entangled into conflicting strategies? How can they avoid becoming totally dependent from the interests and the designs of competing great powers?

I keep these and similar questions in mind since a three months tour through China in spring 2016, when as Inspector General of the German Foreign Office I had to inspect our embassy in Beijing and our consulates general throughout China. During my tour I visited Chengdu in landlocked Sechuan province, where a Chinese official proudly informed me about the regular train service between his province and the city of Duisburg in Germany. He was surprised by my question "Why Duisburg?" and immediately gave the answer: "Of course Duisburg! It is the inland port of Rotterdam!" During the following conversation I realized that my Chinese interlocutor fully understood the details of the geo-economic landscape and the infrastructure of Western Europe.

Visiting two weeks later China's top institution of higher education, Beijing University, I asked the head of the German department: "Which text are you reading with your graduate students?" Her answer was: "The 'Political Dialogue' by Leopold von Ranke". Although this text is one of the most important documents of German political thought in the 19th century it is little known in Germany itself. And when shortly afterwards a deputy minister in Beijing told me that he and his wife, a successful entrepreneur, had carefully studied Karl Marx, he confessed that "Das Kapital" had been the inspiration for his wife's successful business career.

Now I began to understand how carefully classical German texts like Ferdinand von Richthofen's "The Silk Roads" and Carl von Clausewitz' "On War"

(Yu Tiejun 2011) were read in China. Their political and economic teachings were not only studied. They were analyzed, reviewed, skillfully combined and finally integrated into a larger strategy. In this comprehensive context and in a new, contemporary environment they became instruments of operational planning and practice.

Before my eyes I saw a rough sketch of China's strategy and tried to understand how the country utilizes all available means to achieve desired ends. How does a great power with a history of more than two thousand years adapt to the complexities of contemporary policy-making and a changing global distribution of power and wealth? Since I was not trained to engage in philosophical disputes and moral debates, my answer is a very simple interpretation of China's strategy, its main objectives, its strengths and weaknesses. The perception reflects realistic main-stream thinking. However, while your conference will discuss technical and economic issues, you should also remember that even these so-called non-political problems are in reality linked to collective ambitions and emotions.

In my view, the main elements of China's long-term plan became evident since the day the country joined the WTO, the World Trade Organization, at the end of 2001. The strength of China's current position lies in the coordinated and systematic approach that characterizes a grand strategy (Gaddis 2018). Beijing's global outreach covers five critical areas, namely the economic, political, scientific/technological, military and cultural domains. In 2013, China's new leadership under Xi Jinping publicly branded the core elements of the strategy as a coherent geopolitical program under the banner of "One Belt – One Road" or "Belt and Road Initiative" (Johnson 2016). In 2017, the initiative was incorporated into China's constitution with the clear objective to create until the middle of the century a revised global order which secures China's interests and matches Beijing's worldview. Nevertheless, China's weaknesses and vulnerabilities remain critical. They are the lack of natural resources, serious regional imbalances, ethnic strife in border provinces and, in the long-run, the dangers of a petrified authoritarian system.

Out of the most important instruments of China's strategy I will discuss in detail only the so-called "New Silk Road", the economic belt along a transportation network through Western China, Central Asia and finally across the whole Eurasian-African landmass. But even more important is the so-called "21st Century Maritime Silk Road". The volume of sea transport will remain substantially higher than the volume of land transport and the costs much lower. Within the framework of China's grand strategy, infrastructure investments along the coast and on land will include the worldwide construction of artificial islands, ports, canals, railroads, tunnels and airports. These projects will open new trade and transport options. At the same time, they will facilitate direct or indirect control of major transit corridors and of maritime trade routes.

China's strategic objectives and its operational instruments clearly reflect the vital interests and concerns of a rising great power that depends on the import of raw materials and the export of manufactured goods. The recent accident of a container ship in the Suez Canal demonstrated how China depends on a few geo-strategic choke points. The Suez Canal remains a key transport artery between producers in China and consumers in Europe (Global Times, 2021).

4. Western vulnerability and American threat assessment

But the international debate on strategic risks, vulnerability and resilience had started long before the incident in the Suez Canal, the Covid-19 pandemic or shortages in the imports of drugs, pharmaceutical material and vaccines. In the United States and also in the European Union the growing strength of China was already watched for many years with mixed feelings and growing concern.

On the one hand, both the European Union and the United States want to preserve the liberal world order. From the perspective of the United States this also means the continued guarantee of its unique, hegemonic status as the world's lead nation. On the other hand, both actors increasingly realize that even within the existing international environment China is catching up quickly and will be able to implement its grand strategy step by step.

The members of the European Union certainly have reasons for concern. In the Brussels headquarter the extreme weakness of governance structures is evident during every crisis the European Union is facing. Its economic effectiveness and social attractions are declining. A joined political and strategic position vis-à-vis Beijing's grand strategy does not exist. Some member states in Central and Eastern Europe are participating in the 17 plus 1 format initiated by Beijing. Italy and Greece have joined the Belt and Road Initiative. And although Paris and Berlin are ambivalent, Germany keeps in mind the immense Chinese market and its importance for the export and investment interests of its companies.

On the other side of the Atlantic, Washington is confronted with the consequences of imperial overstretch and a permanent, structural trade deficit. The Trans-Pacific Partnership (TPP) was thought to bring countries around the Pacific closer to the United States by reducing their dependence on China. The TPP trade agreement between Australia, Brunei, Canada, Chile, Japan, Malaysia, Mexico, New Zealand, Peru, Singapore and Vietnam was signed in February 2016. But Donald Trump, the newly elected president, withdrew the presidential signature immediately after his inauguration in January 2017. The agreement was not ratified and did not enter into force. The domestic debate on TPP demonstrated, that even before the Trump presidency, the United States started to tear itself apart economically, politically and socially.

Already in 2007, on the eve of the international financial crisis, a study was published that addressed strategic concerns on the increasing Western dependency on Asia. The authors were high ranking officers of major NATO countries. Their study "Towards an overall strategy in an uncertain world – Renewing the transatlantic partnership" (Naumann 2007) revealed a wide range of regional and global risks. It predicted that the strategic challenges of the 21st century would emerge as multi-dimensional threats. According to the study's assessment Western societies were not prepared for a sudden and drastic collapse in vital supply that might be caused by major unrest affecting Asia's high-tech industry, for example in Bangalore, the global center for the inhouse software of major Western companies. For the authors the vulnerability of the West through the new dependence on the services and production of Asia was as strong as the European dependence on the oil of the Middle East.

In 2021 the global threat assessment has, at least in Washington, moved much farther. At the beginning I mentioned that the organizers of the conference had chosen the right moment to discuss a crucial topic you may call the question of the decade. This was not only a polite remark. It was also a specific reference to the annual report issued by the Director of National Intelligence of the United States exactly ten days ago on April 9, 2021 (U.S. 2021). The document, the first official threat assessment under President Biden's new administration, identifies the United States' key adversaries and competitors. However, it notably excludes an assessment of their vulnerabilities and vital interests.

According to the current report, China is the top threat to the interests of the United States. The intelligence community in Washington evaluates Beijing's increasingly competitive relationship with the United States as part of an epochal geopolitical shift. China wants to return into the center of world politics and will thus remain the main competitor of the United States. Beijing uses its coordinated strategic tools to expand China's economic, political, and military presence. Washington expects that the Chinese leadership will consistently promote major infrastructure projects throughout the world with the help of the "Belt and Road Initiative" and the so-called "21st Century Maritime Silk Road". At the same time, Beijing wants to establish in its near abroad effective and exclusive control over major maritime trade routes in the South China and East China Sea.

The 2021 threat assessment signals remarkable continuity and increasing concern. Already in September 2018 an Interagency Task Force had presented a report to President Trump under the title "Assessing and Strengthening the

Manufacturing and Defense Industrial Base and Supply Chain Resiliency of the United States" (U.S. 2018). This report was accompanied by a classified "Action Plan" which included direction to the Department of Defense. It specifically focused on technologies necessary to win a protracted cold war. There is no doubt: The United States and China are upgrading their own resilience and preparing for protracted Sino-American competition. Washington focusses on the Indo-Pacific. The Quad, a platform for strategic coordination among the United States, Japan, Australia and India, facilitates intelligence sharing and informal military coordination. The recent meeting of President Biden and the prime minister of Japan as well as renewed efforts to bring the Republic of Korea on board fit into the picture. But will the competing great powers recognize their mutual vulnerability? Will they accept that neither Washington nor Beijing will have the monopoly of global hegemony? Will they be satisfied with a status of interdependence and a guarantee that both sides will have full cover insurance for their homeland security?

5. In the shadow of great power competition

The Sino-American competition will throw a dark shadow over international relations in the years to come. Possible consequences will be discussed during your conference. At the same time, the competition of great powers highlights the need for closer cooperation among smaller countries like the Republic of Korea and Germany. For more than five decades they have cooperated as close friends and partners. They share common interests. When they compete on global markets they do so as friendly competitors, because they understand their mutual concerns.

In the political domain, the Republic of Korea and Germany both are concerned about the perspectives of a Sino-American competition that might escalate into a confrontational antagonism. In their best interest is an international system based on generally accepted rules and procedures, consistent multilateralism and de-escalation in conflict situations. This also remains true when we enter the economic domain. Here an internationally coordinated approach to the construction and diversification of strategic infrastructure seems necessary. During the last two centuries too, many conflicts broke out over the direct or indirect control of major transit corridors or maritime trade routes. They were the result of increasing political tensions and legal disputes.

Therefore, the status of the world's key strategic infrastructure should, where ever possible, be regulated in internationally accepted, multilateral agreements or regimes. During the cold war, arms control regimes and confidence building measures were successfully negotiated in international fora like the CSCE, the Conference on Security and Cooperation in Europe. The regime of the Non-Proliferation Treaty is controlled by the IAEA, the International Atomic Energy Agency in Vienna. Could the classical approach of multilateral negotiations and agreements, which was so successful in the second half of the 20th century, not be repeated in the domain of strategic infrastructure and trade routes? Should the Republic of Korea and Germany as endpoints of a new silk road not take the lead to formulate the necessary initiatives, for example in the framework of the G 20?

Let me be more specific. Freedom of navigation is not only the cornerstone of international maritime trade, it is indispensable for the vital interests of export driven national economies like the Republic of Korea and Germany. During my tenure in Seoul, the first round of a Korean-German dialog on maritime security took place. Together both sides discussed not only the rights of navigation on the high seas, but also the passage in international straits like the Bosporus and the Dardanelles. Since 1936 the Montreux Convention regulates the control of these straits and guarantees the free passage of civilian vessels in peacetime. The Montreux Convention could be put into question by the Istanbul Canal project which in the interpretation of the Turkish government will not be subject to the terms of the 1936 regime (Lund 2021). This is only one example for the challenges international freedom of navigation might face in the future. Negative impacts on maritime trade and the consequences for Korean and German interests are evident.

The International Tribunal for the Law of the Sea was established as an intergovernmental organization in 1982. It is based in Hamburg and its current president is the Korean judge Paik Jin-hyun, an eminent scholar of international maritime law. Both in Germany and in Korea the knowledge and the expertise for a joined initiative are available. Both countries should become pro-active and launch together with like-minded partners an initiative that decreases potential threats to international trade by strengthening the multilateral approach to maritime security. As far as Germany is concerned, it should in addition promote within the European Union common infrastructure projects that stimulate the European vision and offer concrete material advantages for the young generation through jobs and economic growth. A coherent, strategic European infrastructure project could not only balance China's grand strategy but also renew Europe's optimism at a time when many Europeans are asking themselves: Why are the Chinese building a train route from Budapest to Belgrade and not the members of the European Union? How long do we have to wait for a European Marco Polo project for the 21st century?

6. Innovation along the New Silk Roads

Finally, Korea and Germany should avoid the shadows of great power competition by cooperating in the domain of innovation and technology. Here both countries are, according to international rankings, lead nations in their own right. Of course, every ranking method has its advantages and disadvantages. But if we take for example the "Bloomberg Innovation Index 2019" (Bloomberg 2019), Korea was ranked as number 1, followed by Germany as number 2. Based on six factors, namely investment in research and development, production, high-tech-companies, numbers of patents, university graduations and relevant research personal, the Bloomberg ranking at least indicates the innovation capacities of both countries. Direct investment in joined research and development projects make both countries less dependent in strategic domains. They could become more secure from political and physical shock waves that might temporarily interrupt their connections and supply chains. In critical situations both countries could thus become stabilizing factors in an otherwise fragile environment.

References

Bild (2021) *Sommer im Garten in Gefahr.* 28 March 2021, www.bild.de/news/inland/news-inland/nach-corona-jetzt.

Bloomberg (2019) *Bloomberg Innovation Index 2019.* www.bloombergquint.com/global-economics/germany-nearly catches korea....

Farrow, R. (2018) *War on Peace. The End of Diplomacy and the Decline of American Influence.* New York: W.W.Norton & Company.

Gaddis, J. (2018) *On Grand Strategy.* New York: The Penguin Press.

Global Times (2021) *Suez clip a test for China-Europe trade.* 30 March 2021. www.globaltimes.cn/page/202103/1219868.shtml

Johnson, C. (2016) *President Xi Jinping's "Belt and Road" Initiative. A Practical Assessment of the Chinese Communist Party's Roadmap for China's Global Resurgence.* Washington: CSIS. www.csis.org/analysis/president-xi-jinping%E2%80%99s-.

Lund, A. (2021) *An Unconventional Canal: Will Turkey Rewrite the Rules for Black Sea Access?* Stockholm: Swedish Defense Research Agency. https://www.foi.se/rapportsammanfattning?reportNo=FOI%20Memo%207528

Naumann, K., et al. (2007) *Towards a Grand Strategy for an Uncertain World. Renewing Transatlantic Partnership.* Lunteren: Noaber Foundation.

PricewaterhouseCoopers (2020) *Macroeconomic Impact of the COVID-19 in China and Policy Suggestions*. www.pwccn.com/en/covid-19/macroeconomic-impact-covid1.

U. S. (2018) *Assessing and Strengthening the Manufacturing and Defense Industrial Base and Supply Chain Resiliency of the United States. Report to President Donald J. Trump by the Interagency Task Force in Fulfillment of Executive Order 13806*. Washington, D.C.: Office of the Under Secretary of Defense for Acquisition and Sustainment/Office of the Deputy Assistant Secretary of Defense for Industrial Policy. https://media.defense.gov/2018/oct/05/2002048904/-1/-1/1/assessing-and-strengthening-the-manufacturing-and%20defense-industrial-base-and-supply-chain-resiliency.pdf

U. S. (2021) *Annual Threat Assessment of the US Intelligence Community*. Washington, D.C.: Office of the Director of National Intelligence. www.dni.gov/files/ODNI/documents/assessments/ATA-2021.

Yu Tiejun (2011) *The Western Master and Bible of War – Clausewitz and his "On War" in China*. Pommerin, R. (ed.): *Clausewitz goes global. Carl von Clausewitz in the 21st Century* (pp. 42–59). Berlin: Limes.

Duyeon Kim

Belt and Road in the new geo-political competition: China, the United States, Europe and Korea

1. Introduction

China under Xi Jinping is seeking to reshape international rules, norms, and institutions to gain political and economic influence under the guise of providing global public goods for mutual gains. Beijing's official narrative of the Belt and Road Initiative (BRI) is that it is a "generous gift to humankind, with China not seeking unilateral gains but rather working for common prosperity and shared benefits" (Rolland 2017, 93). Behind the official rhetoric, however, is a country that "forcefully asserts its presence on the global stage," notably through one of its most ambitious and signature foreign policy by providing infrastructure and economic development around the world (Economy 2018). Domestic aims are certainly central to BRI with Beijing determined to boost its own economy to achieve a "moderately prosperous society" by 2021, which is the centennial anniversary of the Chinese Communist Party (USC 2017). Beijing has in effect revived its historical Silk Road and updated it to fit the 21st century context to create external conditions favorable to its rise. Its global aims are to secure energy resources, mitigate terrorist threats, strengthen its influence in the region, and counter U.S. presence in Asia (Rolland 2017, 94). In doing so, China is undermining the rules-based liberal international order and rewriting codes of conduct.

In June 2020, China's Foreign Affairs Ministry announced that the coronavirus (COVID-19) pandemic "seriously affected" about 20 percent (or one-fifth) of BRI projects, citing travel and border restrictions disrupting supply chains as well as "local measures" to combat the pandemic (Reuters 2020). In many countries, medical systems have collapsed or neared the brink of collapse while medical supplies have depleted, compounding increasing debt levels among many BRI partners that were already at high risk of debt distress before the pandemic (Bandiera and Tsiropoulos 2019; Nolan and Leutert 2020). The pandemic might have slowed down the BRI, but Beijing has also accelerated its Health Silk Road (HSR) and Digital Silk Road (DSR) to expand and promote BRI (Lee 2021). China has also reportedly surpassed its pre-pandemic economic activity after the country's own vaccines last year, self-reported at a 79 percent efficacy rate, enabled daily life to return to mostly normal (Dou 2021; Kuo 2020).

Against this backdrop, the United States, Europe, and South Korea must navigate unchartered territory, which China seeks to create in its image. They must identify ways to not only defend the rules-based international order but prevent their respective economic interests from colliding with their shared values and interests. The BRI particularly challenges South Korea's hard-won democratic values that Seoul continuously pursued and promoted after transitioning from its own military dictatorship. Under its current leftist government, South Korea's democratic liberal values already clash frequently with its deferential approach to China, hoping to score foreign policy gains and avoid Chinese economic backlash (Easley 2020). Seoul's choices regarding BRI could either exacerbate or mitigate this phenomenon over time. Such prospects are not exclusive to South Korea, but one that could reverberate globally and determine the codes and standards that govern international relations and world order.

This chapter begins with a brief discussion on the BRI's implications for the economic interests, security, and values of the United States, Europe, and South Korea. The second section narrows the lens on South Korea by analyzing the benefits for Seoul if it joined the Quadrilateral Security Dialogue's activities as one way to deal with China's rise and associated assertiveness. This chapter concludes by highlighting the need for the United States, Europe, South Korea, and Asia writ large to work together to achieve shared interests, purposes, and goals.

2. Belt and Road initiative: Effects on economic interests, security, and values

Indo-Pacific and Trans-Atlantic allies and partners are facing similar dilemmas with China's rise: how to cooperate with Beijing to reap economic benefits while maintaining strong security ties with the United States. However, doing business with China comes at a cost, which is a shared challenge among allies and partners: coercion, unfair trade practices, disinformation, cyber insecurity, and Beijing's pursuit for geopolitical and technological dominance. China's Belt and Road Initiative in particular—as well as signing up for the Regional Comprehensive Economic Partnership and expressing interest in the Comprehensive and Progressive Agreement for Trans-Pacific Partnership—has economic, strategic, and political implications for the United States, Europe, and South Korea.

Rather than helping to close an infrastructure gap in developing countries and contributing to global economic development, BRI in practice undermines macroeconomic stability, promotes exclusive dependence on Chinese technology, favors Chinese companies in major markets' playing field, contributes to environmental problems, and draws countries into its economic and political orbit (Sacks 2021). China's apparent goal to dominate digital networks and technology increases the chances of its surveillance on states, companies, and individuals. BRI further helps Beijing take advantage of its economic influence to punish countries that are at odds with Chinese interests while convincing countries to promote its positions on the global stage. China has already been attempting to peel European Union members away from the unity and cohesion of the Union while trying to lure the EU away from the United States.

Many challenges await as the EU navigates its complex yet vital partnership with China and its position amid the U.S.-China strategic competition. The EU (as well as Australia) has already proven to be a good example for other countries to follow in standing up for shared values and interests. The EU raised human rights at EU-China summits and should continue to do so to not only stand up for democratic values, but to take steps to prevent becoming a pawn between the U.S.-China power game as well (Novotna 2019). The 2020 EU-China Investment Agreement, however, will pose challenges for, if not entirely prevent, Brussels to continue to voice human rights and fully protect its sovereignty, even though the agreement must still be ratified by the European Parliament. Beijing is widely expected to, for example, break its pledge to "work towards" ratifying international labor conventions as free trade unions, for example, are unimaginable in China's system. The investment agreement handed Beijing a diplomatic and strategic victory, which has prompted widespread criticism that it allowed China to drive a wedge between the United States and Europe (Ewing and Myers 2020; Rachman 2021).

This game of "divide and conquer" is all too familiar for Asian countries. China has long sought to divide the United States and its Asian allies and partners while taking a confrontational approach through economic and political coercion when it feels provoked (Pak 2020). For example, Beijing imposed economic sanctions on South Korean companies in retaliation against Seoul receiving the U.S. High Altitude Area Defense batteries (Lim and Ferguson 2019). In response, Seoul agreed to refrain from participating further in America's regional missile defense system. At the same time, Beijing has also regularly enjoyed exploiting perceived fissures between the United States and its Asian allies (Glaser and Mastro 2019; Pollack 2016). For example, China hosted a trilateral ministerial meeting with South Korea and Japan in Chengdu in 2019 (Li 2019). China's hand is particularly evident in the incumbent South Korean Moon Jae-in government as it refused to join the "Free and Open Indo-Pacific" during the Trump administration as well as the Quadrilateral Security Dialogue among the United States, Japan, India, and Australia. Seoul does not want to antagonize China by joining these initiatives among democracies. Beijing has also reportedly nudged Seoul to support its national security law for Hong Kong (Baek and Kim 2020).

The United States has a critical interest to not only encourage and pressure Beijing to improve BRI governance standards, but to also provide an alternative, more appealing economic vision to China's ambitious foreign policy initiative. It is in America's interest to foster stability and peaceful change. The Biden administration's first choice of conduct will likely be stable, predictable, and peaceful methods.

Beijing, meanwhile, will likely further accelerate its BRI efforts amid its competition with the United States, which is expected to also intensify over the coming years. It is only natural and understandable that some countries, particularly middle powers in Asia and Europe, feel pressured to choose a side between the United States and China and are concerned about potential repercussions if they do so. It would certainly be the wish of many countries to maintain a degree of ambiguity and foreign policy autonomy, so that they can enjoy and benefit from sound relations with both the United States and China and avoid retaliation from Beijing. South Korea is a prime example of a country that maintains "strategic ambiguity" in its relationship with China (Kim 2021). The reality, however, is that countries will need to take a stand—however big or small the degree of the direction that needle points to—for their respective national interests and to strengthen their national security.

3. The BRI, South Korea, and the Quad Plus

China's Belt and Road Initiative places South Korea in a precarious situation both domestically and internationally. It provides South Korea with many business opportunities but it also entails significant geopolitical, security, and values risks. While there is no explicit mention of Korea in BRI documents, it can conceptually connect Korea to Europe. The BRI's China, Mongolia, and Russia Economic Corridor, or the Heilongjiang Silk Road Belt, can parlay Korea's New Northern Policy, Russia's new East Asian Policy, and "maritime logistics connectivity of ports and shipping networks in the East Sea Economic Rim… in which development of trade transit transport corridor is critical in [the] northeast Asian region" (Lee 2018). As such, some experts see three conceptual ways the BRI can connect China, Korea, and Europe: through south-west bound maritime routes, the Trans-China Railway and Trans-Siberian Railway, and China's Polar Silk Road (Lee 2018).

South Korea is one example of a country experiencing predicaments amid China's rise and U.S.-China strategic competition. It faces a consequential decision: whether to join the Quadrennial Security Dialogue or Quad Plus activities. It is a question that is perhaps harder for the current progressive Moon Jae-in government whose ideology and national identity, supported by its domestic constituents, are underpinned by its quest for greater autonomy from big foreign powers, particularly the United States and Japan.

South Korea's choice will be a decisive factor in determining both the future of U.S.-South Korean relations and South Korea's standing in East Asia. South Korea would benefit from joining the Quad Plus for three main reasons. First, it would help protect South Korea's survival and security amid future uncertainties as the strategic landscape of the Indo-Pacific region evolves. This is especially important for a country that has historically faced threats to its survival by a rising power. The U.S. alliance is surely the bedrock of South Korea's security and growth, but the Quad would reinforce and strengthen it.

Chinese economic retaliation is always a concern for South Korea, understandably so. However, membership in the Quad would actually strengthen South Korea's leverage vis-à-vis China. It will be more difficult for Beijing to coerce and economically retaliate against South Korea if Seoul stands with the Quad (Chun 2021). It is much easier for Beijing to coerce and divide and conquer when countries act alone. As such, it is important for allies and like-minded countries to work together and formulate joint responses to common challenges with common purposes. Standing up for one's values and interests, rather than hiding them, signifies one's strength and power.

Second, joining the Quad early would provide Seoul a chance to voice and reflect its positions as the Quad makes decisions on its detailed objectives, principles, and modus operandi. While the Quad is still in its nascent stage, it is expected to be the centripetal force that leads the future security order in the Indo-Pacific region. South Korea has a vital interest in the sea lanes that cross through the South China Sea and Indian Ocean as they are integral to the country's economy. This alone should be enough reason for Seoul to want a seat at the table. At the same time, South Korea's participation in the Quad could also be an opportunity for Seoul to promote and garner support for its foreign policies.

Third, the Quad would help temper excessively confrontational behaviors by any of its members while competing with China (Chun 2021). Quad participants certainly share a common interest to keep China in check, but none of them would desire being pulled into a major conflict. As such, instead of viewing the Quad as a gateway to major confrontation or even conflict with China, South

Korea would benefit by regarding its participation in it as an opportunity to contribute to ensuring regional stability.

More importantly, however, the objectives of the Quad transcend far beyond checking just one country. They stand to support and protect a free and open, rules-based Indo-Pacific. It is a grouping of shared values and interests. As a vibrant democracy, South Korea has every reason to join the Quad. It would be another opportunity to demonstrate in action, its country's hard-fought values and system boasted by South Korean leaders. The three reasons outlined above may resonate for other countries as they too grapple with similar dilemmas when figuring out their own future course and global standing.

4. Conclusion

China is undeniably a major global player. An individual and global strategy based solely on containment is certainly not the answer. Democratic and like-minded countries will need to compete in some areas and cooperate in other areas with China—a feat that is far easier said than done. The United States, Europe, and Asia must engage and compete with China on their terms, based on mutual respect and understanding without compromising values such as democracy, rule of law, and human rights as well as best practices including fair and open trade and reciprocity. These are certainly challenging tasks whose playbook and manual need to be written along the way.

For the next four years, the U.S.-China relationship is set to be complex. In contrast with the former Soviet Union and other European partners, mechanisms of crisis prevention, confidence building, and habits of cooperation are not built into the U.S.-China relationship, which transcends the political-military arena to involve every aspect of American life. Decades of habits of cooperation with Europe and Asian allies and clear codes of global exchange while further strengthening U.S.-EU cooperation will be vital in ensuring that Beijing does not threaten the prosperity and security of Americans, Europeans, and South Koreans any further. In particular, such cooperation can help defend a rules-based international order and human rights as well as strengthen areas of trade and technology. In these senses, Transatlantic partnerships with Asian allies and like-minded partners will be just as important. It is essential to connect European allies and partners with Asian allies and partners, which will serve as a multiplier effect in defending and promoting common interests, purposes, and values.

There are certainly innate cultural differences between Asia and Europe. It will take time to not only connect but familiarize Asian and European partners with each other. A coordinated response and system can be constructed thanks to shared interests and values. At the same time, a sharper focus on shared interests and goals could drive cooperation with like-minded countries that are not full-fledged democracies. Economic reliance on China will likely cause states to become more vulnerable to Chinese pressure. A global consensus seems to have already formed that economic overdependence on one country can actually constrain states that seek a more autonomous foreign policy.

The economic reasons with security implications should be enough cause for the United States, Europe, Korea, and other Asian countries to, for example, work together to diversify supply chains and business activities. The United States could also partner with advanced economies and strengthen multilateral organizations to meet the needs of BRI and developing countries. For example, they could provide affordable interest rates for governments in debts due to BRI, and offer technical support for BRI countries to better vet projects related to environmental sustainability (Lew et al. 2021; Ratner 2018). They could also work together to develop digital technology partnerships and trade to reduce and mitigate vulnerabilities to national security and personal privacy posed by Chinese technologies and digital networks while working to ban and eventually replace Chinese digital and telecommunications technologies. These are just a few examples of potential areas of cooperation and partnerships from a list that is undoubtedly extensive because of the expansive, dense, and intricate web of economic interconnections that BRI has already and will continue to create. The task at hand may be daunting and challenging to say the least, but it is one that is necessary to prevent a revisionist power from dictating the terms of international trade and relations.

References

Baek, Hee-youn, and Sarah Kim (2020): "Beijing Consults Seoul on Hong Kong Security Law." *Korea JoongAng Daily*, May 27. https://koreajoongangdaily.joins.com/2020/05/27/diplomacy/China-Chinese-Embassy-Foreign-Ministry/20200527192300119.html.

Bandiera, Luca, and Vaileios Tsiropoulos (2019): A Framework to Assess Debt Sustainability and Fiscal Risks under the Belt and Road Initiative. In *Policy Research Working Paper 8891*: World Bank Group.

Chun, Yung-woo (2021): "Four Reason Why South Korea Should Join the Quad." *Chosun Ilbo*, March 15, Opinion. https://www.chosun.com/opinion/chosun_column/2021/03/15/gaud5gzquna67bsprzvyqlhrxi/.

Dou, Eva (2021): "China's Economy Is Roaring Back, a Year After Coronavirus Shutdown." *The Washington Post*, April 16. https://www.washingtonpost.com/world/asia_pacific/china-gdp-growth-coronavirus-economy/2021/04/15/659185a6-9d93-11eb-b2f5-7d2f0182750d_story.html.

Easley, Leif-Eric (2020): "Shaping South Korea's Middle-Power Future." *East Asia Forum*.

Economy, Elizabeth (2018): "China's New Revolution: The Reign of Xi Jinping." *Foreign Affairs*, May/June.

Ewing, Jack, and Steven Lee Myers (2020): "China and E.U. Leaders Strike Investment Deal, but Political Hurdles Await." *The New York Times*, December 30. https://www.nytimes.com/2020/12/30/business/china-eu-investment-deal.html.

Glaser, Bonnie, and Oriana Skylar Mastro (2019): "How an Alliance System Withers." *Foreign Affairs*.

Kim, Duyeon (2021): "Washington and Seoul Must Heal Their Alliance." *Foreign Affairs*.

Kuo, Lily (2020): "China Approves Sinopharm Coronavirus Vaccine, the Country's First for General Use." *The Washington Post*, December 31. http://css.washingtonpost.com/world/asia_pacific/coronavirus-vaccine-china-sinopharm/2020/12/30/1cc4be9e-4a62-11eb-97b6-4eb9f72ff46b_story.html.

Lee, Dong-gyu (2021): The Belt and Road Initiative after COVID: The Rise of Health and Digital Silk Roads. In *Asan Issue Brief*: Asan Institute for Policy Studies.

Lee, Paul Tae-woo (2018): "Connecting Korea to Europe in the Context of the Belt and Road Initiative." *KMI International Journal of Maritime Affairs and Fisheries* 10 (2): 1–12.

Lew, Jacob J., Gary Roughead, Jennifer Hillman, and David Sacks (2021): China's Belt and Road: Implications for the United States. In *Independent Task Force Report No. 79*: Council on Foreign Relations.

Li, Ruoyu (2019): "Trilateral Summit Signals Chances of Thaw." *Global Times*, December 26. https://www.globaltimes.cn/content/1174889.shtml.

Lim, Darren J., and Victor Ferguson (2019): "Chinese Economic Coercion during the THAAD Dispute." *Open Forum*.

Nolan, Jack, and Wendy Leutert (2020): "Signing Up or Standing Aside: Disaggregating Participation in China's Belt and Road Initiative." October. https://www.brookings.edu/articles/signing-up-or-standing-aside-disaggregating-participation-in-chinas-belt-and-road-initiative/.

Novotna, Tereza (2019): Of Pandas and Elephants: The EU is Positioning Itself between China and the US after the April 2019 EU-China Summit.

Pak, Jung (2020): Trying to Loosen the Linchpin: China's Approach to South Korea. In *Global China*: Brookings Institution.

Pollack, Jonathan D. (2016): Order at Risk: Japan, Korea and the Northeast Asian Paradox. In *Asia Working Group Paper 5*: Brookings Institution.

Rachman, Gideon (2021): "Europe has Handed China a Strategic Victory." *Financial Times*, January 4. https://www.ft.com/content/2d759671-0b1d-4587-ba63-7480990f0438.

Ratner, Ely (2018): "Geostrategic and Military Drivers and Implications of the Belt and Road Initiative." 115th Congress Hearing on China's Belt and Road Initiative: U.S.-China Economic and Security Review Commission, January 25.

Reuters (2020): "China Says One-fifth of Belt and Road Projects 'seriously affected' by Pandemic." *Reuters*, June 19. https://www.reuters.com/article/us-health-coronavirus-china-silkroad-idUSKBN23Q0I1.

Rolland, Nadege (2017): *China's Eurasian Century? Political and Strategic Implications of the Belt and Road Initiative*: The National Bureau of Asian Research.

Sacks, David (2021): "Countries in China's Belt and Road Initiative: Who's In And Who's Out." *Asia Unbound*, March 24. https://www.cfr.org/blog/countries-chinas-belt-and-road-initiative-whos-and-whos-out.

USC (2017): "Chinese Communist Party, 2017 Resolution On Amending The CCP Constitution, Oct. 24, 2017." University of Southern California US-China Institute, Last Modified October 24. https://china.usc.edu/chinese-communist-party-2017-resolution-amending-ccp-constitution-oct-24-2017.

Artyom Lukin

Road and Belt, Iron Silk Road and Russian-Chinese geopolitical cooperation and competition

1. The political context

There are at least three major parts of Eurasia – East Asia, Central Asia, and the Arctic – where China's and Russia's geopolitical interests intersect, creating potential for competition and conflict. However, Moscow and Beijing have so far largely been able to keep their differences in key Eurasian zones under control while displaying a significant degree of mutual coordination and collaboration.

East Asia. As a classic great power, Russia tends to view geopolitics in terms of spheres of influence. Moscow is inclined to see continental East Asia as primarily, albeit not exclusively, Beijing's sphere of influence. And Russia is ready, to some extent, to defer to Chinese interests there. Russian deference to China on East Asian issues, albeit somewhat hurting Moscow's great-power pride, makes geopolitical sense. The Kremlin treats Pacific affairs as an area of lower concern than Europe or the Middle East. Mongolia is the only East Asian nation that may receive Russian security protection in case it finds itself in danger of an external aggression.

It is important that Moscow does not see China as a major security risk on Russia's eastern borders and does not expect China to become one in the foreseeable future. Moscow is aware that Chinese military preparations are directed primarily toward Taiwan and the Western Pacific, not against the Russian Far East. Not sensing any major menace from China, Moscow chooses not to engage in balancing China in East Asia. On the most important issues of contemporary East Asian geopolitics Moscow has either tended to support Beijing or displayed neutrality. On the Korean Peninsula, Moscow has largely played second fiddle to Beijing. On the South China Sea disputes, although Russia's official stance is strict neutrality, some Russian gestures may be seen as backing Beijing. For example, following the July 2016 Hague tribunal ruling that rejected China's claims to sovereignty over the South China Sea, Putin expressed solidarity with China. Russian weapon sales are helping China alter the military balance in the Western Pacific to the detriment of the US and its allies.

Sometimes Russia does act against Chinese wishes in East Asia, demonstrating that it is still an independent actor in the region. One example is Russia's drilling for hydrocarbons in the areas of the South China Sea over which China lays sovereignty claims. The Russian state-owned energy company Rosneft operated on Vietnam's shelf, despite Beijing's displeasure and periodic harassment by Chinese ships. However, in 2020 Rosneft reportedly had to halt its activities in the Chinese-claimed areas after Beijing pressured Hanoi to terminate the offshore development with the Russian oil major (Gavin, 2020). The decision to stop the project was apparently made by Vietnam, not by Rosneft.

The Russian-American enmity pushes Moscow into a confrontational posture toward US alliances in Asia, even though before the Ukraine crisis Russia was generally tolerant of US strategic presence in the Pacific. As long as Moscow perceives Washington as the main adversary, it will continue efforts to weaken the system of alliances that undergird America's global primacy. The thrust of Moscow's policy to undermine US alliances is directed at Europe, but part of the effort is also focused on the Asia-Pacific. Russia's goal of weakening US alliances in Asia is, naturally, shared by Beijing. South Korea seems to be the main target for Russia and China because it is seen as the weak link among the US allies in the Asia-Pacific.

Much of the Russia-Chine military collaboration is focused on the Asia-Pacific. There have been a number of important milestones recently. In 2018, China participated in Russia's Vostok-2018 strategic maneuvers in the Russian Far East. *In July 2019, Russia and China conducted their first joint air force operation beyond their national borders. Russian and Chinese long-range nuclear-capable bombers, accompanied by fighter jets and surveillance aircraft, carried out a patrol over the East China Sea and the Sea of Japan.* In December 2020, Russian and Chinese strategic bombers conducted another joint patrol over *the East China Sea and the Sea of Japan.*

Northeast Asia is currently the most suitable strategic theater to operationalize an emerging military alliance of Moscow and Beijing. Russia and China have a direct presence in the region, where they maintain substantial military potentials that—if combined—can complement each other. And importantly, it is in the North Pacific where they both directly intersect with the US.

That said, with the exception of Northeast Asia, there seems to be little strategic coordination between Russia and China in the rest of the Asia-Pacific (or Indo-Pacific). In Southeast Asia, Russia and China don't compete with each other, but neither do they collaborate in any significant sense. The crisis in Myanmar, triggered by the military coup in February 2021, has shown that Moscow and Beijing may not necessarily be on the same page. While Russia has emerged as the most high-profile backer of the military junta, China's attitude to the coup in Myanmar is more ambivalent. In South Asia, the 2020 border crisis between India and China demonstrated Moscow's willingness to act as a de facto mediator. India may be more interested in the Russian mediation than China. Being the stronger side in the conflict, Beijing would prefer to exclude the involvement of any third parties, including Russia, that might help India offset its relative weakness vis-à-vis China.

Central Asia.[1] When it comes to Moscow-Beijing politics over the post-Soviet space, the most problematic question is certainly about Central Asia, a region composed of five former Soviet republics which shares borders with both Russia and China. Since the nineteenth century, Russia has traditionally considered Central Asia as its sphere of influence. However, in the 2000s China began its economic expansion in the region. It is now by far the biggest trade partner for Central Asian states as well as its largest source of investments. China also set up a small military presence inside Tajikistan, apparently to secure a sensitive area which borders China's Xinjiang region and Afghanistan.

Despite initial misgivings in Moscow, China's economic penetration of Central Asia has not, so far, done any substantial harm to Russian interests. Just like Russia itself, Central Asian "stans" are moving extremely cautiously with respect to Beijing's calls for a free trade area, fearing their economies will be devoured by China. Moreover, populations in Central Asia, particularly in Kazakhstan and Kyrgyzstan, exhibit high levels of Sinophobia. Russia is rather confident the Central Asians are not going to abandon it in favor of China. On the contrary, they may need Moscow even more to hedge against Beijing's rising geo-economic influence.

Multiple predictions by Western analysts that Moscow and Beijing would inevitably clash over Central Asia have thus far been proven wrong. In a stark contrast to the Russian-Western antagonism over Ukraine, Russia and China were able to establish an understanding – and strike a rather stable balance – in Central Asia, whereby Beijing has emerged as the main economic force while Moscow retains the status as Central Asia's chief political-military ally and partner. There will be some irritants, but a clash of Chinese and Russian interests in Central Asia is unlikely in the foreseeable future.

---

1 The following sections on Central Asia and the Arctic draw upon Artyom Lukin. The Russia–China entente and its future. *International Politics.* 2020. https://doi.org/10.1057/s41311-020-00251-7.

The Arctic. Apart from East Asia and Central Asia, the Arctic is another area where Russia and China's interests may, theoretically, come into conflict. Russia lays claims to a significant part of the Arctic Ocean and views it as a sanctuary vital for the country's security and economic interests, as well as for the national identity. China, on the other hand, has been displaying Arctic ambitions, calling itself a 'Near-Arctic state' and seeking to gain access to the Arctic's resources, including through the vision for the Polar Silk Road that would see Chinese ships traversing Arctic routes (Xinhua, 2018).

Until recently, Russia was wary of letting China into the Arctic. But this seems to be changing. The strengthened Russia-China strategic partnership necessitates a more accommodating attitude by Moscow toward Beijing's Arctic aspirations. Furthermore, with a severely reduced access to Western capital and technology, collaboration with China looks like the only realistic option for carrying out major projects in the Russian Arctic that Russia cannot afford to implement on its own due to their huge costs and technological complexity.

In recent years Russian officials have repeatedly stated that Russia is ready for more collaboration with China in the Arctic, with the two countries signing a number of agreements on Arctic projects. So far the most important case of the Russia-China Arctic collaboration has been Chinese participation as the biggest foreign stakeholder in the liquefied natural gas (LNG) projects on Russia's Arctic shore (Humpert, 2019). Russia also hopes to attract Chinese investment into the Northern Sea Route, the Arctic's main shipping artery and a potential maritime corridor between Asia and Europe (TASS, April 2019). The Kremlin is apparently betting it will be able to manage China's rising presence in the extreme North without risking Russian dominance of the Arctic.

2. The economic dimension of the Russia-China relationship

Due to the effect of the coronavirus pandemic, in 2020 China-Russia trade dropped by 2.9 %, amounting to $107.76 bln (TASS, 2021). The contraction was largely caused by the fall in the price of oil, Russia's main export to China. The pandemic also inhibited the operation of transport links between Russia and China. For example, due to the Chinese precautions over covid, the throughput of the Zabaikalsk/Manzhouli railway border crossing, the main Russia-China overland entry point, is now two times lower than pre-covid, while for trucks it is three times lower (Biang, 2021). Despite the covid-related problems in the functioning of the bilateral trade, Russia's economic dependence on China showed a noticeable increase in 2020, with China's share in Russia's foreign trade rising to 18.3 % from 16.7 % a year earlier (Gabuev, 2021). Just a decade earlier, in 2010,

China accounted for 9.5 % of Russia's exports and imports. At the same time, China is far less dependent on trade with Russia, with the share of Russia in China's exports and imports hovering around 2 % (2.3 % in 2020) (Asia Business Blog, 2021). Below I provide an overview of the main areas of Russia-China economic interaction.

Oil. Exports of Russian energy resources, especially oil and gas, to China currently constitute the most important part of the bilateral economic relationship. In 2019 Russia completed a fresh expansion of its Eastern Siberia – Pacific Ocean (ESPO) oil pipeline system (Transneft, 2019), which connects its east and west Siberian fields with China, Russia's Pacific coast, and local refineries. ESPO allows Russia to ship a third of its total oil exports to Asia-Pacific markets, primarily to China (Reuters, 2019). The ESPO system was launched over the past decade. Today, via the ESPO, Russia is shipping 600,000 barrels per day (bpd) directly to China via the Skovorodino-Mohe trans-Amur pipeline link, and also exporting over 600,000 bpd via the oil port of Kozmino on the Pacific coast near Nakhodka, with a substantial part of the Kozmino oil also going to China by tankers (Russia is also shipping 200,000 bpd to China via a pipeline crossing Kazakhstan.). Over the past decade Russia continuously expanded the ESPO system pipeline and by the end of 2019 it reached its full designed capacity of 1.6 million bpd (130 mln tons a year). The Eastern Siberia – Pacific Ocean pipeline was initially scheduled to reach its maximum annual capacity of 130 mln tons of crude by 2030, but, due to the high demand for this route, the project was completed 10 years ahead of schedule (Transneft, 2019).

Even though Russia's oil exports to China are rising, it is notable that there have been no acquisitions by Chinese companies of major upstream oil assets in Russia, including in its Far East. Russia made offers to China about the sale of some major Eastern Siberian oil fields, but negotiations failed to produce deals. The main stumbling block with the Chinese seemed to be over the price of the oil fields. By contrast, India turned out to be a more willing buyer, having purchased a share in the major Vankor oil field in Eastern Siberia.

Natural gas. In December 2019, President of Russia Vladimir Putin and China's Chairman Xi Jinping officially launched a huge pipeline system, the Power of Siberia, that will supply natural gas from the Russian Far East and Eastern Siberia to northeastern China. With the Power of Siberia coming online, Russia was able to begin selling massive amounts of pipeline gas to Asia's largest economy. Until recently, all Russia's export gas pipelines ran west, to Europe. The Power of Siberia trunk line became the first one pumping gas to Asia. The 30-year contract, expected to generate $400 bln for Russia's Gazprom, is the energy company's largest export contract ever. The project has clear geopolitical undertones, accentuating the deepening strategic entente of Russia and China.

The Power of Siberia is quite a feat of engineering, with the pipeline extending over 2,200 kilometers from the Chayanda gas field in the northern region of Yakutia to the Russian border with China where it crosses beneath the Amur river to enter China. The second phase of the project, expected to be completed in 2022, will involve the construction of another branch stretching for about 800 kilometers from the giant Kovykta gas field, located not far west of Lake Baikal, linking it up with Chayanda. The Power of Siberia passes through swampy, mountainous and permafrost areas with extreme environmental conditions, with the lowest winter temperatures along the route ranging from −41 degrees Celsius on the China border to −62 in Yakutia. On the Chinese side, another gas line connects to the Russian system and will eventually stretch another 3,370 kilometers south to Shanghai (Bloomberg, 2019). In 2025, the pipeline is planned to reach its full capacity, supplying to China 38 bln cubic meters of gas annually.

The agreement on the Power of Siberia between the two state-controlled energy behemoths – Gazprom and China's CNPC – was signed in May 2014 during Putin's visit to Beijing. It was hardly a co-incidence that the gas mega deal was clinched in the midst of the Ukraine crisis. The clash with the West over Ukraine may have pushed Moscow to accelerate the gas talks with Beijing that had been dragging on for a decade.

It is anyone's guess how much exactly China will pay for the Power of Siberia's gas. The price formula used in the contract between Gazprom and CNPC is a closely-guarded secret. The whopping $400 bln revenue figure is just an estimate deployed mostly for PR purposes. It is not clear how profitable for Russia the gas exports to China will be, considering that, in order to extract and transport gas for the Power of Siberia project, Gazprom had to build an infrastructure from scratch in the very inhospitable and challenging conditions of Eastern Siberia. The costs involved in the construction of the project's pipelines and the development of remote gas fields were never fully disclosed. The estimates range within $35–40 bln (Vedomosti, 2019). Some Kremlin detractors allege that the Power of Siberia is a geopolitical, rather than commercial, project, which is unlikely to bring profits, except for Putin's cronies whose companies get contracts to build Gazprom's pipelines (Gazeta.Ru, 2019). The reality may be more complex. According to some informed observers, the price for China is similar to what Germany pays for the Russian gas, with the gas price linked to oil (Gabuev, 2019). However, the Power of Siberia will not bring Russia as much profits as its current gas contracts with Europe – and the payback period for the pipeline may be quite long – because the European contracts source gas from Gazprom's fields in Western Siberia where necessary infrastructure was put in place long ago. That said, there is little doubt that the Power of Siberia makes economic sense in the long term, if Russia wants to get a foothold in China's gas market. China has risen to become the world's top importer of natural gas, overtaking Japan in 2018 (Reuters, 2018). As some observers note, China has really just started using natural gas because this hydrocarbon fuel still accounts for just 7-9 % of China's total energy consumption, well below the 30 % gas holds in the fully developed nations like the US (Clemente, 2019).

Apart from unlocking China's gas market, the Power of Siberia is designed to boost the economic development and living standards in the regions in eastern Russia which it traverses. In particular, the Russian government seeks to create a cluster of advanced chemical industry around the Power of Siberia's terminus on the border with China. Gazprom is constructing a gas-processing plant, one of the world's largest. Before sending the pipeline gas to China, the facility will extract from it the more valuable ingredients such as helium, ethane, propane, butane and pentane-hexane that can be further used in petrochemical and other industries (Gazprom, 2021).

The Power of Siberia is going to be followed by a second pipeline that will bring to China natural gas from Western Siberia, Russia's main hydrocarbon province. The initial plan was to build that pipeline through the Altai mountains into China's Xinjiang. In 2019, the plan was changed in favor of a route via Mongolia. Although the pipeline's route will be longer, it should be easier to build thanks to Mongolian steppes and will allow to deliver gas right into China's core industrial areas. The decision to use Mongolia as a transit country may be a sign that Moscow and Beijing do not expect any big troubles from Ulan Bator. Mongolia is unlikely to become another Ukraine. Given that the country is completely sandwiched by Russia and China, there is little risk it could attempt to escape from their geopolitical control.

Coal. Russia has been increasing its coal exports to China. In 2008, Russia's coal exports to China amounted to just 0.3 mln tons. In 2019, they exceeded 30 mln tons, accounting for 14 % of Russia's total coal exports and 10 % of China's coal imports (Ministry of Energy, 2021). Within ten years, Russia aims to increase its China-bound coal exports to 55 mln tons. Two thirds of the China-bound Russian coal is shipped via sea ports in the Russian Far East, with the remaining part going through railway border crossings, mainly the Zabaikalsk – Manchuria.

Electric power. Russia started small-scale electricity exports from the Far East (via the Amur Territory) to China in 1992. In 2011 Russia and China built a more powerful inter-state transmission line across the Amur River near Blagoveshchensk, allowing the Russian Far East to considerably increase electricity supplies to the neighboring Heilongjiang. However, in recent years the volume of Russian electricity exports to China has been stagnating and even somewhat decreasing. In 2018, the Russian Far East exported 3,109 mln kWh to China, 6.3 % down compared to 2017 (Inter RAO, 2021). In 2019, the volume again dropped somewhat, to 3,000 mln kWh, which constitutes 0.004 % of China's total electricity consumption, earning Russia roughly 130 mln USD. Inter RAO, Russia's state-owned exporter of electricity, has expressed concern and disappointment that China is refusing to take more electric power from the Russian Far East, leaving the inter-state transmission infrastructure underutilized (TASS, June 2019). The possible reasons for China's reluctance to buy more electricity from Russia include the slowing economic growth in China, reducing demand for electric power.

Agriculture. Agriculture is seen as a major promising area of cooperation between Russia and China. Food is now Russia's second biggest export item to China after oil (Gabuev, 2020). However, Russian and Chinese interests do not completely coincide when it comes to agriculture. Russia would like to export a broad range of its foodstuffs to China, such as milk, pork, poultry etc., whereas the Chinese side is almost exclusively focused on one product – soybeans – which is considered a strategic imported commodity. Beijing views Russia as one of the alternatives to soy imports from the US, even proposing to form a "soybean industry alliance" with Russia (Wu, 2020).

Chinese imports of Russian soybeans have been rising, but Russia still accounts for a fraction of China's soy imports, which is mostly due to Russia's limited capacity to substantially increase the production of soy beans. In 2018, Russia sold 810,000 tons to China (Amur.Info, 2020), while China's total imports of soybeans stood at 88 mln tons valued at $33 bln (Expert-Business, 2019). Some Chinese agriculture traders admit Beijing sees soybean imports from Russia mainly as a political move rather than economic necessity, meaning there is little urgency for China to invest in Russia's agriculture (Amur.Info, 2020).

A major stumbling block in the Russia-China agriculture trade is Beijing's continued refusal to allow imports of Russian pork. If the Chinese pork market were open to Russia, it would give a boost to Russian meat industry. Moscow is unhappy with China's reluctance to allow Russian pork. Possibly as a retaliatory move, in 2019 Russia suspended imports of citrus fruits and some other fruits, such as apples, from China, citing phytosanitary concerns. Russia also halted imports of a range of Chinese aquaculture products (Rosselkhoznadzor, 2019).

Transport. There have been some significant advances in the development of transport infrastructure connecting Russia and China. Two new trans-border bridges across the Amur River – one for vehicles and the other for railway trains – are the most significant accomplishment in this respect. They will become the first ever permanent bridges linking Russia and China across their main natural boundary, the Amur.

The automobile vehicle bridge, which links the Russian city of Blagoveshchensk and Chinese Heihe, was ready in the spring of 2020, but is still not in operation due to the coronavirus restrictions. When fully operational, the toll bridge will be able to handle 630 trucks, 154 buses and 68 cars a day (Kommersant, 2019). The bridge will allow an eight-fold increase in the cargo traffic turnover between Blagoveshchensk and Heihe, from the current 500,000 tons to 4 mln tons (Amurskaya Pravda, 2019).

The rail bridge across the Amur, linking Nizhneleninskoye on the Russian side with Tunjiang on the Chinese side, is in the final stages of construction, expected to be completed in 2021. Its initial capacity is 5.2 mln tons a year, which can be expanded to 20 mln tons. The bridge will mostly be used to export to China commodities from the Russian Far East, mainly coal, iron ore, and timber.

It is significant that both bridges were constructed on the basis of parity. China did the construction work on its side of the border, while Russia was responsible for the building on its side. The funding also came from both China and Russia. In the case of the Nizhneleninskoye-Tunjiang railway bridge, China and Russia, respectively, financed their halves of the project. Regarding the Blagoveshchensk – Heihe bridge, the financing scheme was more complicated. China fully funded its half of the bridge, while the construction on the Russian side was financed through a specially-created Russian-Chinese company that got a loan from a bank in Heilongjiang. Russia itself did not spend any public money on the bridge (Kommersant, 2019). The Heilongjiang authorities initially demanded that the entire bridge be built by Chinese companies, given that the financing was provided by a Chinese bank. However, the Russian side did not agree to this demand, insisting that the Russian side of the bridge should be built by Russian contractors (Amurskaya Pravda, 2019). Such a stance reflects Russia's emphasis on equality with China in the face of China's superior economic capabilities.

While China has invested money in the trans-border bridges, it is still reluctant to commit to transport infrastructure projects inside the Russian territory. Despite efforts by Russian authorities to attract Chinese investment into the development of transport infrastructure, China has not yet spent a single yuan on transport infrastructure projects in Russia. A case in point is the continued absence of Chinese investments in the international transport corridors Primorye-1 and Primorye-2 that are mainly designed to give the provinces of Heilongjiang and Jilin direct access to Russian ports on the Sea of Japan's (East

Sea) coast. Russian Vice Premier Yuri Trutnev, who leads negotiations with China over the Primorye-1 and Primorye-2, has repeatedly expressed disappointment over the lack of "a clearly formulated position" by Chinese on the development of the corridors (Trans.Ru, 2019). Even though China keeps saying it is interested in transport corridors via the Russian Far East, it avoids taking any specific commitments with respect to investment or the volume of Chinese cargos to pass through the corridors. One major reason for Chinese reluctance to finance Russian infrastructure projects is China's desire to have ownership and management control over them, which Russian authorities are unwilling to grant.

Russia's does benefit from China's Belt and Road thanks to the role of Russia's rail network as an important link in the China – Europe overland freight routes. In 2020, the total number of freight trains from China to Europe rose 50 % – and was up sevenfold since 2016 (Financial Times, 2021). Most of this China-Europe traffic goes via Kazakhstan and Russia, because these two Eurasian countries provide the shortest land route from China to Europe. In 2020, the volume of traffic between China and Europe via the Russian railways doubled (Gazeta. Ru, 2020). The Evergiven accident in March 2021 that temporarily blocked the Suez Canal highlighted the importance of alternative routes, including the trans-Eurasian continental corridors, for global trade.

Russia also hopes to capitalize on the Northern Sea Route (NSR) as the Arctic waters are expected to become more navigable with the global warming and technological advancements. Russia's ambitions seem to be compatible with China's Polar Silk Road (Reuters, 2021). However, as with other Russia's mega projects in the sphere of transport, China is not in a hurry to fund the expensive infrastructure required to turn the NSR into a major commercial sea lane.

3. Conclusion

Being the largest, and trans-continental, Eurasian country, Russia occupies an important place in China's BRI. One of the BRI's main land routes includes Russia, while the Polar Silk Road will potentially traverse the Russian-controlled Arctic waters. In recent years there has been a noticeable rise in shipments from China to Europe, and in the reverse direction, using the rail routes via Russia. However, despite the increase in its trans-continental freight traffic going via Russia, China still refrains from investing in the upgrade of Russia's transport networks such as railroads, ports and highways. China's unwillingness to fund Russia's transport infrastructure, including those transport corridors that are directly relevant to the BRI, can be explained by several reasons. First, China exhibits general reluctance to invest in Russia's economy due to the perceived relatively high risks associated with doing business in Russia that are not, in most cases, offset by profit margins. In other words, the risks are relatively high while potential profits are not that high. This is exacerbated by the almost decade-long stagnation of the Russian economy which is not seen as a particularly attractive and promising market by Chinese businesses. Second, Russia's insistence on parity and equality with China and its refusal to grant Chinese companies special terms, similar to those they get in many other countries who are in need of infrastructure investments, is another major inhibition. Moscow's refusal to sign a bilateral BRI agreement with China might also be a reason why Beijing has not yet invested a single yuan in BRI-related projects in Russia.

References

Amur.Info (2020) "Businessmen in China do not see soybean exports from the Russian Far East as promising." (In Russian). January 20, 2020. https://www.amur.info/news/2020/01/20/166543

Amurskaya Pravda (2019) "The construction of the Russian part of the Amur bridge is finished." (In Russian). November 29, 2019. https://www.ampravda.ru/2019/11/28/092484.html

Asia Business Blog (2021) "Interview with Russia's former trade representative to China." (In Russian). April 2021. https://asiabblog.com/2021/04/china-russia-trade/

Biang (2021) "The throughput of traffic at the Manzhouli border crossing has been reduced." (In Russian). April 19, 2021. https://biang.ru/ru/politics/propusk-transporta-na-mapp-manchzhuriya-iz-za-pandemii-zanizhen-v-3-raza,-na-zhdpp-%e2%80%93-v-2-raza-%e2%80%93-torgpredstvo.html

Bloomberg (2019) "How Russia-China gas pipeline changes energy calculus." November 25, 2019. https://www.bloomberg.com/news/articles/2019-11-25/how-russia-china-gas-pipeline-changes-energy-calculus-quicktake

Clemente, Jude (2019) "China Is The World's Largest Oil & Gas Importer." Forbes. October 17, 2019. https://www.forbes.com/sites/judeclemente/2019/10/17/china-is-the-worlds-largest-oil--gas-importer/#39e2dc9f5441

Expert-Business (2019) "China's foodstuffs market: new opportunities for the Russian agribusiness." August 7, 2019. https://expert-business.ru/researches/macro/agb_ch_2019

Financial Times (2021) "China embraces rail to transport goods to Europe." March 28, 2021. https://www.ft.com/content/8bcd9ded-b094-4562-8766-d7250ac4851b

Gabuev, Alexander (2019) November 28, 2019. https://twitter.com/AlexGabuev/status/1198927912566702080

Gabuev, Alexander (2020) "The impact of the pandemic on the exports of Russian foodstuffs to China." July 3, 2020. https://www.kommersant.ru/doc/4399754

Gabuev, Alexander (2021) "Europe and the Russian-Chinese entente." (In Russian). March 19, 2021. https://carnegie.ru/2021/03/19/ru-pub-84128

Gavin, James (2020) "Vietnam battles for IOCs as China turns up the heat." Petroleum Economist. August 18, 2020. http://admin.petroleum-economist.com/articles/upstream/exploration-production/2020/vietnam-battles-for-iocs-as-china-turns-up-the-heat

Gazeta.Ru (2019) "Putin and Xi launched Power of Siberia." (In Russian). December 2, 2019. https://www.gazeta.ru/business/2019/12/01/12841694.shtml

Gazeta.Ru (2020) "The Russian Railways set records in freight traffic amid the pandemic." (In Russian). December 21, 2020. https://www.gazeta.ru/business/2020/12/21/13409210.shtml

Gazprom (2021) Amur Gas Processing Plant. https://www.gazprom.com/projects/amur-gpp/ . Date of access: April 24, 2021.

Humpert, Malte (2019) "China Acquires 20 Percent Stake in Novatek's Latest Arctic LNG Project." High North News. April 29, 2019. https://www.highnorthnews.com/en/china-acquires-20-percent-stake-novateks-latest-arctic-lng-project

Inter RAO (2021) "Trading." (In Russian). https://www.interrao.ru/activity/traiding/. Date of access: April 24, 2021.

Kommersant (2019) "In the Amur Region, the construction of the Russian part of the bridge to China is completed." (In Russian). November 29, 2019. https://www.kommersant.ru/doc/4173966

Ministry of Energy (2021) "What is the future of Russia's coal in China?" (In Russian). https://minenergo.gov.ru/node/16340. Date of access: April 24, 2021.

Reuters (2018) "China overtakes Japan as world's top natural gas importer." November 12, 2018. https://www.reuters.com/article/china-japan-lng/china-overtakes-japan-as-worlds-top-natural-gas-importer-idUSL4N1XN3LO

Reuters (2019) "As Russia expands Pacific pipeline, a third of oil exports go East." November 29, 2019. https://www.reuters.com/article/us-russia-oil-exports/as-russia-expands-pacific-pipeline-a-third-of-oil-exports-go-east-idUSKBN1XV1LB

Reuters (2021) "China pledges to build 'Polar Silk Road' over 2021–2025." March 5, 2021. https://www.reuters.com/article/us-china-parliament-polar-idUSKBN2AX09F

Rosselkhoznadzor (2019) “Federal Service for Veterinary and Phytosanitary Surveillance has held talks with the Customs Administration of China.” (In Russian). December 30, 2019. https://fsvps.gov.ru/fsvps/news/33664.html

TASS (2019) “Russia’s ambassador to China: Russia and China have real prospects for cooperation in the Arctic.” (In Russian). April 20, 2019. https://tass.ru/ekonomika/6353386

TASS (2021) “The trade turnover between Russia and China dropped by 2.9%.” (In Russian). January 14, 2021. https://tass.ru/ekonomika/10455547

Transneft (2019) “Transneft brings Eastern Siberia — Pacific Ocean oil pipeline to maximum capacity.” November 27, 2019. https://en.transneft.ru/newsPress/view/id/25213?re=en

Trans.Ru (2019) “The presidential representative: the upgrade of the transport corridors in Primorsky Krai is progressing at a slow pace.” (In Russian). February 6, 2019. https://trans.ru/news/predstavitel-prezidenta-v-dfo-modernizatsiya-transportnih-koridorov-v-primorskom-krae-realizuetsya-medlenno

Vedomosti (2019) “The launch of Power of Siberia will help Gazprom to reduce the dependence on Europe.” (In Russian). December 3, 2019. https://www.vedomosti.ru/business/articles/2019/12/02/817690-zapusk-sibiri

Wu, Wendy (2020) “China calls for ‘soybean industry alliance’ with strategic partner Russia.” South China Morning Post. August 26, 2020. https://www.scmp.com/news/china/diplomacy/article/3098980/china-calls-soybean-industry-alliance-strategic-partner-russia

Xinhua (2018) “China’s Arctic Policy.” January 26, 2018. https://www.chinadailyasia.com/articles/188/159/234/1516941033919.html

Jagannath Panda

China's BRI diplomacy: What it means to India and India's rise

1. Introduction

India and China share a complex, if not tumultuous, relationship that has regularly been depicted in repudiating terms ranging from conflict and containment to competition and cooperation. The Doklam standoff in 2017 and the Galwan Valley clash of 2020 only underscored the continued saliency and centrality of their boundary dispute in tensed bilateral ties. At the same time, factors like China's 'iron brotherhood' with Pakistan (Ministry of Foreign Affairs of the People's Republic of China 2021), the rapid development of China's maritime force in the Indian Ocean (Becker 2020), and China's 'charm offensive' and 'wolf warrior' diplomacy (Kurlantzick 2007; Zhu 2020) are seeking to tilt the power balance of the region in Beijing's favor. In face of such imperatives, India has initiated its own efforts to adjust its competition-cooperation complex with China in the Indo-Pacific. New Delhi has not only sought to improve bilateral ties via its Act East Policy (AEP) and multilateral collaborations, like with Japan, the United States and Australia via the Quadrilateral Dialogue (Quad), but also made attempts to enhance its domestic infrastructure along the border and build its global presence as a leader.

Prior to their current tensions, the India-China developmental partnership endured through informal summits like the 'Wuhan Spirit', 'Astana Consensus' and 'Chennai Connect' between Chinese President Xi Jinping and Indian Prime Minister Narendra Modi. Boundary talk mechanisms—like the special representatives dialog, confidence building treaty of 1996 and Working Mechanism for Consultation & Coordination (WMCC)—were put in place to ensure open dialogue and prevent their border dispute from becoming the defining factor of their bilateral relationship. On a pragmatic side, China is India's biggest trade partner. Strategically, the two nations are members of the BRICS (Brazil, Russia, India, China, South Africa), the Shanghai Cooperation Organization (SCO) and the Asian Infrastructure Investment Bank. Yet, both sides are on a quest for great power identity and are therefore highly concerned with protecting their national interest, national security and national sovereignty. Notably, such quests remain at odds with each other, particularly as India's democratic system and observance to a rules-based regulatory framework stand in the way of China's rise, which to an extent, remains contingent on the success of the Belt and Road Initiative (BRI). It is in this context that the BRI, announced by Chinese President Xi Jinping in 2013 during his visits to Southeast Asia and Central Asia (The State Council of the People's Republic of China 2015) has been opposed and rejected by India, particularly owing to the China-Pakistan Economic Corridor's hindrance to India's sovereignty and territorial integrity while passing through the disputed Pakistan Occupied Kashmir region.

Regarded as Xi's flagship project, the BRI consists of two parts: The Silk Road Economic Belt (SREB) and Maritime Silk Road (MSR), with the former associated with land routes and the latter with sea route. As per the Chinese government, the BRI 'promote[s] orderly and free flow of economic factors, highly efficient allocation of resources and deep integration of markets by enhancing [the] connectivity of Asian, European and African continents and their adjacent seas' (The State Council of the People's Republic of China 2020). Essentially, as the Chinese claims, the BRI is built upon the notions introduced by China's ancient silk trade route of the Han dynasty (206 BCE–220 CE) that connected China to Europe through India, Pakistan, Afghanistan and Central Asia. Under this initiative, Beijing plans to build connectivity infrastructures such as massive highways, rail and telecommunication networks, ports, pipelines and shipping routes, among others; these projects boast of estimated costs as high as hundreds of billions of dollars, and pass through several strategically and economically key nations so as to gain access to critical and emerging markets and establish a wide supply chain network with China at its center.

In the post-COVID-19 world order, particularly, amidst intensifying great power competition and changing regional and global power dynamics, infrastructural advancement has taken on new and expanded significance. The Asian Development Bank (ADB) in 2018 assessed Asian infrastructural deficiency to rest at US$459 billion (Sungsup and Zhigang 2018). Further, a Moody's report predicted that investments in the Asia Pacific infrastructural domain will be 'increasingly diversified' post-COVID-19 (Moody's 2020). These will include an expansion in investments by developing economies in public health infrastructure with a unique focus on Asia's demographic patterns; China's BRI will therefore need to evolve in line with such new imperatives to expand its focus from traditional connectivity infrastructure to new avenues such as public health projects. Whether it can successfully incorporate this element within its purview will dictate the success or failure of the initiative in the coming time.

The COVID-19 pandemic witnessed the BRI projects around the world halted, leading to major setbacks in timeline. The Payra power plant in southern

Bangladesh (Hossain 2020), the Port City venture in western Sri Lanka (CHEC Port City Colombo 2020), and different undertakings along the China Pakistan Economic Corridor (CPEC) were deferred citing disturbances caused due to the movement of Chinese labor and gear (Ali 2020). Moreover, in the post-pandemic period, China's budgetary needs (and those of BRI participant nations) are likely going to change fundamentally. For the first time since Deng Xiaoping opened the nation to economic reform in 1978, China's GDP shrunk by 6.8 percent in the primary quarter of 2020 (Li, Detrixhe, and Li 2020). Although the Chinese economy has recovered since then (it grew by a record 18.3 percent in Q1 of 2021) (BBC 2021), the dip did unveil social unrest in China and a need to ensure domestic growth; Beijing will thus likely be exceedingly cautious about new fiscal ventures and unwilling to spend unrestrainedly in the future. Rather, China's focus will be to attain massive growth that gives it an edge over the US as it prepares for increased and stiffer competition. Likewise, the pandemic will leave its imprint on South Asian economies which will be forced to re-evaluate their priorities and reallocate funds to more urgent matters—like public health. Notably, China is already confronting demands for debt alleviation (Aamir 2020b). In South Asia, Maldives has tried to renegotiate its obligation to China while Bangladesh has asked China to consider conceding instalments over 'debt-trap' fears (The Eurasian Times 2020).

Amidst delays to the BRI, India's take on the venture and its response to the same can be moulded strategically to shape the emerging post-pandemic architecture. This paper/chapter seeks to look at how China's BRI is shaping post-COVID-19; it assesses how India's response to the same has emerged over the years and how it may shift in the coming times. Further, the chapter analyses how India's own infrastructure projects can manage the post-pandemic containment of the BRI corridors.

2. India's BRI chip

The BRI aims to interface China with Central Asia, Russia, Southeast Asia, South Asia and Europe via territorial connections and Oceania, Southeast Asia, South Asia, and East African coastal districts through maritime routes. Beijing had introduced six explicit economic corridors (see, Tab. 1) that form networks constituting the BRI and developed supporting worldwide monetary foundations, for example the AIIB and the Silk Road Fund (SRF), to back planned projects. The sheer massive scale of the BRI has naturally brought about critical geo-financial and geo-political reactions from the international community. On the off chance that Beijing can effectively execute its arrangement, the BRI holds the guarantee of completely changing its position in the region and globally and introducing entirely new power dynamics. Despite the fact that there is a profound geo-political nuance attached to this contention, its primary key characteristic is geo-economical. Via BRI, which many countries view with caution, President Xi aims to create a 'community of common destiny', which has become a pillar of Chinese foreign policy in recent years (Xinhuanet 2017). In this context, the BRI is a centralized project that is governed by top Chinese political leadership with Xi Jinping at its helm which aims to further the CCP's grand strategy for the nation (Rolland 2019). The BRI seeks to create a Sino-centric world order with a consistently growing geographic scope that combines economic and strategic policy goals. At the onset, BRI focused on connectivity with Eurasia; now, it incorporates Oceania, Latin America, Africa and the Arctic (Ibid.). BRI's five key focuses are (European Bank for Reconstruction and Development n.d.) trade, coordinating policy, building infrastructure connectivity, finance integration and people-to-people connectivity focused on culture. The 'rejuvenation of the Chinese nation' has led to the venture's convergence with the foreign policy and strategic interests of China, making it one with Beijing's international treaties. This has prompted concerns over BRI's 'debt trap' (Hornby and Zhang 2019) policies, adverse environmental impact fallouts, non-transparent transactions and the unilateral trade dominance in favor of China.

The possibility of such an outcome has put states like India on alert to Beijing's underlying ambitions, as reflected in their responses to the BRI. India has long been severely critical of the BRI; its policy towards the initiative shifted from a non-endorsement in its early years (when the project was shrouded in uncertainty) to an outright opposition post the CPEC highlighted in its response to refuse an invitation to join the first forum for the project in 2017 (Ministry of External Affairs 2017). It is not a supporter of the project and probably never will be. In 2019, New Delhi refused to attend the BRI summit for the second time in a row—this led to Chinese reassurances at the forum that the BRI was 'not an exclusive club' with Xi vowing to look into debt concerns, environmental policies and corruption dangers within the projects (Chaudhury 2019). India's External Affairs Minister S. Jaishankar recently reiterated India's longstanding position on the BRI with a direct rejection, stating: 'BRI rethink, the answer is no' (The Economic Times 2019a).

Simply put, the Indian government does not endorse the BRI amidst speculation that the initiative is not what China claims it to be. New Delhi likely sees the BRI (with CPEC as its flagship corridor) as an initiative to disregard India's sway and dismantle its regional power. India's tepid response to the BRI is based on multiple factors: threat to Indian sovereignty via CPEC which passes through

Tab. 1: Six Major Economic Corridors of Belt and Road Initiative

1	The New Eurasia Land Bridge Economic Corridor (NELB)	It is an international rail-passageway, alternatively referred to as 'Second Eurasia Land Bridge' Links the Pacific and the Atlantic by connecting Chinese coastal cities Lianyungang and Rizhao to Netherland's Rotterdam and Belgium's Antwerp
2	The China-Mongolia-Russia Economic Corridor (CMREC)	Idea proposed in 2014; in 2016, it became the first multilateral cooperation project to become part of BRI It has two distinct pathways: One running from China's Beijing-Tianjin-Hebei to Hohhot in Inner Mongolia, further extending to Mongolia and Russia while the other runs from China's Dalian, Shenyang, Changchun, Harbin and Manzhouli to Russia's Chita
3	China-Central Asia-West Asia Economic Corridor (CCWAEC)	Follows the general trajectory of ancient Silk Road for majority of its modern tracks Links China to the Arabian Peninsula Runs from China's Xinjiang via Alashankou and joins railway networks of Central Asia and West Asia
4	China-Indochina Peninsula Economic Corridor (CICPEC)	Covering mainly the Greater Mekong-sub region, its aim is to boost China-ASEAN connectivity Runs west from China's Pearl River Delta along Nanchong-Guang'an Expressway and the Nanning-Guangzhou High-speed Railway via Nanning and Pingxiang to Hanoi and Singapore Guangxi has opened international rail line from Nanning to Hanoi; this corridor connects China to Indochina Peninsula via Vietnam, Cambodia, Thailand, Myanmar and Laos
5	China-Pakistan Economic Corridor (CPEC)	BRI's flagship project; comprises highways, pipelines, optic cables and highways and has highest level of BRI investment Main goal is to build economic connect running from Kashgar in Xinjiang, China to Gwadar port in Pakistan Connects SREB and MSR
6	Bangladesh-China-India-Myanmar Economic Corridor (BCIMEC)	Proposed jointly in 2013 by India and China to link the huge markets of both countries and enhance regional inter-connectivity Conspicuously dropped from the list released by China post 2nd BRI Forum in 2019

the disputed Gilgit Baltistan region; absence of transparency; lack of open dialog prior to its creation; the undue influence it gives to Beijing in terms of comprehensive national power (CNP) calculations; and threat of potential militarization of BRI projects to support China's developing military existence in the Indian Ocean Region (IOR) accentuating the 'String of Pearls' strategy. Moreover, New Delhi stresses that BRI undertakings may prompt debt-trap, corruption, political instability, ecological issues, and instability in its immediate neighborhood. Although it remains too early to judge the impact and outcomes of BRI projects, early indications of its engagement laying a 'debt trap' in certain nations has prompted a discussion of emerging Chinese 'neo-colonialism' in the region.

Moreover, to New Delhi, BRI is a unilateral, state-centrist venture by China. BRI does not endorse a consultative approach that follows universal norms; hence, it expunges without discussion on project decisions with stakeholders; for instance, China's unilateral approach to CPEC has adversely affected its ties with India and made the project come across as a threat to India's sovereignty (The Economic Times 2018). Nonetheless, China and India have relatively strong economic ties that both wish to further and benefit from. At the 2019 Shanghai Cooperation Summit (SCO), President Xi remarked that 'India and China are opportunities, not a threat, to one another' (Lee 2019). Indian Prime Minister Narendra Modi, in his 2018 Shangri-La Dialogue keynote address, spoke about how India is looking to create an 'inclusive' Indo-Pacific that 'includes all nations in this geography as also others beyond' (Ministry of External Affairs 2018). This idea does not entirely rule out engagement with China, but rather looks to build a power-parity relationship with the economic power while challenging its aggressive and belligerent tactics (Panda 2016). Thus, New Delhi has become a part of other more open and universalist China-centered projects like the Asian Infrastructure Investment Bank (AIIB); New Delhi's engagement with such structures demonstrates its commitment to inclusivity in the Asian geopolitical landscape.

Of the six BRI corridors, BCIM-EC and CPEC directly impact India. While CPEC is discussed in detail in this chapter, as it is voiced as one of India's biggest concerns over BRI, BCIM-EC has become a victim, so to say, of BRI geopolitics. India's refusal to attend the first and second BRI Forums led to the BCIM-EC's visible removal as a BRI corridor in the Joint Communiqué of the Leaders' Roundtable of the BRF held in 2019 (Xinhuanet 2019). Despite this omission, there is little official clarity on whether or not it is still a part—or key corridor—of BRI; the BCIM-EC was subsequently included in the 'The Belt and Road Initiative Progress, Contributions and Prospects' released by the Leading Group for Promoting the Belt and Road Initiative of the Communist Party of China (CPC) (Belt and Road News 2019). The BCIMEC connects Kunming in China's Yunnan province with the Indian city of Kolkata, passing through cities like Mandalay in Myanmar and Dhaka in Bangladesh. Although it can be a critical advantage in enhancing India's connectivity aspirations, the same does not supersede national security. While it is framed as a benign infrastructure project, New Delhi is deeply concerned that the BRI outreach in South Asia and amongst the Indian Ocean littoral states could prove to be a security threat for India. New Delhi has so far maintained considerable influence over this region as a 'security provider', and is therefore generally perceived as its backyard. India is uneasy that the BRI will advance Beijing's presence and sabotage India's impact over the region.

New Delhi's explicit criticism of the CPEC is drawn primarily on national security concerns. Being old diplomatic, political and strategic partners, China and Pakistan share what is often referred to as an 'iron brotherhood' (Du 2014). CPEC has resulted in strong sovereignty and security concerns for India as it seeks to link Pakistan to Xinjiang in China by road. To achieve this goal, CPEC passes through Gilgit-Baltistan in Pakistan-administered Kashmir which India holds an historical claim. New Delhi therefore argues that the undertaking abuses Indian sovereignty by building infrastructure through the (Pakistan-controlled) Kashmir. Speaking at the second Raisina Dialogue in New Delhi in 2017, Prime Minister Modi said that 'connectivity in itself cannot undermine or override the sovereignty of other nations', highlighting the key disfranchisement India holds in respect to the BRI (Ministry of External Affairs, Government of India 2017). While the issue of sovereignty is referred to as the main justification for not supporting the BRI, another key factor is India's stress over the international ramifications of the initiative. In this context, China's push to promote the BRI within India's neighborhood and India's staunch opposition to the same, have only escalated Sino-Indian rivalry in South Asia and the Indian Ocean locale.

3. The CPEC angle

Chinese media has described the CPEC as 'a 3,000-kilometer network of roads, railways and pipelines to transport oil and gas from southern Pakistan's Gwadar Port to Kashgar city, northwestern China's Xinjiang Uygur autonomous region' (National Health and Family Planning Commission 2015). Proposed by Chinese Premier Li Keqiang in May 2013 during his visit to Pakistan and touted as the flagship corridor under the BRI, MoUs for the CPEC's long-term plan were signed the same year (Global Times 2020). The initial low scale of the corridor got a huge boost during Xi Jinping's visit to Pakistan in 2015. It was during the same visit that both nations agreed on a '1+4' structure of the corridor, where CPEC would form the core with Gwadar Port, energy, transport infrastructure and industrial cooperation, forming its four surrounding key areas. Implementation of CPEC is guided by the 2017–2030 Long-Term Plan, unveiled in 2016 (The News 2017). China-Pakistan ties have evolved into an 'all-weather strategic cooperative partnership'; CPEC is at its core (The State Council 2018).

Notably, CPEC is the only BRI corridor defined in strictly bilateral terms. Chinese investments along the CPEC have three major focus areas: to prove that its development model can be exported, to use Islamabad in strategic competition with Washington and New Delhi, and to showcase China's attractiveness as a cooperative partner to the world. Throughout China-Pakistan partnership, restraining India has been a focal point of convergence; with India and US drawing closer and China-Pakistan synergy only growing, the India-Pakistan conflict has the potential to become a proxy-war zone for US-China. The trade and connectivity boost expected through the CPEC will provide China room to economically develop its backward East, especially the Xinjiang province, which has not seen economic prosperity comparable to other Chinese regions. Beijing believes that such growth is crucial to mitigate the militancy and separatism related to the East Turkestan independence movement by the Uighurs in the Xinjiang region. Furthermore, Chinese strategic community also believes that involving Pakistan in this corridor is advantageous because Islamabad can, in return for Chinese economic generosity, and through its influence in the Islamic Jihadi network, lobby against East Turkestan cause in the neighborhood.

The Gwadar Port is key to China's 'string of pearls' strategy across the Indian Ocean that involves crucial commercial ports with Chinese stakes as well as Beijing's military base in Djibouti. One of the key objectives of this strategy is to not just secure China's sea lines of communications but also suppress India's growing strategic heft in the Indian Ocean, which is key to the future of the Asian order. Given China and Pakistan's all-weather strategic partnership, the Gwadar Port could very well be used as a Chinese naval base, which would put the PLA in the vicinity of strategically significant locations (like the Strait of Hormuz). This will also enable China to provide complementary assistance to its deployed missions in Djibouti base, which is located in close proximity to Gwadar. Such a prominent presence of the Chinese military in India's backyard is a major source of concern for India's territorial integrity and strategic autonomy; and presents a direct challenge to the Indian Navy in the region.

Further, by letting the corridor pass through the contentious region of Gilgit-Baltistan, China is trying to not just satisfy its ally Pakistan but also challenge India's dominant role in the region, perhaps as a way to reassert its own superior position and re-enforce the lack of power parity between the two states. Also, as the CPEC passes through Karakoram ranges, China intends to upgrade the Karakoram highway as part of the project. Geopolitically, this region is important as it is geographically close to the Daulat Bel Oldie in Ladakh, India, and the Pangong Tso are region which formed site for India-China clash in 2020.

Realizing Pakistan's need for economic development and investments (CPEC n.d.) amidst the growing chasm between Washington and Islamabad, Beijing has seized a key opportunity and built upon its historic partnership with Pakistan via CPEC. Pakistan's economy has become inherently and unsustainably dependent on China. Given the nature of non-feasibility and unsustainability of BRI projects due to their debt-trap nature, Pakistan seems to be rapidly moving towards becoming a debt-laden vassal state of China, if it has not already (Business Standard 2021). This will allow Beijing to have even more influence over Pakistan, which is also a key nuclear power with intermediary military capabilities in the region.

Moving forward, talks are already on-going for translating China-Pakistan synergy into a regional partnership, primarily by expanding China's engagement with other South Asian nations and initiating joint projects between China, Pakistan and other partners. For instance, on July 27, 2020, China, Pakistan, Afghanistan and Nepal had a quadrilateral meeting where China has put forward two proposals under BRI: first, extending the CPEC to Afghanistan; second, working on an economic corridor with Nepal, called the Trans-Himalayan Multi-dimensional Connectivity Network (Krishnan 2020). Furthermore, China recently signed a 25 year-long economic deal with Iran—which some reports have valued at $400 billion (Fassihi and Myers 2021) thus eclipsing the size of CPEC—with potential investments in port development at Strait of Hormuz, $280 billion in Iranian oil and gas industry, and $120 billion in developing production and transportation infrastructure (Aamir 2020a). Although this $400 billion figure has been strictly refuted (Scita 2019), the deal is nevertheless significant and can be seen as an attempt by China to bring both Iran and Pakistan close under its strategic umbrella. Additionally, China may also be attempting to form a strategic 'golden ring' involving Russia, Turkey, Iran, and Pakistan, with the possibility of also linking 'Gwadar and Chabahar to China by rail through Pakistan' (Said 2020; Shakeel 2020). The Iran deal thus comes as a blow to India as it has been working on the Chabahar project for a while as it was supposed to be its gateway to Afghanistan and Central Asia with the assistance of Iran (Duggal 2021). These developments assume even more significance in the context of previous reports of problems in India-Iran Chabahar collaboration (Haidar 2020); although these issues were resolved, they demonstrate China's growing presence in the region, and how it could impact India's own strategic outreach. CPEC's extension to Afghanistan and potential strategic proximity to Tehran would give China huge influence over Kabul—on both civilian government and Taliban—as American establishment looks to increasingly vacate the region.

4. China's BRI posturing amidst COVID-19: Health Silk Road

At the side-lines of the thirteenth National People's Congress (NPC), Chinese State Councillor and Foreign Minister Wang Yi expressed that 'impact of COVID-19 on the Belt and Road cooperation is temporary and limited', further adding that the pandemic will just 're-energize Belt and Road cooperation and open up new possibilities' (CGTN 2020). The BRI has clearly noticed deferrals and delays in view of pandemic instigated guidelines. More obstacles are likely as countries grapple with outbreaks of the virus. The episode has shown BRI's failure to act as a 'global development strategy' (Chatzky and McBride 2020) that looked for advancement of maintainable development under commonly advantageous procedures. With public health and health infrastructure gaining prominence, the AIIB delivered in March 2020 an official document that anticipated that the key needs for the post-pandemic world will revolve on investments in public health infrastructure (Asian Infrastructure Investment Bank 2020). In the midst of such aggravations and trying to steer away from the anti-China outlook that has arisen around the world, Xi's 'mask diplomacy' and 'vaccine diplomacy' has prompted the rejuvenation of a 'Health Silk Road' (HSR).

Xi uncovered the plan of making a HSR in a telephonic conversation call with the Italian Prime Minister Giuseppe Conte in March (Ministry of Foreign Affairs of the Pepople's Republic of China 2020). The HSR comes as Xi's attempt to rebuild the quickly dissipating global trust in China by situating the state as an innovator in worldwide public health. The medical aid sent by China to countries demonstrates this account of China's good samaritan act. Such posturing endeavors show that the BRI's part in building a worldwide medical services framework is essential, and that China is prepared to lead the pack based on its success in navigating the pandemic by controlling the outbreak within months. Numerous times, this rhetoric has been espoused (almost as a clinical guide) by Chinese government officials and organizations that are a part of BRI globally—like the China Communications Construction Company (CCCC) and Huawei; private endeavors like Alibaba Foundation have likewise taken an interest in large-scale COVID-19 clinical aid adventures.

The idea of a HSR is not new; since 2015, China has shown energetic interest in moulding general wellbeing administration universally under the BRI's ambit. The objective has been to 'establish health cooperation networks among neighbouring countries and those on the Road and Belt' (National Health and Family Planning Commission 2015). In 2017, Xi used the term HSR in Switzerland while signing an MOU with the World Health Organization (WHO) on the development of such a Road (Baijie 2017). The beginning of the

COVID-19 pandemic has allowed China the chance to bring this vision to the forefront.

In the post-pandemic era, the HSR can be critically beneficial in realizing the BRI goals and giving the initiative new life for the new, and dramatically changed times (Lancaster, Rubin, and Rapp-Hooper 2020). It can have a significant impact in reviving homegrown political help for the CCP, legitimizing its standard globally. Beijing's clear outreach through assistance (with mask and vaccine diplomacy for instance) to various countries signals to the Chinese people that the state is responding to the pandemic in a trustworthy way. Besides, the HSR presents a framework through which Beijing may choose to rebrand BRI, which Xi will most likely do in view of COVID-activated monetary mishaps. As China restarts its economy, which was giving indications of slowdown pre-COVID, it will likely be unable to muster similar levels of resources for new BRI corridors or projects. Also, BRI countries are already facing financial crises of their own, casting doubts on whether they will be prepared to undertake massive infrastructure projects or bear the heavy debt that follows. In this context, to remain relevant in the post-pandemic world, the BRI must be updated and rebranded; HSR could offer a useful banner in this regard.

Moreover, the HSR could find significant commonalities with China's Digital Silk Road (DSR). As US-China tech competition intensifies, digital innovation and outreach are likely to form central objectives in China's strategic ambit. Further, the tech domain has received a veritable boost in the post-pandemic period amidst a search for alternatives to physical connectivity. Beijing's focus on the DSR as a connectivity ambit will be drawn on such factors. The HSR and DSR could be combined in areas such as development and exchanging of new tech in tackling the pandemic; as developing nations look to invest in upgrading their public health infrastructure, a focus on such areas could help revitalize the BRI. Notably, this shift would also help the BRI stand out from its competing ventures that have recently gained traction in the region—such as the US-Japan-Australia led Blue Dot Network (BDN) (Basu 2020).

5. India's rise and BRI

In Beijing's perception, an 'India challenge' is not synonymous with an 'American challenge'. Nonetheless, India's rise is arguably Beijing's biggest concern in Asia. Xi views the American presence on the global stage as a deterrent and a test for China's own power—that is, one focused on countering China's influence operations and negating successful promotion of its thoughts. Concurrently, India's rise, based on its democratic thoughts and commitment to upholding a rules-based order, comes as a phenomenon contradicting and hindering China's ascension to great power status in Asia and in the Indo-Pacific. In other words, Chinese perception on American presence in the Indo-Pacific is more a contest of authority to shape the global order while India's rise is seen as more of a challenge to obstruct China's Asian unipolarism. The difference can be drawn along the lines of status dilemmas (Xiaoyu 2019); the US-China great power rivalry shapes a global status dilemma for Beijing while the India-China balance of power shapes a regional status security outlook. Status politics directly shapes Beijing's quest for a 'great power identity' (Rozman 1999); parallel to the same, status recognition also holds a central position in national identity aspirations of China as a state (Lao 2019). Furthermore, this status manoeuvring both domestically and internationally boosts the security dilemma (Shiping 2009) conundrum leading to a Cold War like situation—not just between US and China, but also between China and India on a regional platform.

In essence, China is increasingly perceiving India through a more competing and contesting prism that disturbs its own ascendance to power. China's unilateral actions—be it along the India-China border or via the establishment of Xi's flagship Belt and Road Initiative (BRI)—have received sharp rebuke from New Delhi. India's commitment to the creation and sustainability of a multipolar Asia further highlights a key perceptual gap that exists between the two Asian giants, which is only further compounded by their increasing gap in power. With both India and China being led by excessively nationalist and populist leaders since 2014, the erstwhile equation of continuity in ties despite changes has shifted. While Prime Minister Modi has imbibed a pragmatic power-partner parity with China that looks to balance engagement with equilibrium by focusing on economics (Panda n.d.), the security threats Beijing poses to New Delhi have received strong militarist replies. Examples of this were seen during the 2017 Doklam standoff and the 2020 Galwan clash. Despite Xi's initial emphasis that India and China, in their mutual direction towards multipolarity, must emerge as 'global partners having strategic coordination' and working towards 'an Asian century of prosperity' (Xi 2014), India-China relations have transitioned into a period of uncertainty, from decoupling and disengagement being common narratives shaping ties.

At the same time, Xi's outlook towards India takes into account beyond the challenges India brings to China, particularly, the mutual dependency of both states on each other. A successful second informal summit between the two leaders in 2019 highlighted their 'common objective of working for a peaceful, secure and prosperous world' in a 'rules-based international order' that is also 'inclusive' (Ministry of External Affairs 2019). However, such a statement has been relegated as mere rhetoric rather than a substantial and realistic commitment based on shared values. With heightening tensions and stressed flashpoints between both states since the past year, India's evolutionary revisionism has come to stand in stark contrast to China's revolutionary revisionism—a difference that has also helped greatly in shaping US outlooks towards both states. Rather than a multipolar order, what China has sought to promote with its frequently belligerent actions is a regional order driven by unilateral Chinese interests and the 'Xi Jinping Thought'(Xiang 2018). India's construct of a multipolar Asia, underpinned by liberal democratic values, therefore threatens China's unipolar regional worldview. India has largely balanced this outlook by acknowledging the importance China holds in the globalized world order (Chinoy and Panda 2020); participation in the AIIB and SCO while rejecting BRI are examples of such strategic balancing.

In the post-Galwan and the emerging post-pandemic order, India's strategic balancing outlook will undergo a visible change, especially in the Indo-Pacific region. India's 'inclusive' approach is likely to imbibe an increased national security and 'pointed alignment' paradigm (Panda 2020)—already observable in New Delhi's active participation in the Quad, Quad Plus and the Quad Leadership Summit. For instance, Prime Minister Modi has echoed India's vision of creating a 'free', 'open' and 'inclusive' Indo-Pacific by ideating the Indo-Pacific Oceans Initiative (IPOI) (The Economic Times 2019b). The Initiative marks a focus on securing strategic maritime boundaries while highlighting India's willingness in dealing with Chinese aggression in the region. The proposal seeks to 'create partnerships' that will bind together interested nations in areas such as maritime security, trade, sustainable use of marine resources, and disaster prevention measures (Time Times of India 2019). IPOI builds on Security and Growth for All (SAGAR) and by creating a cooperative platform that actualizes Indo-Pacific principles into action furthers India's Indo-Pacific vision in a direct extension of its AEP. Moving forward, the IPOI will gain critical importance in India's foreign policy and act as a central platform for practical action with India's Indo-Pacific partners (especially Japan and Australia) for the security of the region.

It is important to note that for Xi, the penultimate goal—made increasingly clear as CCP's centennial celebrations approach—is to build a China that stands foremost amongst the world powers. This is highlighted under Xi's concept of 'national rejuvenation' and the creation of a 'moderately prosperous society' within the prism of his 'Chinese Dream'. In other words, Xi envisions a China that is no longer constrained by bilateral pacts or international norms that it signed onto at a time when it had a diminished voice on the global stage; rather, Xi wants to bolster China's economic, militarist and even territorial expansion—as seen along the India-China border as well as in 'unification' goals vis-à-vis Hong Kong and Taiwan—in order to build a powerful Chinese state that can dictate the international order. The BRI is centrifugal to these ambitions; however, post-Galwan, India's appeasement of China is no longer a preferred policy option in New Delhi. Hence, India's vocal if not action-driven potential responses to BRI's growth could greatly shape the region's push towards containing China. India's inclusion in initiatives like the BDN or opening of negotiations vis-à-vis the Regional Comprehensive Economic Partnership (RCEP) to fulfill New Delhi's demands must be accentuated.

References

Aamir, Adnan (2020a): "China-Iran deal overshadows Pakistan Belt and Road project," *Asia Nikkei*, July 21, 2020, https://asia.nikkei.com/Spotlight/Belt-and-Road/China-Iran-deal-overshadows-Pakistan-Belt-and-Road-project.

Aamir, Adnan (2020b): "BRI Debt Relief Requests Present an Economic Dilemma for China", China-US Focus, June 13, 2020, at https://www.chinausfocus.com/finance-economy/bri-debt-relief-requests-present-an-economic-dilemma-for-china#:~:text=Pakistan%20asked%20for%20debt%20relief,million%20in%20annual%20cash%20flows.

Ali, IIrfan (2020): "Impact of Covid-19 on CPEC", Modern Diplomacy, June 15, 2020, at https://moderndiplomacy.eu/2020/06/15/impact-of-covid-19-on-cpec/.

Asian Infrastructure Investment Bank (2020): "Impact of the Coronavirus (COVID-19) and Its Implications for Infrastructure Priorities," Background Document, AIIB, March 25, 2020, https://www.aiib.org/en/news-events/news/2020/_download/Background-Impact-of-Covid-19-and-Implications-on-Infrastructure-Priorities.pdf.

Baijie, An (2017): "WHO, China sign pact establishing 'health Silk Road'," *China Daily*, January 19, 2017, https://www.chinadaily.com.cn/business/2017wef/2017-01/19/content_27993857.htm.

Basu, Nayanima (2020): "Blue Dot Network — US answer to China's Belt & Road Initiative that India's 'interested' in," *The Print*, March 10, 2020, https://theprint.in/theprint-essential/blue-dot-network-us-answer-to-chinas-belt-road-initiative-that-indias-interested-in/378457/.

BBC (2021): "China's economy grows 18.3% in post-Covid comeback," April 16, 2021, at https://www.bbc.com/news/business-56768663.

Becker, Jeffry (2020): "China Maritime Report No. 11: Security China's Lifelines across the Indian Ocean," *CMSI China Maritime Reports, China Maritime*

Studies Institute, December 2020, at https://digital-commons.usnwc.edu/cgi/viewcontent.cgi?article=1010&context=cmsi-maritime-reports.

Belt and Road News (2019): "Leading Group for Promoting the Belt and Road Initiative of the Communist Party of China (CPC)", April 23, 2019, at https://www.beltandroad.news/report_19832742#:~:text=Belt%20%26%20Road%20Initiative%3A%20Progress%2C%20Contributions%20and%20Prospects%20–%202019,-By&text=The%20Belt%20and%20Road%20Initiative%20originated%20in%20China%2C%20but%20it,is%20open%20to%20all%20partners.

Business Standard (2021): ANI, "China's debt-trap diplomacy: Pak to seek debt relief for power projects," February 25, 2021, https://www.business-standard.com/article/international/china-s-debt-trap-diplomacy-pak-to-seek-debt-relief-for-power-projects-121022500125_1.html.

CGTN (2020): "Wang Yi: COVID-19 only to strengthen, re-energize BRI cooperation," *CGTN*, May 24, 2020, https://news.cgtn.com/news/2020-05-24/Wang-Yi-Coronavirus-to-strengthen-and-re-energize-BRI-cooperation-QKOTpIJpkc/index.html.

Chatzky, Andrew; and McBride, James (2020): "China's Massive Belt and Road Initiative," Council on Foreign Relations, January 28, 2020, https://www.cfr.org/backgrounder/chinas-massive-belt-and-road-initiative.

Chaudhury, Dipanjan Roy (2019): "Beijing tries to woo India after BRI summit snub", *The Economic Times*, April 27, 2019, at https://economictimes.indiatimes.com/news/defence/beijing-tries-to-woo-india-after-bri-summit-snub/articleshow/69066815.cms?from=mdr.

CHEC Port City Colombo (2020): "Is the 'Health Silk Road' a 'debt-trap' of China's BRI for Sri Lanka?", (Pvt) Ltd., April 25, 2020, at https://www.portcitycolombo.lk/press/2020/04/25/is-the-health-silk-road-a-debt-trap-of-china-s-bri-for-sri-lanka.html.

CPEC (n.d): Pakistani Economy: An Appraisal http://cpec.gov.pk/brain/public/uploads/documents/CPEC-and-Pakistani-Economy_An-Appraisal.pdf.

Du, Youkang (2014): "Paradigm of bilateral cooperation", *China Daily USA*, February 19, 2014, at usa.chinadaily.com.cn/epaper/2014-02/19/content_17291875.htm.

Duggal, Mahima (2021): "What the China-Iran Strategic Cooperation Pact Means for India," *The Diplomat*, April 9, 2021, at https://thediplomat.com/2021/04/what-the-china-iran-strategic-cooperation-pact-means-for-india/.

European Bank for Reconstruction and Development (n.d.): "Belt and Road Initiative (BRI)", at https://wwwHorn.ebrd.com/what-we-do/belt-and-road/overview.html.

Fassihi, Franz; and Lee Myers, Steven (2021): "China, With $400 Billion Iran Deal, Could Deepen Influence in Mideast," *The New York Times*, March 27, 2021, at https://www.nytimes.com/2021/03/27/world/middleeast/china-iran-deal.html.

Global Times (2020): "China-Pakistan: A journey of friendship (1950–2020)", May 21, 2020, at https://www.globaltimes.cn/content/1189007.shtml.

Haidar, Suhasini (2020): "The Hindu Explains | Why is India out of the Chabahar rail project?," *The Hindu*, July 19, 2020, at https://www.thehindu.com/news/international/the-hindu-explains-why-is-india-out-of-the-chabahar-rail-project/article32126361.ece.

Hornby, Lucy; and Zhang, Archie (2019): "Belt and Road debt trap accusations hound China as it hosts forum", *Financial Times*, April 24, 2019, at https://www.ft.com/content/3e9a0266-6500-11e9-9adc-98bf1d35a056.

Hossain, Emran (2020): "Payra power plant set to become economic burden on Bangladesh", New Age Bangladesh, March 14, 2020, at https://www.newagebd.net/article/102134/payra-power-plant-set-to-become-economic-burden-on-bangladesh#:~:text=Payra%20power%20plant%20set%20to%20become%20economic%20burden%20on%20Bangladesh,-Emran%20Hossain%20%7C%20Published&text=The%20Payra%20power%20plant%20project,the%20commercial%20operation%20will%20begin http://mofa.gov.pk/pakistan-and-china-diplomatic-relations/.

Krishnan, Ananth (2020): "China chairs meet with Afghan, Pak., Nepal Foreign Ministers," *The Hindu*, July 27, 2020, https://www.thehindu.com/news/international/china-chairs-meet-with-afghan-pak-nepal-foreign-ministers/article32206906.ece.

Kurlantzick, Joshua (2007): *Charm Offensive: How China's Soft Power is Transforming the World* (New Haven: Yale University Press, 2007); Zhiqun Zhu, "Interpreting China's 'Wolf-Warrior' Diplomacy," *The Diplomat*, Ma 15, 2020, at https://thediplomat.com/2020/05/interpreting-chinas-wolf-warrior-diplomacy/.

Lancaster, Kirk; Rubin, Michael; and Rapp-Hooper, Mira (2020): "Mapping China's Health Silk Road," Council on Foreign Relations, April 10, 2020, https://www.cfr.org/blog/mapping-chinas-health-silk-road.

Lao, Ning (2019): "Identity, Role Conception, and Status Dilemma: A Socio-Psychological Account of China-US Relations," *China Quarterly of International Strategic Studies 5* (3), 2019, 343–372, https://doi.org/10.1142/S2377740019500180.

Lee, Jeong-ho (2019): "China and India offer 'opportunities, not a threat, to one another' President Xi Jinping tells Prime Minister Narendra Modi", *South*

China Morning Post, June 14, 2019, at https://www.scmp.com/news/china/diplomacy/article/3014498/china-and-india-are-opportunities-not-threat-one-another.

Li, Jane; Detrixhe, John, and Li, Jane (2020): "The coronavirus outbreak might be nearly over in China, but economic hardship is not", Quartz, April 17, 2020, at https://qz.com/1839062/china-gdp-contracts-6-8-percent-in-first-quarter-due-to-coronavirus/.

Ministry of External Affairs (2017): "Inaugural Address by Prime Minister at Second Raisina Dialogue, New Delhi (January 17, 2017)", January 17, 2017, at mea.gov.in/Speeches-Statements.htm?dtl/27948/Inaugural_Address_by_Prime_Minister_at_Second_Raisina_Dialogue_New_Delhi_January_17_2017.

Ministry of External Affairs (2018): "Prime Minister's Keynote Address at Shangri La Dialogue", June 1, 2018, at https://www.mea.gov.in/Speeches-Statements.htm?dtl/29943/Prime+Ministers+Keynote+Address+at+Shangri+La+Dialogue+June+01+2018.

Ministry of External Affairs (2019): Government of India, "2nd India-China Informal Summit," October 12, 2019, https://www.mea.gov.in/press-releases.htm?dtl/31938/2nd+IndiaChina+Informal+Summit.

Ministry of External Affairs, Government of India (2017): "Official Spokesperson's response to a query on participation of India in OBOR/BRI Forum," May 13, 2017, at https://www.mea.gov.in/media-briefings.htm?dtl/28463/Official_Spokespersons_response_to_a_query_on_participation_of_India_in_OBORBRI_Forum.

Ministry of Foreign Affairs of the People's Republic of China (2021): "Wang Yi Attends the Launch Ceremony in Celebration of the 70th Anniversary of China-Pakistan Diplomatic Relations," March 2, 2021, at https://www.fmprc.gov.cn/mfa_eng/zxxx_662805/t1858237.shtml.

Ministry of Foreign Affairs of the People's Republic of China (2020): "President Xi Jinping Talked with Italian Prime Minister Giuseppe Conte over the Phone," March 16, 2020, https://www.fmprc.gov.cn/mfa_eng/zxxx_662805/t1756887.shtml.

Moody's (2020): "Coronavirus will drive funding diversity for APAC infrastructure projects", June 29, 2020, at https://www.moodys.com/research/Moodys-Coronavirus-will-drive-funding-diversity-for-APAC-infrastructure-projects--PBC_1235860.

National Health and Family Planning Commission (2015): "Major Health Exchange and Cooperation on the Belt and Road Initiative," National Health and Family Planning Commission, December 18, 2015, http://www.chinadaily.com.cn/m/chinahealth/2015-12/18/content_22774412.htm.

Panda, Jagannath (n.d.): "Narendra Modi's China policy: between pragmatism and power parity."

Panda, Jagannath (2016): "Narendra Modi's China policy: between pragmatism and power parity", *Journal of Asian Public Policy 9* (2), March 31, 2016, at https://www.tandfonline.com/doi/abs/10.1080/17516234.2016.1165334.

Panda, Jagannath (2020): "[Asia's Next Page] A Moving Partnership of Consequential Democracies," *Japan Forward*, September 28, 2020, https://japan-forward.com/asias-next-page-a-moving-partnership-of-consequential-democracies/.

Rolland, Nadège (2019): "A Concise Guide to the Belt and Road Initiative", *The National Bureau of Asian Research*, April 11, 2019, at https://www.nbr.org/publication/a-guide-to-the-belt-and-road-initiative/.

Rozman, Gilbert (1999): "China's quest for great power identity," *Orbis 43* (3), Summer 1999, 383–402, https://doi.org/10.1016/S0030-4387(99)80078-7.

Said, Islamuddin (2020): "Iranian envoy proposes new alliance of 5 countries," Anadolu Agency, February 5, 2020, at https://www.aa.com.tr/en/middle-east/iranian-envoy-proposes-new-alliance-of-5-countries/1724935.

Scita, Jacopo (2019): "No, China Isn't Giving Iran $400 Billion," *Bourse & Bazaar*, September 20, 2019, at https://www.bourseandbazaar.com/articles/2019/9/20/no-china-isnt-giving-iran-400-billion.

Shakeel, Hira (2020): "Emergence of Golden Ring Axis: Alliance of China, Russia, Turkey, Pakistan and Iran," Pakistan House, November 26, 2020, https://pakistanhouse.net/emergence-of-golden-ring-axis-alliance-of-china-russia-turkey-pakistan-and-iran/; "India-Iran-Afghanistan Axis Against Pakistan?," *South Asia Investor Review*, July 10, 2020, at https://www.southasiainvestor.com/2020/07/india-iran-afghanistan-axis-against.html.

Shiping, Tang (2009): "The Security Dilemma: A Conceptual Analysis," *Security Studies 18* (3), 2009, 587–623. doi: https://doi.org/10.1080/09636410903133050.

Sujan, Chinoy and Panda, Jagannath (2020): Panda (ed.), *Asia between Multipolarism and Multipolarity* (New Delhi: KW Publishers, 2020), https://idsa.in/system/files/book/asia-multipolarism-book.pdf.

Sungsup, Ra and Zhigang Li (2018): "Closing the Financing Gap in Asian Infrastructure", Asian Development Bank, June 2018, at https://www.adb.org/sites/default/files/publication/431261/swp-057-financing-gap-asian-infrastructure.pdf.

The Economic Times (2018): "CPEC violates sovereignty: India tells China", July 12, 2018 at https://m.economictimes.com/news/defence/cpec-violates-sovereignty-india-tells-china/articleshow/57296736.cms.

The Economic Times (2019a): "India won't join BRI, its concept won't apply to us: Jaishankar", October 4, 2019, at https://economictimes.indiatimes.com/news/politics-and-nation/india-wont-join-bri-its-concept-wont-apply-to-us-jaishankar/articleshow/71441347.cms?from=mdr.

The Economic Times (2019b): "PM Modi proposes Indo-Pacific Oceans Initiative", November 5, 2019, at https://economictimes.indiatimes.com/news/politics-and-nation/pm-modi-proposes-indo-pacific-oceans-initiative/articleshow/71915838.cms.

The Eurasian Times (2020): "Maldives Could Relinquish Control Of An Island As Chinese Loan & Pressure Mounts?", September 18, 2020, at https://eurasiantimes.com/maldives-could-relinquish-control-of-an-island-as-chinese-loan-pressure-mounts/.

The News (2017): "Implementation of CPEC is guided by the Long-Term Plan", The News, December 18, 2017, at https://www.thenews.com.pk/latest/257655-cpec-long-term-plan-launched.

The State Council (2018): The People's Republic of China, "China, Pakistan to upgrade all-weather strategic partnership," November 3, 2018, at http://english.www.gov.cn/premier/news/2018/11/03/content_281476374207750.htm.

The State Council of the People's Republic of China (2015): "China unveils action plan on Belt and Road Initiative", March 28, 2015, at english.www.gov.cn/news/top_news/2015/03/28/content_281475079055789.htm.

The Times of India (2019): "PM Modi proposes new initiative to secure maritime domain in Indo-Pacific", November 4, 2019, at https://timesofindia.indiatimes.com/india/pm-modi-proposes-new-initiative-to-secure-maritime-domain-in-indo-pacific/articleshow/71910705.cms.

Xi, Jinping (2014) "Towards an Asian century of prosperity," *The Hindu*, September 17, 2014, https://www.thehindu.com/opinion/op-ed/towards-an-asian-century-of-prosperity/article6416553.ece.

Xiang, Bo (2018): "Backgrounder: Xi Jinping Thought n Socialism with Chinese Characteristics for a New Era," *Xinhua*, March 17, 2018, http://www.xinhuanet.com/english/2018-03/17/c_137046261.htm.

Xiaoyu, Pu (2019): "One Mountain, Two Tigers: China, the United States, and the Status Dilemma in the Indo-Pacific," *Asia Policy 14* (3), July 30, 2019, https://www.nbr.org/publication/one-mountain-two-tigers-china-the-united-states-and-the-status-dilemma-in-the-indo-pacific/.

Xinhuanet (2017): "Xinhua Insight: Xi's world vision: a community of common destiny, a shared home for humanity", January 15, 2017, http://www.xinhuanet.com//english/2017-01/15/c_135983586.htm.

Xinhuanet (2019): "Full text of joint communique of leaders' roundtable of 2nd BRF", March 27, 2019, at www.xinhuanet.com/english/2019-04/27/c_138016073.htm.

Zhiqun Zhu (2020): "Interpreting China's 'Wolf-Warrior' Diplomacy," The Diplomat, May 15, 2020, at https://thediplomat.com/2020/05/interpreting-chinas-wolf-warrior-diplomacy/.

Part II: Both Koreas and the Belt and Road Initiative

Ralph M. Wrobel[1]

Kim Jong-un's Byungjin policy: Support or obstacle for economic convergence on the Korean Peninsula?

1. Introduction

While reunification remains a long-term goal for both governments on the Korean peninsula, economic convergence – in concrete a transformation of the North Korean centrally planned economy to some market economic approach – is a necessary precondition for more cooperation and a peaceful development. Already in the beginning of the new millennium a few economic reforms brought some changes of North Korea's economic system. At the same time "sunshine policy" – an explicit cooperation approach of the South Korean government to the North (1998–2008) – led to several economic cooperation projects. First, the Kaesong Industrial Complex must be mentioned as central project (Wrobel 2014). But also, a Trans-Korean Railways Project allowing rail freight to travel between South Korea, North Korea, Russia and China is discussed continuously because it can be hoped to halve the time taken to transport freight from South Korea to Europe. Such a link of South Korea to the "Iron Silk Road" which already connects China and Europe would be a great support for South Korea's economic development. Additionally, it could be seen as symbol of "Peace in the Korean Peninsula" (Lee/Chung 2020, 1–2).

But cooperation with North Korea is difficult for the South. North Korea's leader Kim Jong-un is well known for his missile tests and his successful nuclear program. After two summits with US president Trump in 2018 and 2019 as well as several inner-Korean summits with South Korea's president Moon Jae-in gave hope for a more peaceful development in Northeast Asia, relations between North Korea and the West world cooled down again since the US didn't support the abolishment of the UN sanctions on North Korea without a nuclear disarmament in the country. But simultaneously to nuclear armament Kim Jong-un adopted an increasing extent market economic approaches to improve the supply of goods in the country. As Lankov mentioned in 2017, Kim Jong-un's policy

1 The author thanks Ms. Na Jinsook, Dong-A University Busan, for the review of the Korean transcriptions.

can be described as "*combination of quiet and largely unrecognizable market-economic oriented reforms, with an aggressive pursuit of a nuclear arsenal*" (Lankov 2017, 26). Does that give hope for a further economic cooperation between both Koreas? The basic ideological approaches in North Korea, "*Juche*" (autarky) and "*Songun*" (military first), actually do not allow any marketization. But, when Kim Jong-un took power in 2011 he announced a political change in North Korea, a new ideology called "*Byungjin*" (parallel development). On a plenary meeting of the Central Committee of the Workers Party of Korea in March 2013 Byungjin was described as "*a new strategic line on carrying out economic construction and building nuclear armed forces simultaneously*" (Kwon 2019, 311). From 2018 on, Byungjin is even replaced by several successor ideologies respective policies basing upon it.

Therefore, this paper asks if North Korea's ideological approaches, its economic reforms and its current economic institutions allow any economic cooperation with South Korea. It is assumed that North Korea must reform its ideology as well as its economy at least like the People's Republic of China or Vietnam in the first years of transformation to do so. Can we observe a gradual transition from centrally planned economy to a market economy in North Korea, somehow? In concrete, is North Korea following the Chinese or the Vietnamese model? To answer these questions, first the ideological and economic transformation process in the East Asian Communist Party dictatorships China and Vietnam will be introduced briefly as a benchmark. Then, the development of North Korean basic ideologies – Juche, Songun and Byungjin – will be analyzed. As can be shown ideology in North Korea is much more crucial for the stability of the North Korean regime than for China's or Vietnam's Communist Party. Then, the gradual transformation process and the in reality developed economic institutions in North Korea will be examined. At all, it is to be found out if Kim Jong-un's ideological change and his economic policy is a hope for further economic reforms in North Korea towards a functioning market economy and a basis for further economic cooperation on the Korean peninsula.

2. China and Vietnam as models for North Korea

Market economies are able to attain a higher GDP per capita by functioning market incentives and freedom of entrepreneurs and consumers. Therefore, market institutions are necessary for economic growth. Which institutions in detail, was already developed as basic theoretical approach of "Ordnungspolitik" by the German economist Walter Eucken (1952/90). His ideas include a regulatory framework of constituting principles like a functioning price system, monetary stability, private property, open markets and others (Wrobel 2011: 48–54). Such a regulatory framework is an example for what North (1990, 3) described broadly as institutions, "the rules of the game in a society" or more formally "the humanly devised constraints that shape human interaction". When he focussed on the structure of property rights and the presence and perfection of markets he brought Eucken's ideas into a completed theory. Building upon, Acemoglu/Robinson (2012) introduced the idea of "inclusive institutions" as fundamental basis for economic growth. As they pointed out when markets are missing or ignored gains from trade are unexploited and resources are misallocated. Additionally, they explain why "inclusive political institutions" give rise to economic growth, or in other words, why democratic institutions are supporting economic growth in a society. This was inspired by North et al. (2009)'s "Open Access Order" characterized by inclusiveness, equality and diversity which enables societies to flourish and prosper. Also, Western "modernization theories" like Lerner (1958) and others agree that democracy and market institutions like property rights have to be combined to foster economic growth and establish a flourishing society. This approach is also manifested in the works of Eucken (1950/90), North et al. (2009) and Acemoglu/Robinson (2012). But it is questionable if it can be applied to East Asia, too.

As the examples of China and Vietnam show also a communist party dictatorship can be combined with a market system, successfully. Of course, the result is not a "*Western Style*" market order – or a system of "*inclusive institutions*" as Acemoglu/Robinson (2012) called it – but a hybrid system of state capitalism with elements of both, market economy and socialism. As already Fukuyama (1995, 21) pointed out the main result of Western "*modernization theories*" is correct: "*Economic development tends to be followed by political liberalization*". But if the East Asian style of democracy will be similar to the Western one is questionable. At all, it must be emphasized that these approaches are "*Eurocentric*" and may not fit to East Asia. In contrast, a "*paternalistic form of authoritarianism, which combined capitalism with an authoritarian political system*" should be more appropriate to Confucian based societies as former Singaporean prime minister Lee Kian Yee mentioned once (Fukuyama 1995, 24). The results in China and Vietnam are impressive. While both countries remained politically as one-party-systems, they gradually transformed their economies to market economies with high growth rates in the last decades creating prosperity for a lot of their citizens.

For instance, China introduced market institutions like private property and some freedom of contract already in the late 1970s. The transformation process started with reforms of micro-management institutions like the replacement of collective farming with a household-based system and the introduction of enterprise autonomy. Later, resource allocation was reformed, too. Under the pressure of autonomous enterprises material supplies were delinked from the central plan and retail commerce was gradually deregulated. Already in 1980s Chinese enterprises were allowed to sell parts of their production at market prices (Lin et al. 1996, 213–217). Step by step, markets were opened, mainly by the introduction of Special Economic Zones. Additionally, the Communist Party of China maintained fiscal and monetary stability in the country with an "*iron fist*". On the other hand, in China a huge part of the economy remains in form of State-Owned Enterprises (SOEs) following a Central Plan and the political goals of the Communist Party. Therefore, the price system is not functioning everywhere because of several subsidies – specially to support the export industries. But at all, China shows that introduction of a few of Eucken's principles are already pretty successful to support a gradual transformation process while the final goal is not necessarily a functioning market order in Eucken's sense but may be a hybrid "*Socialist Market Economy*".

Also, in Vietnam the Communist Party decided in 1986 to introduce "*Doi Moi Reforms*", a set of basically gradual institutional changes quite similar to the Chinese one. First steps of reform took place in agriculture by replacing centralized management by cooperatives. Additionally, SOEs were allowed to carry on production on the market outside the limits of the plan. In 1989, subsidies were eliminated introducing a market price system. The Dong was devaluated and pegged to the USD. One year later, a legal framework for private entrepreneurs was introduced. Additional efforts to increase FDI served to introduce new technologies and skills (Adams/Tran 2010, 178–179). At all, China and Vietnam introduced respective allowed at least three basic market institutions already emphasized by Eucken (1952/90) during their reforms: 1) markets and a functioning price system, 2) entrepreneurship and private property in means of production, and 3) open markets by establishment of Special Economic zones. They added macroeconomic stability, too.

In contrast to countries like South Korea, Singapore or Taiwan, both by communist parties dominated regimes had the problem to explain the obvious contradiction between well working capitalist reality and socialist ideology which is of highest relevance for the stability of the political regime. In China, the ideological basis for this transformation was given by Deng Xiaoping when he mentioned "It doesn't matter whether a cat is black or white, as long as it catches mice". This quota shows an enormous pragmatism of the Chinese economic reform policy (Formica 2017, 19). Obviously, since the end of the 1970s China's communist party could keep the contradiction small between communist ideology and economic reality. The new economic system is officially called "Socialism with

Chinese characteristics" (Zhōngguó tèsè shèhuìzhǔyì, 中国特色社会主义) or simply "Socialist Market Economy". Nowadays, the Communist Party describes the "Socialist Market Economy" in China as a "socialist economic system at the preliminary stage" (MOFCOM 2004). Therefore, "China, as a socialist country, should persist in public ownership as the base of the socialist economy" (ibid.) beside private enterprises. Additionally, social measures were supplied by the state. In this way, market incentives could be combined with state ownership and the leadership of the Communist Party. The ideological foundation of Doi Moi reforms in Vietnam is similar to China. Vietnam is "firmly holding on the socialist orientation". Therefore, the Communist Party in Vietnam calls this economic system a "socialist-oriented market economy" (Kinh tế thị trường theo định hướng xã hội chủ nghĩa) (Surhone et al. 2010) With one-party rule, strict censorship, minimal dissent and a strong top-down system of control beside its opening to the world markets especially Vietnam is a very attractive model for North Korea. What remains is the question if such a transformation policy like in China or Vietnam is also possible in North Korea with its strong dogmatism in ideology.

3. North Korean ideologies over time

3.1. Juche – The idea of Autarky

After World War II the Korean peninsula was divided into South and North Korea. While first was protected by the US the latter became a communist party dictatorship under the rule of the "*great leader*" Kim Il-sung. At all, the North Korean society and especially economy was organized along lines similar to all other socialist states. But Kim Il-sung further developed the basic ideas of Marxism-Leninism integrating his own ideas of Korean self-reliance, called Juche. Literally "*juche*" (주체) means "*subject*", meaning the subject thinking and acting to master the world (Seliger 2004, 78). For the first time Kim Il-sung used the term in 1955. Later it was translated into political practice as "*a state of mind and position of a person capable of carrying out policies by himself without outside influence*" (Dobrzeniecki 2019, 119). Juche includes several different elements like "*jaju*" (자주), independence in politics, "*jarip*" (자립), self-sufficiency in the economy, and "*jawi*" (자위), self-reliance in national defence. Later also the principle of "*suryeong*" (수령), the leadership and the representation of the masses by a strong leader, was added (ibid., 121).

From the first beginning, the concept of Juche was used to justify extremely high levels of central command and autarky in the economic system. As the historical experience of the Soviet Union – especially in the Stalin era – has shown in this way the use of central determined economic targets and the ideological mobilization of the labor force were possible. Also, a high level of collectivization of agriculture was a result of the Juche approach in North Korea. Later Juche ideology allowed Kim Il-sung to move away from the Soviet model in some important respects. For instance, he could defend his essentially Stalinist methods of command in the economy at a time when Khrushchev was moving in new directions within the Soviet Union itself (McKay 2005, p. 88). Later, in the 1960s, Juche has been interpreted as the guiding through for military self-defence and as the principle of political independence. In 1970, Juche ideology was introduced as the guiding principle of the Worker's Party along with Marxism-Leninism, and two years later it became the leading guideline in the new communist constitution of the Democratic People's Republic of Korea (DPRK) (Seliger 2004, 78–79). In 1992, the remaining connections to Marxism-Leninism were completely removed from the North Korean constitution and Juche became the status of a moral or religious system providing the ideological justification for the hereditary succession of power of the Kim dynasty. Therefore, until now Juche is much more for North Korea than Maoism has ever been for the Chinese Communist Party (Dobrzeniecki 2019, 121).

In economic terms, Juche ideology is responsible for the seclusion and autarky of the North Korean economy. North Korea tries to produce a little bit of everything it needs until nowadays. Factories and farms in the country are producing everything feasible, but nothing efficiently. Therefore, the quality of commodities is suspect and the quantity insufficient (Brown 2018a). Additionally, North Korea maintains its "*closed door*" policy to protect the country against outside mass media as well as interaction with the outside world as extension of its information control policy. This is of highest importance for the stability of the regime (Hong/Cho 2018, 499). According to a survey in 2016, more than the half of North Koreans are estimated to support Kim Jong-un and have pride for the Juche ideology (Kim 2018, 25). Therefore, Juche is still basis of the North Korean regime's policy and basis for the people's attitude. But that makes economic reforms in north Korea already quite complicated.

3.2. Songun – Military first

When Kim Jong-il took power after the dead of his charismatic father Kim Il-sung in 1994 he had to fear a coup d'état although his succession has been planned for twenty years. Therefore, so secure his position as leader of the country, Kim Jong-il prioritized the new Songun policy (actually: seongun, 선군), which means "military first". By this way, he secured the loyalty of the military leaders while the military became the main pillar of his power. Hence, in North Korea the armed forces were even more influential than in any other socialist state in recent history (Armstrong 2013, 115). In contrast, during Kim Jong-il's rule the North Korean Workers' Party became step by step less important. The last party congress before 2016 took place in 1980. Instead, the National Defence Commission and other military decision-making bodies were given priorities under Kim jong-il (Seliger 2020, 9).

As a result, the military could establish an own economic sector within North Korea, especially in the monopoly area of foreign trade (including trade in arms and illegal goods as drugs). This economic sector existed outside the central plan. Until now, it is a completely integrated economic system, including farms and mines up to facilities to manufacture uniforms and weapons. The administrative structures, including foreign trade firms, are separated from the rest of the economy. Additionally, it has privileged access to technology and imports (Wrobel 2007, 485). To this day, many North Korean export companies, e.g. in the fishery and seafood sector, are under the control of the military. Therefore, the foreign trade sector is highly monopolized and far away from market structures (Seliger 2020, 8).

While in 1998 Kim Jong-il emphasized again – for a short period – the economic development as fundamental to achieve a "*strong and prosperous great nation*" (gangseong daeguk, 강성대국) (Hong/Cho 2018, 498), Songun became more important for the North Korean regime in the new millennium, again. After the Iraq War (2003–2011) and the US intervention in Libya (2011) the regime felt its security threatened by the US and other Western states. Therefore, it worked towards a nuclear arsenal to defend the country against US military attacks (Hong/Cho 2018, 501). In 2003, Songun was even put on the level of Juche. The military replaced the Worker's Party as vanguard of the revolution (Armstrong 2013, 116). Formally, Songun was never abolished in North Korea but as official ideology it became less important. Nevertheless, the military in North Korea is still economically active in several sectors. This is quite similar to China and may be no basic hindrance of economic reforms.

3.3. Byungjin: The two pillar policy – And its successors

In contrast to his grandfather Kim Il-sung also Kim Jong-un cannot maintain his legitimacy only through Juche policies which were based on Kim Il-sung's charisma. Like his father, Kim Jong-un had to find other forms of legitimation for his regime. This desperately requires a foundation as strong socialist country by a good economic development to secure the stability of the regime (Hong/Cho 2018, 502). Therefore, in his New Year's Address 2013 Kim Jong-un repeated his father's idea of strong and prosperous great nation (Han/Joo 2014, 134). Then, he announced a move to "Byungjin" Policy (actually: byeongjin, 병진) meaning "*parallel development*" or "*parallel advancement*" in March 2013. This refers to the approach of his grandfather Kim Il-sung and focusses on nuclear armament and economic development. While the nuclear armament shall defend the regime against attacks from abroad – mainly the US – economic development is of highest importance for the regime to ensure support of the local population (Lankov 2017, 26). Officially, Byungjin was described as "*the manifestation […] and will to complete the revolutionary cause of Juche through a path of self-reliance, military-first and socialism*" (Han/Joo 2014, 135). That way, Kim Jong-un could integrate Juche and Songun into his Byungjin policy as predecessors. Already this shows the path dependency of all ideologies respective resulting policies in North Korea.

After stabilizing his power in North Korea and the successes in the development of nuclear weapons Kim Jong-un started to focus more on the economy. As response to UN sanctions and China's economic power the regime added also "*Chagangryeok*" (jangagryeok, 장악력) principle, the power to survive through its own efforts, to the Byungjin line, in the end of 2015 (Kim 2016, 2). When Kim Jong-un attained his goal to establish North Korea as nuclear power he could shift to start negotiations on the abolition of the UN sanctions in early 2018 (Shin/Moon 2019, 38). Therefore, in April 2018 Kim Jong-un officially ended the Byungjin line and declared the "*final victory*" (choehu seoungni, 최후 승리) of his policy approach. Instead he emphasized his commitment to economic and scientific development (Global Security 2018). This new ideological reversal is known as "Economy First" (gyeongje useon, 경제 우선) strategy. This can be seen as a 100 percent ideological turnaround from "Military First" to "Economy First" (Seliger 2020, 9–10), or as change of strategy within Byungjin line. However, after having achieved one pillar of the Byungjin line, the development of a nuclear program, Kim Jong-un emphasized to accomplish the other pillar, the economic development (Kwon 2019, 324). That gave hope that North Korea is maintaining its marketization and is following the Chinese or Vietnamese model of gradual transformation.

But after the failure of summits with US president Trump in 2018 and 2019 Kim Jong-un had to change his ideological program, again. While North Korea – obviously – was able to build nuclear weapons, which can threaten the Western world, Kim failed in negotiating a compromise on nuclear disarmament and abolition of economic sanctions. At all, the North Korean regime is caught in a bind: Either they will abandon protection of the regime by the nuclear missiles or they have to accept the long-term maintenance of UN sanctions. Kim Jong-un reacted by announcing a "*frontal breakthrough*" (jeongmyeon dolpa, 정면돌파) in the beginning of 2020. On 1 January – instead of a New Year's address from the leader – North Korea's state-run "*Rodong Sinmun*" reported that Kim called upon the party to "*turn out in the offensive for [a] frontal breakthrough to foil the enemies' sanctions and blockade by dint of self-reliance*". Thereby, he focussed on the economic "*front*" which he described as a "*battle between self-reliance and sanctions*" (Lee et al. 2020). This indicates that Kim Jong-un intends to maintain "*Byungjin*" policy focussing on economic and nuclear development at the same time while a recourse to Juche and Chagangryeok is also obvious. Ideologically, Kim Jong-un's "*frontal breakthrough*" borrows from his father's "*Defensive March of Suffering*" against the devasting famine in the 1990s. But Kim Jong-un's approach is more future oriented and must be understood as an "*Offensive March of self-reliance based on the confidence of nuclear deterrence*" (Koh 2020). Obviously, UN sanctions have hurt North Korea's economy hard but the regime decided to return to Juche finding an own way out of the bind. Therefore, Kim Jong-un's possibilities to copy the transformation path of China or Vietnam is reduced while it still leaves a window open for additional economic reforms.

4. The hybrid reality of economic development in North Korea

4.1. Economic reform approaches

Reforms on the microeconomic level

In the early 1990s North Korea's Public Distribution System (PDS) began to break down at the onset of famine. Several years later, the government shifted responsibility for cooperative farms to local governments. This measure induced already a modest rise in production. Therefore, the July 2002 reforms explicitly called for a continuation of the PDS and did not change anything in the agricultural sector (Hale 2005, 836). But at the same time, the government reduced the size of work-units and granted cooperative farms the authority to establish detailed production plans. Additionally, farmers were leased land of 400 pyong (1,320 square meters) per family and given independence in production. Also, they were permitted to sell their production on private markets. The success of this measure was limited because of the small area of privately used land (Wrobel 2007, 492). First reforms in the industrial sector were already done in 2001 by Kim Jong-il, too. Most important was the alteration of the economic management system, including the alteration of the wage structure for factory employees. Additionally, a new responsibility was placed on factory managers for paying such wages. Also, unprofitable enterprises were shut down and the number of Party officials in the factories was reduced drastically (Wrobel 2007, 491). The North Korean government emphasized "*autonomy under central control*", while continuing the setting of production quotas and refusing to give managers the ability to hire and fire workers. On the other hand, formerly government-run restaurants and stores were transformed into in fact private entities (Hale 2005, p. 834).

Only, under the Byungjin line further reforms were done. On 28 June 2012, Kim jong-un announced a set of instructions for the agricultural and industrial sector (so-called "*6.28 measures*"), followed by the "*5.30 measures*" on 30 May 2014. Already the "*6.28 measures*" implied that farmers should – from now on – work in small teams of 3–6 persons instead of larger ones (10–25 members) (Hong 2018, 29). These changes enabled families to register as work team. Additionally, under the new system farmers did not receive fixed grain rations anymore but had to deliver 70 percent of their last harvest to the state while they could keep 30 percent for themselves. From 2014 on that changed to 60 respective 40 percent. These measures can be seen as a reintroduction of a traditional household-based agriculture combined with taxes. The parallels to China and Vietnam in its first reform steps are obvious. As a result, North Korean farmers can sell a huge amount of their harvest themselves on "*farmers markets*" for market prices, nowadays. But on the other hand, it must be emphasized that the collective farm units themselves were not dismantled, in contrast to China where collective farms were abolished in 1984 (Gray/Lee 2015, 11–12). The real changes were not accompanied by formal rules. A private property of land was explicitly not established what is in line with the ideological approaches in North Korea and similar to the situation in China, too.

The "*6.28 measures*" and "*5.30 measures*" were also giving really great autonomy to industrial managers. Among others, they were allowed to attract private investments (Park et al. 2018, 25). Additionally, they were given permission to buy raw material and spare parts from the market paying market prices. This is also quite similar to the first reform steps in China and Vietnam. Additionally, North Korean managers are allowed to pay their workers as much as they consider as appropriate. These "*bonuses*" may be far larger than basic wages (Lankov 2017, 29). At least, compared to the token salaries of the past they are setting incentives and are opening consumption possibilities. In the commerce and service sector business participation through personal investment in the fields of transportation, stores, convenience services and restaurants were allowed. Additionally, the private investors got the autonomy to hire workers and the duty to pay 10–20 percent of profits to the state (Hong 2018, 29). But these reforms actually represent acceptance of an already established practice because factories were already working outside the plan (Gray/Lee 2015, 14). Also, these reforms in the industrial sector are quite similar to that in China or Vietnam during their early stages of gradual economic reforms, but the scope may be quite limited in comparison to those (Ward et al. 2019, 543).

Additionally, to these reforms, a symbol of the centrally planned system was reformed, too. The "*5-year National Development Strategy*" substituted the regular "*5-year plan*" in 2016. As a result, central planning authorities in North Korea lost some importance. But market reforms remain ambiguous. At the same time a strong emphasis on localization is characterizing the Kim Jong-un era. Following "*Chagangryeok*"-first principle factories and businesses in North Korea should "*localize their raw materials, commodities, and facilities for production based on their own power, technology, and resource*" (Hong 2018, 23–25). At all, already a few years ago North Korea was not more a Stalinist Central Planned economy but became a poorly developed market economy characterized by extensive government intervention and a heavy but inconsistent regulation (Lankov 2016, 3). Therefore, Kim Jong-un was described as the "*most pro-market leader in North Korean history*" (Lankov 2017, 26). But the reform process on the microeconomic level stopped in 2016. No further reforms were done since then. Until today, North Korea developed only an economic system of informal market institutions as it usually develops during a transitional period of gradual transformation. No introduction of a legal framework for private entrepreneurs can be observed in North Korea. Therefore, in current North Korea there are growing discrepancies of the official centrally planned economy and spontaneous markets. Only the first steps of Chinese and Vietnamese microeconomic reforms were copied but without further continuation and formalization.

Reforms on the macroeconomic level

Macroeconomic reforms in North Korea show the constantly changing leadership's view of the developing private sector. Under Kim Jong-il, from the 1990s to 2001, the existence of free markets was simply ignored. The private economy was tolerated as a necessary evil. Then, in 2002 and 2003, the government's policy underwent a fundamental change starting to conduct economic reforms to stimulate the private economy (Lankov 2016, 10). On July 1, 2002, the North Korean government raised the official price of goods it provided, including food, transportation, and electricity, to better reflect the actual cost of their production. By this way, all elements of government subsidization were eliminated (Hale 2005, 825). But these price reforms were a case of state introduced inflation (Wrobel 2007, 493). Therefore, these reforms were rolled back in 2004. Between 2005 and 2009 the government even took steps to undermine the private economy. This anti-market campaign culminated in the 2009 currency reform.

In December 2009 a currency reform was officially introduced to stop inflation and eliminate illegal black markets in the country. North Korean citizens were allowed to convert their old currency to the new currency during seven days at variable rates and in limited quantities. This reform caused unrest which forced the government to relax the strict limits and to offer subsidies as compensation. On the one hand, this reform can be seen as a trial to stop inflation, but on the other hand it was an attempt to reassert control over the evolving private economy, again (Beauchamp-Mustafaga 2012, 70). Obviously, the economic processes were seen as threats to the regime stability by questioning the basic ideologies in the country. In fact, the main result of the currency reform was a rising "*dollarization*" or actually "*yuanization*", a rapid spread of the use of foreign currency – mainly Chinese RMB – in North Korea (Kim 2020, 2). From the first beginning, the use of foreign currency was tolerated by the regime but under Kim Jong-un it was even accelerated. To stabilize the monetary system the North Korean regime decided in 2013 to peg the Won in fact at 8,000 Won to the USD. Since then, the black-market exchange rate was no longer deemed illegal and became the basis for mainly all transactions in the North Korean economy (Koen/Beom 2020, 14). This is quite similar to the Vietnamese case in the 1980s. As long as the public has the confidence that the Central Bank can support this rate with reserves in USD and RMB inflation can be kept small (Brown 2018b, 330). To absorb this circulating currency several measures were introduced, e.g. inducing savings in foreign currency or activating the use of foreign currency-based cards (Hong 2018, 27). At all, monetary stability could be achieved by this policy (see Fig. 1).

For decades, North Korea had a single-bank system completed in 1976 with the integration of the Commercial Bank into the Central Bank of the DPRK. But in 2014, Kim Jong-un decided to separate the functions of a commercial bank from the Central Bank, again. But it is dubious if this reform is working in reality. After all experiences with monetary reforms North Koreans fear to deposit money at banks. Because most of the North Korean's incomes are officially illegal they are reluctant to disclose their property to any state agency (Park et al. 2018, 35–36). On the other hand, the regime under Kim Jong-un adopted some capitalist measures to attract the private-owned funds of its citizens. First,

Fig. 1: Market Exchange Rate, North Korean Won per USD. Source: Koen/Beom (2020), 15.

the regime released an announcement that no one will be asked where the money is from North Korean citizens are paying in a bank account. Also, interests are payed for cash deposits. Second, electronic payment cards are increasingly common, mainly the "*Jonsong Card*" (jeonseong kadeu,전성 카드), launched by the Central Bank itself (Park et al. 2018, 40). The introduction of payment cards shows a further transformation of the North Korean economic system to a market-oriented consumerism.

But it is questionable if all these macro-level reforms are "*sophisticated enough to constitute a complete policy package*" (Hong 2018, 28). Although, these reforms are in line with Kim Jong-un's Byungjin policy because they offer more consumption possibilities to the growing middle class in North Korea, especially Pyongyang. But they keep still ideas like Juche in consideration. So, the whole banking sector is still under state control, the payment system is national, only. First is quite similar to China while an only national payment system does not support economic exchange with abroad. Therefore, an opening-up of the North Korean financial sector cannot be observed.

Reforms of international economic relations

Like in China, the development of "*Special Economic Zones*" (SEZ) has been part of North Korea's efforts to attract foreign capital since several decades. Already in 1984, after visits to China by Kim Il-sung, North Korea introduced a Joint Venture law apparently modeled on China's to attract Western capital. And already in 1991, a first SEZ has been established in the Rajin-Sonbong (라진선봉) area – briefly called "*Rason*" – within the so-called Golden Triangle between Korea, China and Russia (Wrobel 2007, 488). That was North Korea's first attempt to copy the Chinese reforms of foreign trade relations (Gray/Lee 2015, 6). During "*Sunshine Policy*", the political rapprochement between North and South Korea in the beginning of the new millennium, the focus shifted more to the by South Korea financed SEZs in Kaesong (개성) and in Kumgangsan (금강산). While South Korea established an Industrial Complex in Kaesong with several South Korean firms investing here and creating jobs for North Korean workers the SEZ in Kumgangsan remained a Tourism Zone for South Korean tourists, only (Wrobel 2014, 128). After several quarrels between both Koreas both SEZs were closed in 2005 respective 2016 (Koen/Beom 2020, 23).

After Kim Jong-un took power in North Korea the development of new forms of SEZs was pushed forward. The new "*Economic Development Zones*" shall be small-sized specialized economic zones, promoted and constructed under the leadership of local governments with possibilities for North Korean enterprises to participate (see Fig. 2). As of the end of 2015 already 21 Economic Development Zones were established (Hong 2018, 48). Main goal was to attract investments by Chinese entrepreneurs. But the development of these SEZs is very limited. A main handicap are UN sanctions since 2006 which were tightened with a resolution of the Security Council in 2017 for the last time (Koen/Beom 2020, 21–28). These sanctions include all kinds of an arms embargo, a ban on certain financial transactions and technical training etc., a freeze of funds and other financial assets, a luxury good embargo, and an explicit textile, seafood and fuel ban. Additional sectoral sanctions forbid North Korea to sell coal, iron, other metals, food and agricultural products, machinery and electrical equipment etc. Also, North Koreans are not allowed to work abroad. According to SEZs the resolution prohibits explicitly "*the opening, maintenance, and operation of all joint ventures or cooperative entities, new and existing, with DPRK entities or individuals*" (Security Council Committee 2018, 10). Therefore, with sanctions getting stronger, the North Korean authorities started to emphasize the "*Chagangryeok*"-first principle, again. As a result, the drive to develop the new established SEZs is declining (Hong 2018, 48).

But also, without UN sanctions the progress of North Korea's SEZs would be limited because of a lack of willingness of foreign investors to spend money for projects in a country considered as instable political area. Additionally, the risk of re-nationalization of private investments in North Korea is still high

Fig. 2: Economic Development Zones in North Korea (2014). Source: Ministry of Land, Infrastructure and Transport (2014). The National Atlas of Korea, 50.

(Lankov 2017, 30). A very good example is the nationalization of the Kaesong Industrial Complex in 2016. A further example is Orascom, an Egyptian enterprise building up a network for mobile phones in North Korea (Lankov 2017, 30). While sanctions can be seen as main reason for a lack of openness of the North Korean economy, also internal factors play an important role. The lack of international trust in North Korea's economic and military policy hinders an opening of the country like China or Vietnam decades before. But also, Juche ideology or the "*Chagangryeok*"-first principle are obstructing all attempts in the country to open its economy. At all, the North Korean reform attempts under the Byungjin line to open the country to foreign investors as well as clients are limited compared to the reforms in China or Vietnam decades ago.

4.2. Resulting private market institutions

Marketization: Private markets without legal framework

While Juche, Songun and Byungjin are still the basic official ideologies in North Korea and economic reforms are quite limited it must be stated clearly that the country's economy is already a hybrid system consisting of elements from the orthodox Soviet-style centrally planned economy with certain Asian characteristics on the one hand and market structures on the other hand. The development to this hybrid structure can be shown by the origin of the farmer's markets (jangmadang, 장마당), actually "*market grounds*".

When the public distribution system collapsed in the beginning 1990s and the people suffered from a huge famine local markets developed spontaneously to supply the majority of population with food. First, private markets were tolerated under Kim Jong-il until he decided for anti-market policies again, culminating in the 2009 currency reforms (Lankov 2017, 29). But in 2010, the markets in North Korea had to be restored, again (Kim 2018, 6). Later, these markets became more organized as "*general markets*". As a result, the number of markets has grown within the last years. While in 2010 only about 200 general markets operated in North Korea, after Kim jong-un's takeover of power the number increased enormously. In 2016 about 400 markets were estimated to be active. And as of early 2019, some 500 general markets were in operation across the country. These general markets are housed in permanent buildings and can be identified by satellite images (Koen/Beom 2020, 29–30). It is assumed that about 85 percent of consumer goods supplied on the markets have their origin in China. Because these markets are regulated and taxed, additionally, so called "*frog markets*" developed where traders carried their goods in suitcases disappearing immediately when police shows up (Seliger 2020, 5). Here, shoppers are also able to purchase rice which is actually prohibited to be sold in the general markets (Xiang 2019, 1764). Nowadays, all these markets are of highest importance for the supply of goods in North Korea. Kim Jong-un in particular changed the regulation of the jangmadang. While in the past a direct regulation was usual nowadays the focus is more on regulation on tax revenues through stall fees (Kim 2018, 6). The results of reforms in the agricultural sector and the rise of private markets are obvious. The improvement of North Korean food supply was remarkable. This was not only benefitting privileged inhabitants but also the poorest farmers in the countryside. For several years, famine was not more a part of daily life in North Korea (Lankow 2017, 31).

Also, an unofficial labor market developed in North Korea during the last years. Actually, every citizen with exception of students, soldiers and seniors is assigned to a workplace by the government and required to work there (Park et al. 2018, 29). But the development of private markets and entrepreneurs who are running private businesses (see next chapter) led to a rising demand for labor force in the North Korean private sector, too. On the other hand, in some SOEs fewer than 50 percent of employees have real work to do. Therefore, some employers exempt workers from going to work and social mobilization in exchange for a set monthly payment to the factories. These workers are known as "*8.3 workers*". This name originated from Kim Il-sung's announcement dated 3 August 1984. It encouraged the production of consumer goods "*using by-products and waste in a self-reliant way*" (Kim 2010, 29). The absent workers earn money in the private sector, maintaining their factory employee status. The advantage for the public companies is a financial support for government contributions or social mobilization tasks (Park et al. 2018, 27–28). In this way, a hybrid labor market developed in North Korea consisting of a centrally planned working schedule for every citizen on the one hand, and an absolute free "*hired and fired*" labor market in the private sector. Because of the macroeconomic reforms both labor markets are disintegrating more and more. The huge gap between official and market exchange rate of the North Korean Won destroys the last incentives to work in the official sector. There, wages are mostly paid in North Korean Won and only equivalent to a few USD a month at the market exchange rate, even if they give access to goods and services at state prices as well as social benefits. Instead, incentives are high to use the workplace property for private purposes or to undertake other jobs on the side, paid in hard currency (Koen/Beom 2020, 15).

While the number of jangmadang is rising and an unofficial labor market is developing due to the nature of the North Korean ideology as self-reliant socialist state official markets are impossible to be formed. Additionally, markets are a place where North Koreans can learn about market economy and capitalism. Therefore, for the regime all markets are a potential threat which can change the consciousness and ideological framework of the people (Kim 2018, 6). On the other hand, if Kim Jong-un is able to accompany the process of marketization by some successful reforms he can enhance his legitimacy and consolidate his power (Hanssen/Song 2019, 4). But marketization did not yet lead to further systemic transformations because it was not accompanied by economic liberalization and opening to the world (Kim 2018, 9). In contrast, marketization in North Korea remains in its first stage. A legal framework for private markets is still missing in the country.

Privatization: Entrepreneurs without private property

Hybrid institutions can also be found in the North Korean service sector as well as in the consumer goods industry. The reason is a "*cold privatization*" of means of production which is also well known from the wild phase of privatization in other socialist countries. In North Korea the private use of military trucks for transportation services or the unofficial use of machines of SOEs for the production of consumer goods sold on the private markets are good examples (Seliger 2020, 6). While private ownership of cars is somehow allowed in North Korea, it is subject to many restrictions. Therefore, most North Koreans prefer to register their private cars as the property of government agencies (Lankov 2016, 12).

Like in other transformation countries of the past also in North Korea the former nomenclature is in charge of the new market economy. In North Korea they are called donju (돈주), literally "*money masters*", which means all people with capital to invest. Generally, they cannot be understood as opponents of the regime because they are rather identical or at least closed to them. Therefore, the new private sector is dominated by people from the worker's party, the military, and the security services, either in form of personal identity or at least by bribery. Their activities are focussing mainly on the liberalized service sector like restaurants, transportation or private education, e.g. language teaching (Seliger 2020, 6–7). Nowadays, about 200,000 private entrepreneurs are expected to conduct businesses in North Korea (Lee 2019, 121).

Private money is also required by the state in the construction sector. For instance, Kim Jong-un is encouraging SOEs to search for private investors supplying private capital. Additionally, newly-build houses in Pyongyang are sold to the highest bidders, with money from the sales paying back to the private investors who supported the projects. The results are visible. Beside the new houses where apartments are sold for USD 100,000 and more expensive boutiques are opened in Pyongyang (Lankov 2017, 30–31). But the lack of formal market institutions is obvious in this sector, too. Still, private home ownership is officially prohibited in North Korea, even though this prohibition has not been enforced during the last two decades. Additionally, because of the absence of a functioning banking system, real estate investments are a favorite way of private entrepreneurs to maintain their savings (Hong 2018, 35).

Foreign trade is another business activity for the donju. Although the state has an official monopoly on foreign trade, already in the late 1990s several more or less private trade firms came into existence. First of all, fish and seafood became the most important export products in the last 30 years. Production and export of these goods can be described as "*private-public-partnership*". While most fishing vessels have private owners (although they are registered as the property of a fishing cooperative) the export of pollock and squid is managed by a foreign trade firm established by a government agency. Because the last needs some hard currency to pay the fishermen they have to line up private investors, who are usually hired officially to work for the agency (Lankov 2016, 9). Of course, these activities are made more difficult by the UN sanctions which are focussing on seafood in concrete, for instance.

Nowadays, a fusion of the private and the state sector in North Korea is visible. State-run companies are interacting with the private sector frequently. While they sell their products to semi-legal enterprises, they buy raw materials and spare parts from them. This includes benefits for both sides. For SOEs it is a way to raise funds and make profits, for the donju it provides a quite safe way to run their own businesses (Lankov 2016, 11). But at the same time, the North Korean regime still prohibits all citizens from owning private property and means of production (Koen/Beom 2020, 32). A conflict between real economic needs and the ideological fundament of the North Korean society must be seen as main reason. While banning individuals from owning means of production is a key element of the country's socialist planned economy and its basic ideologies, marketization in a necessary evil to survive. Here one can observe a fundamental difference to China and Vietnam which were much more pragmatic in this case.

Additionally, capital accumulation and transfer are growing problems for the evolving private as well as for the semi-private and liberalized state firms in North Korea. For instance, state-run firms borrow money from the private entrepreneurs because bank loans are almost impossible to obtain (Lankov 2016, 11). But added to services in currency exchange and loans a private financial system has developed in North Korea – beside the Central Bank and its branches. A quite evenly-developed inter-regional network of local marketplaces allows money transfer anywhere in the country. Each region now has so-called "*mulju*" (물주), trade masters, who also offer banking services. The result is an unofficial inter-regional remittance system within the country as well as across the Chinese border. Actually, the system originated from an unofficial trade settlement system between North Korea and China. It allows businessmen to order products simply by phone call having their orders delivered – not only within North Korea but worldwide. In the last decades a three-way settlement system among North Korea, China and a third-party country developed. The transfer system is quite similar to other remittance systems through unofficial mediators, such as the Arabic "*hawala*" (ة ل ا و ح). The only difference to the hawala system in Islamic countries is that the money passes through China and North Korean businessmen get the money in foreign currency instead of the local one (Park et al. 2018, 37–38).

At all, donju's influence in the North Korean economy is rising since Kim Jong-un took power, at least since 2014 when he legalized some types of private investments (Park et al. 2018, 29). Therefore, the donju's economic activities will continue. It may happen that the management reforms lead to permitting the establishment of private companies. That would be a legalization of the de facto privatization of means of production. If realized by the regime, it will be a significant change in North Korea's economic system (Hong 2018, 28). But a further fundamental shift of ideology would be necessary to implement such reforms, indeed.

5. Conclusion

In fact, the private sector in North Korea could be estimated to account for 30–50 percent of the country's GDP several years ago (Lankov 2016, 3). Basis are some microeconomic reforms in the agricultural sector and in the management of SOEs from the first years of Kim Jong-un's rule (2012–2014). But the resulting market institutions – jangmadang (markets) and donju (entrepreneurs) – are only the result of a spontaneous development, not of an active reform process initiated by the regime. Therefore, formal institutions like private property rights are not yet established in the country. Main obstacles for further reforms are the importance of strict ideologies like Juche for the regime stability, a lack of ideological pragmatism and the UN sanctions. Especially, as Kong (2014, 73) already pointed out; the risk aversion of the North Korean regime permits only an ultra-cautious reform strategy. The effects of the ideological underpinning of the system include an "*excessive restriction of the development of grassroots capitalism; entrenchment of the wasteful economics of militarization and the perpetuation of international isolation*". (ibid.) Following this interpretation, North Korea tries only a "*systemic adjustment*" by adopting partial reforms – mainly consisting of informal institutions – to fix immediate economic problems.

On the other hand, it can be argued that in North Korea evolved something like a "*mixed economy of an unusual sort*" (Ward et al. 2019, 533). The real existing informal institutions can be interpreted as first step of an evolving "*capitalism from below*" where capitalism grows out of the plan alongside the state sector in special industries opened up to start-ups run by private individuals (Naughton 1995, 8–13). Some observers already stated that North Korea is implementing the same reforms like China in the late 1970s or early 1980s. For instance, Lankov (2017, 27) sees "*striking similarities*" between Kim Jong-un's

Byungjin policy and the reform policy of the Deng Xiao-ping era from 1978 to 1989. But if in North Korea emerged a "*developmental dictatorship*" as he (2017, 26) proposed is questionable. While Kim Jong-un sees the success of reforming communist countries like China and Vietnam and knows that his regime cannot survive in the long run without economic success, he must be aware of ending like the sorry fates of Ceausescu and Ghaddafi.

Additionally, in North Korea ideology had – and still has – almost religious function. Since the outbreak of the corona virus pandemic in 2020 the ideological underpinning in North Korea changed again. North Korean peoples' economic activities are shrinking, even the size of smuggling through illegal markets are reduced. These changes hit hard the new class of donju as well as the political elite in Pyongyang (Cho 2020, 4). As a result, Kim Jong-un's political position became more difficult. That seems to be the beginning of a huge backward step for economic reforms. For instance, during the annual session of the North Korean parliament, the Supreme People's Assembly, on January 17, 2021, self-reliance, self-sufficiency and import substitution were mentioned again as key economic policies in the country. Additionally, the prime minister stressed "*the need to restore the state's control in the economy*". And a "*return to central planning*" instead of decentralization was announced (Frank 2021). In other words, Juche seems to be back as key approach of North Korea's economic policy. Therefore, it must be expected that the reform process in North Korea under Kim Jong-un will remain moderate or – as these announcements show – will be even driven back. At all, Kim Jong-un is trapped between short-term regime stability and nuclear armament on the one hand and economic reforms bringing some regime stability in the long term. Economic cooperation on the Korean peninsula is therefore only a long-term prospect.

References

Acemoglu, D./Robinson, J. (2012): Why Nations Fail – The Origins of Power, Prosperity and Poverty, London.

Adams, F. Gerard/Tran, Anh Le (2010): Vietnam: From Transitional State to Asian Tiger? Issues of the Vietnamese Economic Transformation Experience, in: World Economics, Bd. 11, 2, S. 177–197.

Armstrong, Charles K. (2013): Ideological Introversion and Regime Survival: North Korea's "Our-Style Socialism", in: M. Dimitrov (ed.): Why Communism Did Not Collapse: Understanding Authoritarian Regime Resilience in Asia and Europe, pp. 99–122.

Beauchamp-Mustafaga, Nathan (2012): Prospects for Economic Reform in North Korea, in: China Perspectives, No. 2012/4, pp. 70–72.

Brown, William (2018a): Special Report: North Korea's Shackled Economy (2018), The National Committee on North Korea, online: https://www.ncnk.org/resources/briefing-papers/all-briefing-papers/special-report-north-koreas-shackled-economy-2018

Brown, William (2018b): North Korea's Economic Strategy 2018, in: G. Rozman (ed.): Joint U.S.-Korea Academic Studies, Vol. 29 (2018), pp. 325–341.

Cho Sungmin (2020): The Corona Virus and Its Likely Impact on North Korea, in: Security Nexus, online: https://www.jstor.org/stable/pdf/resrep24854.pdf?refreqid=excelsior%3A9298b5a533731cf194f453126b5c7d49

Dobrzeniecki, Igor (2019): Juche Ideology in Africa: Its Origins & Development, in: Asiatica Varsoviensia, No. 32 (2019), pp. 117–137.

Eucken, Walter (1952/90): Grundsätze der Wirtschaftspolitik, 6th ed., Tübingen.

Formica, Piero (2017): Scope of the Renaissance, in: ibid. (ed.): Entrepreneurial Renaissance: Cities Striving Towards an Era of rebirth and Revival, Cham.

Frank, Rüdiger (2021): SPA Session: Lowest Official Growth Rate in Decades, in: 38North, online: https://www.38north.org/2021/01/spa-session-lowest-official-growth-rate-in-decades/

Fukuyama, Francis (1995): Confucianism and Democracy, in: Journal of Democracy, Vol. 6.2 (1995), pp. 20–33.

Global Security (2018): "Byungjin" (Parallel Development), online: https://www.globalsecurity.org/military/world/dprk/byungjin.htm

Gray, Kevin/Lee Yong-woon (2015): Following in China's Footsteps? The Political Economy of North Korean Reform, in: The Pacific Review, October 2015, pp. 1–23.

Hale, Christopher D. (2005): Real Reform in North Korea? The Aftermath of July 2002 Economic Measures, in: Asian Survey: A Bimonthly Review of Contemporary Asian Aaffairs, Vol. 45/6, pp. 823–842.

Han Tak-sung/Joo Heon-kyung (2014): Can Catch North Korea Two Rabbits at Once: Nuke and Economy? One Year of the Byungjin Line in North Korea and Its Future, in: The Korean Journal of Defense Analysis, Vol. 26, No. 2, pp. 133–153.

Hanssen, Ulv/Song, Ji Won (2019) Marketization in North Korea: Scenarios for economic, political and social change, SWEDISH INSTITUTE OF INTERNATIONAL AFFAIRS (ed.): UI-Paper 1/2019, online: https://www.ui.se/globalassets/ui.se-eng/publications/ui-publications/ui-paper-no.-1-2019.pdf

Hong Jea-hwan (2018): North Korean Economy in the Kim Jong-un Regime, Korea Institute for National Unification (ed.): KINU Study Series 18–03.

Hong Suk-hoon/Cho Yun-young (2018): North Korea's Transition of Its Economic Development Strategy: Its Significance and the Political Environment Surrounding the Korean Peninsula, in: The Korean Journal of Defense Analysis, Vol. 30, No. 4, pp. 493–512.

Kim Byung-yeon (2010): Markets, Bribery, and Regime Stability in North Korea, EAI Asia Security Initiative Working Paper No. 4, East Asia Institute Seoul.

Kim Kap-sik (2016): Analysis on the 7th Congress of Korean Worker's Party (1): General Review, KINU Online Series 2016.5.11, online: https://www.kinu.or.kr/pyxis-api/1/digital-files/51df001d-b664-438d-8c5c-19db9d65bc30

Kim Philo (2018): The Segmented Marketization of North Korea and Its Sociopolitical Implications, in: Asian Perspective, Vol. 42 (2018), pp.1–31.

Kim So-young (2020): Dollarization of the North Korean Economy: Causes and Effects, Korea Development Institute (ed.): Dialogue on the North Korean Economy, March 2020.

Koen, Vincent/Beom Jinwoan (2020): North Korea: The Last Transition Economy? OECG (ed.): Economics Department Working Papers, No. 1607 (12 May 2020).

Koh Yu-hwan (2020): A 'new path' is Needed, in: JoongAng Ilbo, 2020, Jan. 6, p. 29, also online: https://koreajoongangdaily.joins.com/news/article/article.aspx?aid=3072292

Kong, Tat Yang (2014): The Political Obstacles to Economic Reform in North Korea: The Ultra Cautious Strategy in Comparative Perspective, in: The Pacific Review, Vol. 27 (2014), No. 1, pp. 73–96.

Kwon, Edward (2019): Denuclearization of North Korea: Before and After the Summits, in: The Korean journal of Defense Analysis, Vol. 31, No. 3, pp. 309–328.

Lankov, Andrei (2016): The Resurgence of a Market Economy in North Korea, Carnegie Moscow Center, Moscow.

Lankov, Andrei (2017): Is Byungjin Policy Failing? Kim Jong Un's Unannounced Reform and its Chances of Success, in: The Korean Journal of Defense Analysis, Vol. 29 (1), pp. 25–45.

Lee Inyeop (2019): Can North Korea Follow China's Path? A Comparative Study of the Nexus Between National Security and Economic Reforms, in: Pacific Focus, Vol. XXXIV (2019), No. 1, pp. 102–126.

Lee Je-hun/Noh Ji-won/Hwang Joon-bum (2020): Kim Jong-un Message of Self-reliance and "foiling" Sanctions During Last Party Meeting of 2019, in: HANKYOREH (2 January 2020), online: http://english.hani.co.kr/arti/english_edition/e_northkorea/922940.html

Lee Minha/Chung Suh Yong (2020): Is Trans-Korean Railway Solely a Symbol of Peace in the Korean Peninsula? in: Sustainability 2020/12, pp. 1–13.

Lerner, Daniel (1958): The Passing of Traditional Society, Glencoe.

Lin Justin Yifu/Cai Fang/Li Zhou (1996): The Lessons of China's Transition to a Market Economy, in: Cato Journal, Vol. 16, No. 2, pp. 201–231.

McKay, John (2005): How Significant and Effective are North Korea's "market reforms"? in: Global Economic Review, Vol. 34/1, pp. 83–97.

Ministry of Land, Infrastructure and Transport (2014): The National Atlas of Korea, online: http://nationalatlas.ngii.go.kr/us/index.php

MOFCOM (2004): Socialist Market Economic System, online: http://english.mofcom.gov.cn/article/topic/bizchina/economicsystem/200406/20040600239133.shtml

Naughton, Berry (1995): Growing Out of the Plan: Chinese Economic Reform 1978–1993, Cambridge.

North, Douglas (1990): Institutions, Institutional Change and Economic Performance, Washington.

North, Douglas/Wallis, John/Weingast, Barry (2009): Violence and Social Orders: A Conceptual Framework for Interpreting Recorded Human History, Camebridge.

Park Young-Ja, et al. (2018): Eight Chances in North Korean Economy and Society under the Kim Jong Un Regime, KINU Study Series 18–05, Dec. 2018.

Security Council Committee (2018): Fact Sheet Compiling Certain Measures Imposed by Security Council Resolutions 1718 (2006), 1874 (2009), 2087 (2013), 2094 (2013), 2270 (2016), 2321 (2016), 2356 (2017),2371 (2017), 2375 (2017), and 2397 (2017), 17 April 2018, online: https://www.un.org/securitycouncil/sites/www.un.org.securitycouncil/files/fact_sheet_updated_17_apr_2018_0.pdf

Seliger, Bernhard (2004): The North Korean Economy: Nuclear Crisis and Decline, or Peace and Reform in the Last Asian Dynastic Regime? in: The Korea Economic Institute (ed.): Korea's economy 2004, pp. 77–86.

Seliger, Bernhard (2020): North Korea's Political Economy: Hybrid Economic Institutions and the Contributions of German Order Policy (Ordnungspolitik), Ordnungspolitischer Diskurs 2020–2, online: https://www.econstor.eu/bitstream/10419/215832/1/1694622037.pdf

Shin Gi-wook/Moon, Rennie (2019): North Korea in 2018: Kim's Summit Diplomacy, in: Asian Survey, Vol. 50 (2019), No. 1, pp. 35–43.

Surhone, Lambert, et al. (2010): Socialist-oriented Market Economy: Economy of Vietnam, Doi Moi, Centrally-Planned Economy, Market Socialism, ßetascript Publishing.

Ward, Peter/Lankov, Andrei/Kim Jiyoung (2019): Capitalism from Below with North Korean Characteristics: The State, Capitalist Class Formation, and Foreign investment in Comparative Perspective, in: Asian Perspective, Vol. 43 (2019), No. 3, pp. 533–555.

Wrobel, Ralph (2007): North Korea after the Nuclear Crisis: The Future of the Economic Reforms, in: Post Communist Economies, Vol. 12, No. 4 (2007), S. 483–504.

Wrobel, Ralph (2011): The Social Market Economy as a Model for Sustainable Growth in Developing and Emerging Economies, in: Economic and Environmental Studies, Vol. 12, No. 1 (21/2011), 47–63, pp. 47–64.

Wrobel, Ralph (2014): Ten Years of Kaesong Industrial Complex: A Brief History of the Last Economic Cooperation Project of the Korean Peninsula, in: Economic and Environmental Studies, Bd. 14 (2014), 2, S.125–147.

Xiang, Qifan (2019): The Black Markets of North Korea, in: Modern Economy, 2019/10, pp. 1759–1768.

Bernhard Seliger

The Iron Silk Road and North Korea: Is there any chance to move forward?

1. Introduction: The BRI – Economic integration without the Korean Peninsula?

When in September 2013 Chinese leader Xi Jinping started to promote the "One Belt, one Road" Initiative (short BRI), first in trips to Indonesia and Kazakhstan, and afterwards a flurry of diplomatic activity began, in the original definition of the BRI the Korean Peninsula was not a part of the concept. For participating countries, the promises were tempting: lower logistics costs, access to new markets, joint infrastructure development and joint finance of such projects made them attractive in particular for developing countries. For an overview, see the contributions in Djankov-Miner (2016), Nobis (2017), and OECD 2018, for instance. For a more critical analysis see Parameswaran (2017), or Panda (2018). Over time, new aspects of the BRI emerged, like the possibility of a Health and Digital Silk Road (Lee 2021). But most of all, they all were centered in China. Indeed, as in the past all proverbial ways (and real Roman state streets) were leading to Rome, the BRI saw Beijing like a spider in a net, and all ways leading to Beijing (Fig. 1). However, this quickly changed, and as well South Korea and North Korea were offered parts to play into the concept. First, this was a simple extension of the net, by including ports (Nampo in North Korea, Incheon in South Korea) and potential railway connections to the capital Pyongyang and Seoul. Also, in the main financing agency of the BRI, the Asian Infrastructure Investment Bank (AIIB), South Korea is a prominent member. But South Korea is still wary of being too associated with the BRI concept, given the huge, largely negative impression the initiative made in the main allied country of South Korea, the USA, as a project to create and maintain Chinese dominance (Kung-Pan 2018; Rolland 2020). At the same time, since several decades already South Korea promoted similar infrastructure projects called for example "iron silk road", to link it with European markets, but also to integrate North Korea more into the world economy. However, these ideas, all of which needed a North Korean component, largely ended nowhere due to the inability of North and South Korea to agree on them.

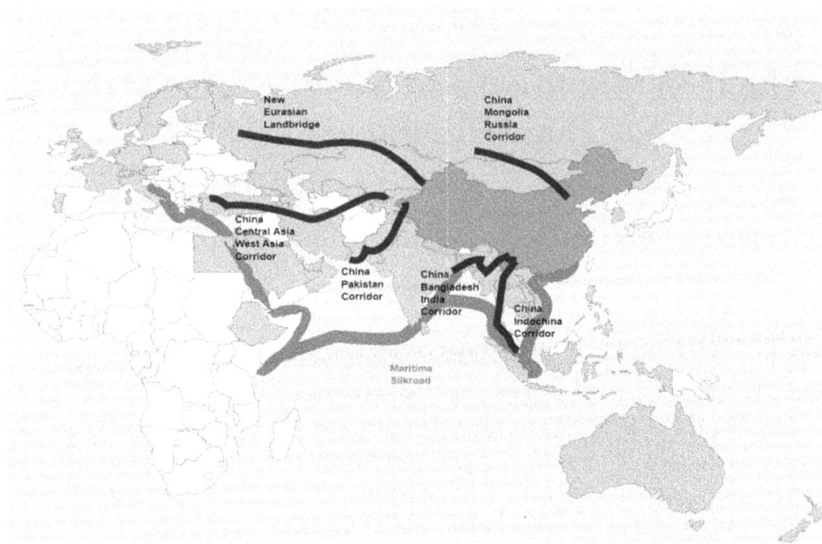

Fig. 1: Main linkages of the One Belt, One Road Initiative. (Source: CC BY SA 3.0, Wikimedia 2021a).

For North Korea, the question of connection to the BRI is not only a question of geo-economics, but also has to be considered from the point of view of the political economy of integration. Since trade with China already now plays an overwhelming role for North Korea, with more than 90 percent of goods imported from there, a closer trade connection seems definitely advantageous. Indeed, the Special Economic Zone policy of North Korea, while also targeting South Korea and originally maybe even the Japanese and world market to become more independent from China, indeed mostly is a policy to make these linkages even closer. At the same time, however, given the overarching goal of regime survival and regime stability, the political effects of closer trade integration, which invariably means less political control and more opening (for example, through faster customs procedures allowing less state intervention, more openness for business people etc.), have to be considered. These effects make North Korea wary of too much integration and an integration process where certain parts of control of the economy are given up. The situation in 2020 and 2021, when the Covid-19 pandemic led to a complete self-isolation of North Korea, is an illustration of this problem: in a closer integrated area, like the European Union, to take it to an extreme, such self-isolation would no longer be possible. This does not mean that North Korea outright rejects the BRI. In certain political circumstances, like in the political thaw with South Korea in 2018, closer integration had had its appeal. That time, for example, North Korea hoped to escape from US and UN sanctions by negotiating with South Korea. In other times, interest in the BRI seems advantageous to reach out to the main protector nation China. But these advances never are complete, and in the North Korean playbook always have to be easily reversible, to remain independent. So, is there a way to coax North Korea into closer integration and opening?

The remainder of this paper looks more in detail into the South and North Korean views on this question. The second part looks at North Korea's integration in the BRI and similar schemes from the point of view of South Korea and China. Given the strong dominance and push of South Korea for such a move, it seems to be justified to first look at it from this angle. The third section then looks into the North Korea view, balancing economic benefits from trade and closer integration with potential political fallout from these policies. The fourth section takes a closer look at the policy of Special Economic Zones and Economic Development Zones of North Korea, one of the signature policies of the past decade, and how they fit into the BRI scheme, followed by some conclusions (5.).

2. North Korea as an object in the Iron Silk Road discussion: South Korean and Chinese views

Considering the economic geography of the Korean Peninsula, it is no wonder that South Korea has a strong interest in the position of its Northern neighbor in Eurasian economic integration. For South Korea, the Eurasian land bridge always was a dream and an important economic goal, given the importance of South Korea's export industry, which could benefit from reduced costs of reaching export markets in Central Asia, Europe and Russia for bulk goods like cars and household appliances. While the maritime connection from South Korea to Europe measures around 25.000 km, with bottlenecks and dangerous places like the Singapore straits, the Horn of Africa and the Suez Canal included, potential train and highway connections would measure less than half, around 12.000 kilometers. Simply looking at time from port to port, if no political borders were there, it would reduce traffic from around 30 days by ship to only 20 days by railway. However, for the time being this land bridge is not competitive, due to technical incompatibilities of infrastructure, delays at numerous customs points, travel through difficult and sometimes dangerous terrain, for example by weather events or political events. For example, Chinese railway freight, though existing for a long time and being modernized under the

BRI, has a minuscule share in total freight, and stagnates (Kenderdine – Bucsky 2020). Specifically for South Korea, it is outright impossible to traverse North Korea. South Korea is in fact an island, and all discussion of using the Eurasian land bridge up to now means for South Korea to bring goods by ship to Russia (Vladivostok) or China and use the Trans-Siberian or Trans-Chinese railway systems, making such a move much more costly and causing delays in time through transshipping. This is one reason why South Korea is highly interested in a North Korean connection with the BRI or other infrastructure projects. The Moon Jae-In Administration tried to prepare for this not only with an active North Korea policy, but also with the "New Northern Policy" aiming at engaging Russia and Mongolia, which has its own version of a New Silk Road, the "Steppe Road" (Song 2019).

The second, equally important reason is political. Since more than 75 years the Korean Peninsula is divided into the socialist North and South Korea, a democracy and market economy. But on both sides, at least the official raison d'être is still the unity of the nation, even if North Korea's elite and South Korea's youth have silently dropped this overarching political goal. While being confrontational in the form of systemic competition most of the time, South Korea by the 1990s realized that a propagation of North Korea's economic development, opening and increased trade would rather benefit them, since it would be – a lesser or larger degree – be related to political opening and the chance for more peaceful relations, and maybe even unification. In this sense, the political schemes for infrastructure development South Korea promoted long before the current Chinese BRI plan all were aiming at making bilateral relations more peaceful, not only for the benefit of South Korea's industry, but also to enhance chances of political rapprochement and, maybe ultimately unification (Lee 2016; Römer 2018).

It is perfectly understandable that such schemes first gained prominence by the early to mid-1990s. In that time, systemic competition, which had been fierce and originally by no way being guaranteed to provide an easy South Korean dominance or victory, clearly was decided: After the breakdown of the Soviet Union and its socialist trading system, which had provided North Korea for decades with massive aid in the form of cheap energy, North Korea suffered from a massive economic crisis, leading to famine and the forced opening to international aid. Later, this period which cost hundred thousands and maybe millions of lives, was referred to as the "arduous march". At the same time, South Korea in the early 1990s not only achieved a largely peaceful transition to democracy, but also rose to the ranks of the world's foremost exporters, a development which culminated in the transition from a "newly industrialized country" to the second

Asian OECD members. Even the severe economic crisis of 1997 and 1998 did barely affect this position.

In particular, from the time of the Kim Dae-Jung presidency, who also tried to emulate the example of *Ostpolitik* of West Germany in the late 1960s and 1970s, there have been constantly proposals for closer logistics and economic linkages proposed which resemble to some extent the current Chinese BRI approach. First of all, this includes the "Iron Silk Road" approach. The Iron Silk Road was the idea to revive the famous medieval trading route, the Silk route, connecting Asia and Europe.

Though, proper speaking, Korea was at best peripheral to the original Silk road, South Korean governments since the administration of Kim Dae-Jung (1998–2002) used it to describe in particular a railway network connecting South Korea to the Trans-Siberian and Trans-Chinese network through North Korea (Fig. 2). In particular, Kim Dae-Jung at the ASEM summit in Copenhagen on September 22, 2002, unveiled the vision of an ever closer European-Asian connection through the Iron Silk Road, made possible by this breakthrough in relations with North Korea, and transcending from a mere reduction in logistics costs to an ever-closer community of spirit. Even the idea of a Korea-Japan tunnel under the sea, similar to the Euro-tunnel linking the United Kingdom to the European landmass, was part of the vision. But integration proposals did not stop there.

Another project gaining track in the 1990s was the Asian Highway Network, or Great Asian Highway. This UN-promoted project originated already in 1959 and saw a first phase throughout the 1960s, but then slowed down, until the UN-ESCAP in 1992 endorsed it as part of the Asian Land Transportation Infrastructure Development (ALTID) project. For the Korean Peninsula, Asian Highway no. 1 is important, a 20557 km road network from Tokyo in Japan to the Turkish-Bulgarian border. It's Korean Peninsula leg reaches from Busan via Gyeongju, Daegu, Daejeon and Seoul to Musan at the inner-Korean border, and from there to Kaesong, Pyongyang and Sinuiju. While South Korea did develop its part of the road network early on, the North Korean road exists, but remains in a less-well developed state, in particular from Pyongyang to Sinuiju. In 2003, the Intergovernmental Agreement on the Asian Highway Network (IGA) was adopted by the Intergovernmental Meeting; the IGA includes Annex I, which identifies 55 AH routes among 32 member countries totaling approximately 140,000 km and Annex II "Classification and Design Standards" (Fig. 3). During the 60th session of the ESCAP Commission at Shanghai, China, in April 2004, the IGA treaty was signed by 23 countries. By 2013, 29 countries had ratified the agreement, including North Korea on October 12, 2012 (UN n.d.). However, signing a treaty on the Asian highway did not automatically lead to improved

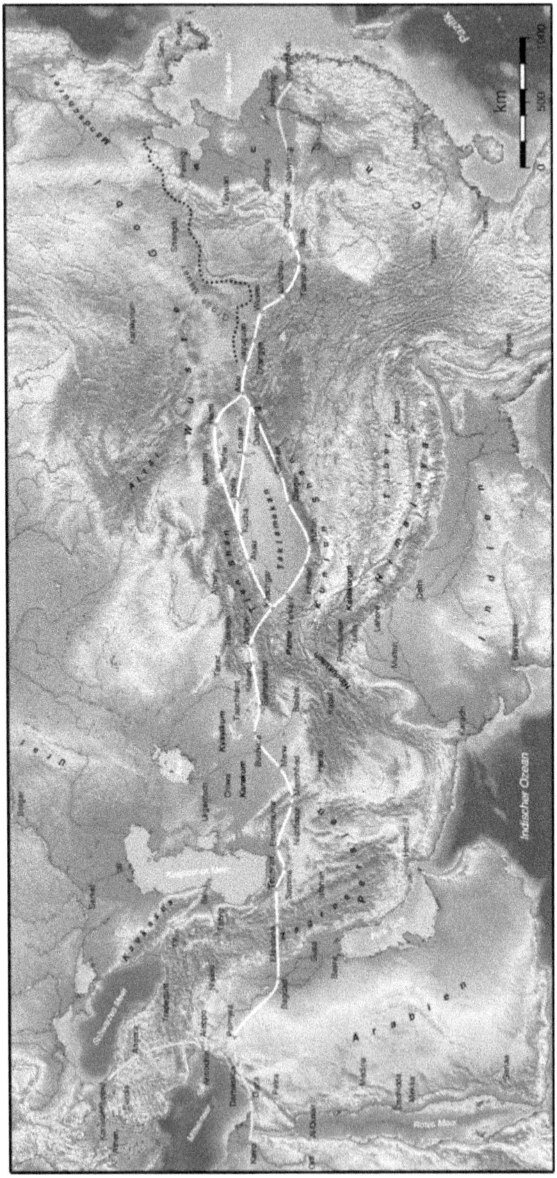

Fig. 2: Main routes of the original silk road. (Source: CC BY SA 3.0, Wikimedia 2021b).

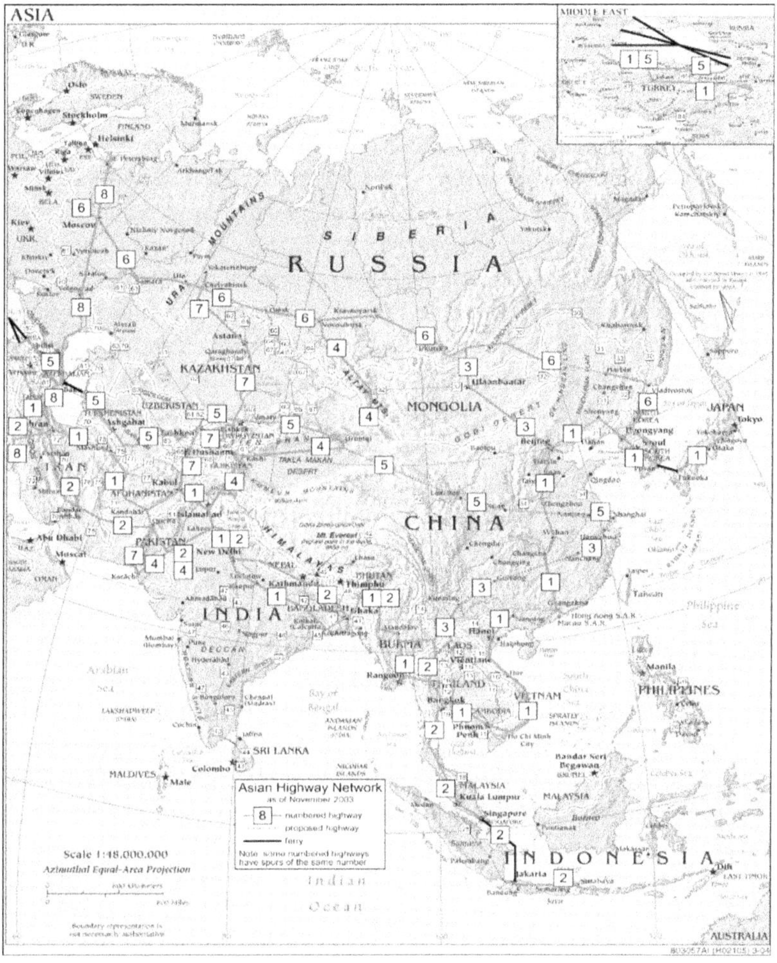

Fig. 3: Asian Highways. (Source: Public domain).

cross-border access, as not only the Korean case shows, where the treaty had no impact at all on the situation of the border, but also other cases like Myanmar or Pakistan. Political sensitivities in all these cases trumped potential economic benefits, and so for Korea the Asian highway remains an elusive dream – though South Korea already erected road signs for the Asian Highway 1 along its route.

Finally, infrastructure development also regarded better linkages in the field of energy (Bermudez 2021). For South Korea, a country practically without any energy sources, but ironically at the same time until recently a main petrochemical industry power and highly dependent on reliable and cheap energy for its industrial base, securing energy had always been an economic priority. One of the ways to become more diversified in energy sources was the project of a gas pipeline from Russian gas fields (in Sakchalin or further West on the mainland) to South Korea via North Korea (Ahn 2010). This project did not only appeal to the Kim Dae-Jung administration during the sunshine policy era of improved relations to North Korea, but also to the subsequent conservative government of Lee Myung-Bak, who took raw material security serious and later again the Moon Jae-In administration in the 2018 thaw of relations to the North. This includes the discussion of the possibility of a Korean Peninsula energy community, similar to the European Coal and Steel Community, Russia is also highly interested in the project to enlarge its customer base. (for a general discussion Blanck 2018)

In practice, however, all three projects, the Asian railway links through North Korea, the Asian highway and the gas pipeline did not come to fruition. Regarding the railway, the biggest advances were made in the time of "Sunshine policy": the newly erected Kaesong Industrial Complex on the North Korean side of the border was connected to South Korea, which invested in the complex – with 130 companies at peak – by road and railroad, and this railroad was used to transport produced bulk goods to the South. Under the 2000 summit agreement between South Korean President Kim Dae-Jung and North Korean leader Kim Jong-Il North Korea connected roughly 15 km of the so-called Kyeungeui railway line from Kaesong station to the DMZ in the north, and the South connected a roughly 2 km long section in the DMZ, together with a two-lane road. All material for the connection came from the South. At the same time, a slightly-less-than-30 km section of the Donghae (East Sea) railroad was restored, from Onjong-Ri in North Korea. To reconnect, hundreds of mines had to been removed, which had been in the area since the Korean war. The Kyeungeui railway line connects Seoul to Kaesong to Pyongang and Sinuiju, and from there to Dandong connects to the Chinese railway network and the Trans-Chinese railway. The Donghae line connects Kangneung in the South to Wonsan in the North, from there via Hamheung and Chongjin to Rason, and from Tumen village further to the Russian railroad network and Vladivostok, the end point of the Trans-Siberian railroad. However, not much more than an opening ceremony for both railroads – in the case of the Donghae railroad there was even no real connection to the further Northern or Southern stations – and some goods transportation to and from Kaesong Industrial Complex happened. A regular rail service never took place. With the thaw of relations in 2018 a renewed inter-Korean railroad project was started, and at one point South Korea pledged to invest up to 40 bn. KRW (around 35 mill. USD) on the North Korean railroad. Some commentators saw this as a way of integrating North Korea into the BRI scheme (Devonshire-Ellis 2018, 2019). However, the South barely could justify an exemption for UN sanctions for a preliminary 10-day joint survey of the North Korean railroad. Afterwards, the project became stalled again.

As for the highway project, though the road physically exists, the impossibility to cross the DMZ renders it useless as an Asian highway project. And finally, the gas pipeline project did come up regularly as a discussion topic among Russia and South Korea in bilateral negotiations, but never made it to a trilateral stage. What could make such infrastructure projects possible? Let us look into the political economy of large-scale infrastructure projects, but without looking at the ramifications for North Korea's political system for a moment (this will be more extensively done in the third section). There are five important issues to consider: First of all, transparency conditions are very important. This concerns costs of building infrastructure, access to infrastructure, costs of maintenance and fee structure. For example, one problem regarding the construction of a gas pipeline is the necessity to lead to through remote regions of North Korea, and North Korea might want to restrict this access. This is in particular also true for monitoring, e.g. of the status of infrastructure, necessary repairs etc. in the case, it cannot be done entirely (for political reasons, or for technical reasons) by the North Korean side alone. Second, there is the question of large-scale upfront investment or sunk costs. The more investment there is, and investment on roads and railroads as well as pipelines is usually very heavy, since most of the investment is not tangible and cannot be recovered in case a deal is broken or getting void for whatever reason, the more there is a strategic incentive for a partner to alter the deal after this initial investment is done. For example, North Korea could at will change the fee structure for the transmission of gas in a gas pipeline or take prohibitively high fees for the use of roads or railroads. Though not completely comparable, in this way, in the past East Germany regulated the number of West German visitors by raising the amount of mandatory exchange of hard West German currency (deutschmark) at an unfavorable rate to the East German mark. Third, there is the question of the nature of payments to North Korea resulting from a project. The best structure to ensure a lasting economic interest in such a project is a constant and long-term stream of payments, rather than a one-off original payment. All projects, roads, railroads and gas pipelines could work in a way to fulfill this condition for successful investment. Fourth, there is the question of how the payment stream is reached, as a politically-bargained lump sum, or as a market-driven amount (maybe, with a politically-guaranteed minimum level to make it more palatable for North Korea). For example, fees for the tourism project by Hyundai Asan in the Kumgangsan mountain were not directly related to the number of tourists, but were negotiated politically. Road and railroad fees, if set market-driven and related to demand, are an incentive for North Korea to provide a sufficient service, and even to provide better services, if they are related to more revenue. Finally, fifth there is the question of the possibility of North Korea to hurt others by non-compliance with its obligations under a treaty. This is closely related to the question of sunk costs. In all, the road, railroad and gas pipeline project, North Korea's role is pivotal. This gives it great bargaining power, once the investment has been done. Therefore, any infrastructure project should consider potential alternatives, even if they are more expensive than the initially offered price by North Korea. For example, rail transport and road transport theoretically could be combined with shipping around North Korea, e.g. from Busan to Vladivostok. With this, time and money would be lost, but the pivotal role of North Korea would be reduced.

Given these considerations, the projects seem to be quite risky. However, the track record of a similar project with the Soviet Union, the gas pipeline projects from the Soviet Union to Austria and Germany, the so-called transgas pipeline, build after 1970 with pipes delivered by West German companies and gas being brought back in return, worked until the end of the Soviet Union twenty years later without problems, and only during the phase of the disintegration of the Soviet Union Ukrainian-Russian gas disputes impaired the performance of the pipeline (Lee 2013). It is very difficult to directly compare this with the case of a potential pipeline or road project on the Korean Peninsula, but at least this shows that even in the times of strong systemic competition, like in the European missile crisis of the early 1980s, such deals could work.

Given South Korean political economy considerations, such a deal even could be economically disadvantageous or costly, if it reduces tensions on the Korean Peninsula and in particular, in the direct border area, and maybe contributes to long-term opening up of North Korea. At the same time, in the current actual situation sanctions are a grave obstacle to this kind of policy and obviously the policy of the Moon Jae-In government to offer large-scale cooperation with North Korea, without caring for the appropriate political conditions, simply by hoping that the nuclear crisis would find a miraculous end, did backfire in the end.

Finally, let us take a short look at China's interest in making North Korea part of the BRI. This interest is again in part economic, in part political in nature.

Economically, North Korea as a potential investment location or as an origin of export goods to be transported via the Chinese rail or road network can be neglected. It is at the most of very local interest in the border area. However, North Korea does offer the prospect of being an important source of raw material, among them coal, iron, seafood, and, to a lesser extent even gold and rare earth. As such, China has a great interest to come to closer economic integration with the North. Also, China could be interested in smooth logistics with South Korea if ever the common road or railroad would lead to increased traffic. Finally, China has also an interest politically in the Northern part of the Peninsula, as a buffer to South Korea with its large stationed US troups. As such, China is interested in stability in the North, and this again might be related to closer economic integration.

3. North Korea as the subject in the Iron Silk Road discussion

As seen above, North Korea has been matter of intense discussions of its neighbors regarding the participation in regional integration projects. Some it rejects outright, others it sometimes pursued, only to give it up again, like the inter-Korean railway projects. With regards to the One Belt, One Road (BRI) initiative, for a long time North Korea did practically ignore its existence. There are only a handful of mentions of it in the largest available data base, KCNA watch (KCNA n.d.), most of which are the same two news of the North Korean government delegation traveling to the BRI conference in Beijing in 2017, with only one longer article dealing with the BRI itself. The Naenara website, a quasi-governmental website, has no mentioning of the BRI. So, there is a great likelihood that an overwhelming part of North Koreans never has heard about it. This might be the reason why the North Korean government delegation which attended the BRI Forum in Beijing in May 2017, headed by Kim Yong Jae, Minister of External Economic Relations, was greeted with considerable interest. However, beside participating, there was no concrete commitment of North Korea to the BRI. And the article of June 2019, which again talks about the same forum, but describes it as something that recently has happened (not usual in North Korea media, which are not exactly too punctual in reporting about events), does not at all view it as something North Korea should be involved in, but merely praises China for bringing together a large number of international organizations and states in the project and closing a lot of deals.

Certainly, purely seen by economic benefits, North Korea stands to gain a lot by integration in the BRI. Disregarding sanctions for a moment, North Korea could expect infrastructure investment from China (for example, the railroad leg from Pyongyang to Sinuiju), South Korea and Russia. Russia since several years has a representative office of the state railroad in Pyongyang. This is mainly dealing with questions of the existing railroad to Rason Special Zone (see more on this in section 4), but also plans for a wholescale renovation of North Korean railway lines by Russia was discussed in the past. Closer economic integration with the neighbors also would fit in with the economic strategy of trade expansion followed by North Korea from the early 2000s, and reinforced so from the start of the reign of Kim Jong-Un in late 2011, until the UN sanctions blocked this path in 2016.

North Korea had been a country run largely on orthodox Soviet central planning lines from 1945 to 1990. In this time, by exploiting the Sino-Soviet rift, they attracted considerable amounts of aid from both sides. In particular, North Korea built up an industry and mechanized agriculture crucially dependent on cheap Soviet oil. When this stopped to arrive, since the new Russian government required hard currency payment for any exports, the North Korean economy collapsed, and by the mid-1990s a famine gripped the country, which claimed hundred thousands, maybe millions of victims. From 1995, being at the brink of complete state collapse, the country opened for international aid goods and for a considerable time, up to one third of the Korean population could only survive thanks to foreign food aid and other aid. By the early 2000s, the situation had somewhat stabilized and North Korea began to develop again an export industry, focusing on sea food first, later some labor-intensive industries like textile, but in particular raw materials like coal, iron and rare earth.

After the collapse of the centrally planned economy, also a new hybrid economic system developed, consisting of three pillars: special enterprises related to the party or army, the so-called people's economy, where central planning was still dominant, and a genuinely new private sector, in particular in the service industries (Seliger 2020). However, these distinctions never were clear, but rather fuzzy: the hybrid economy also brought about hybrid companies: the entire construction sector was run by soldiers, but now you could hire groups of them to work on private projects; military units owning trucks could have logistics companies as a side business of entrepreneurial officers, and a new class of "*donju*", men with money, emerged, not necessary apart from the cadres of the past, but with an interest in private gains. At the same time, the Chinese influence on the economy more and more grew. This was partly a reason of proximity and the huge success of Chinese market reforms. Additionally, the share of non-Chinese exports and imports shrank strongly with the onset of the second nuclear crisis starting from 2002. While North Korea's trade grew, more and more non-Chinese companies grew wary to trade with North Korea, since they feared political entanglement, making North Korea more and more dependent on the Chinese market. While this was first true in the market for goods, North Korea still expanded its export of labor to many countries and regions, including Russia, the Middle East and Africa, and even some European countries.

The increased trade (trade roughly quadrupled between 2002 and 2016) had political side effects: more and more foreign goods entering the country were related to more and more foreign information, brought in by traders, in particular introduced on CDs, DVDs and USB sticks on markets, often in the form of South Korean music, films and other forbidden information. The Sunshine era (2000–2007) had been for many North Koreans the first time when they were confronted with new and more accurate information on South Korea, apart from the domestic propaganda, which painted a negative picture of South Koreans living in poverty and suppression. Now, a new generation of North Koreans grew up knowing about the technological and economic superiority of South Korea. North Korea's propaganda changed, to picture South Korea as rich, but decadent, but this did not help to reduce the attraction of South Korea among young people. New campaigns tried to weed out "anti-socialist" behavior, hairstyles, clothing etc.

At the same time, at least partly the new economy and trade were embraced. North Korea graduated from the extreme poverty of the 1900s and early 2000s, rates of undernourishment sank and in Pyongyang, signs of a new, more affluent middle class became visible. By now, the state had carefully to balance the wishes for more material well-being of a class, on which Kim Jong-Un's regime was dependent, and the fear of more foreign influence. Since after the end of the Sunshine era almost the entire flow of goods and information came from China, also proposals for more and easier trade with China were seen with mistrust. This can best be seen in the fate of the New Yalu River Bridge crossing from Dandong in China to Sinuiju in North Korea, the main entry point for goods and people between both states. From 1937 to 1943, under Japanese occupation, a bridge later called the "Sino-Korean friendship bridge" had been built by the Japanese Empire, which by the 2010s was old and could barely handle increased trade. Since 2011, China built the New Yalu River bridge, which was finished in 2014. Since then, North Korea did not make use of this modern bridge for the next five years, refusing to connect it to the own road network. This shows that in practice, North Korea has a limited interest in better connection to the Belt and Road network of China, though it is economically entirely dependent on it (Silberstein 2019). Also, as Ward (2018) points out, North Korea might be wary of becoming dependent on Chinese debt for infrastructure, by observing how China deals with defaulting countries in Africa and South Asia.

With increased international sanctions from 2016, North Korea became less and less integrated with the world economy, making it maybe the most isolated country in terms of trade openness. While afterwards, for three years still the level of imports from China could be held constant, though exports dwindled and the labor force abroad, with the exception of workers in China, fell almost to zero, making North Korea losing important earnings of foreign currency, since most of the wages of North Korean workers abroad were claimed by the state, the onset of the Covid-19 pandemic brought in late January 2020 the complete isolation of North Korea and subsequently, also trade with China fell to very low figures. This could not, however, eradicate the perceived threat from foreign influence, as renewed ideological campaigns to abstain from anti-socialist behavior in 2020 and 2021 show. Indeed, it might well be that the generation which grew up in relatively more secure economic conditions than the previous ones, and was used to trade and some outside information, in the times of pandemic and renewed economic hardship more obstinately pins its hopes on opening of the economy. This shows the clear limits, the North Korean government has in accepting the Chinese offer of increased economic integration under the BRI, if regime survival is the overarching political goal.

4. North Korea's special economic zone policy, the Iron Silk Road, Belt and Road, and the growing dependence on China

If opening of the whole economy is deemed politically not feasible, there still might be the possibility to promote trade and cooperation in geographically limited, politically controlled special economic zones. This was the recipe for Chinese success in the 1980s and 1990s, when from very limited beginnings zones like Shenzhen became a spectacular success and motor of the Chinese opening and magnet for foreign investment, transforming the zones into industrial giants and high-tech areas. This development did not escape the attention of North Koreans, and indeed several times China promoted this successful model through high-level tours for North Korean cadres. And, for North Korea, this included the dream of a more integrated economy with its two Northern neighbors, China and Russia. Ever since the bold claim by Kim Il-Sung in 1991 that the Rajin-Sonbong area in the utmost Northeast of North Korea would become the "Singapore of the East", there has been a dream of a "Golden Triangle" of co-prosperity between China, Russia and North Korea. The history of Special Economic Zones in North Korea dates back to that year, when the two remote counties of Rajin and Sonbong were merged into the Rason Special Economic Zone. Located at the border to China and Russia and equipped with an ice-free harbor, the zone seemed ideally located as a potential logistics hub of the future: far from the politically dangerous Southern border, close to the neighbors and with one attractive feature, the ice-free harbor, neither of the neighbors had. Though the original idea to create a "Singapore of the North" quickly evaporated and for ten years progress on the zone was very slow, until today Rason SEZ is the only zone, where real progress in terms of foreign involvement, overwhelmingly through Chinese investment and trade, can be seen. Ironically, the geographic location of the zone originally was partly chosen to diversify economic relations and allow North Korea more integration with Russia, and maybe even through the Pacific to foster relations with Japan and other market economies beyond, including the USA. But in the end, Rason became a place overwhelmingly interesting for Chinese investors. While in the first years of its existence, Rason was mainly famous for a casino-hotel, the Emperor (now Imperial) hotel built by a Hong Kong tycoon, with the Chinese development of the former "rust belt", the three Northeastern provinces Heilonggang, Liaoning and Jilin, from the late 2000s also the interest in Rason rekindled, since these provinces lacked a harbor connection to the Pacific. China built a motorway and high-speed train to Hunchun, built a new bridge over the Tumen river to substitute the old bridge from Japanese colonial times and also substituted the 48 km dirt track between the border post Wonjong and Rajin in the Rason SEZ with a modern road. Russia, which under Putin's presidency did not want to stand by, negotiated the long-term lease of pier 3 of Rason harbor and equipped it with an autonomous oil power plant and modern cranes as well as modernized the railway tracks from the border to Rajin harbor to accomodate Russian railway carts.

In November 2015, North Korea claimed that there were 150 foreign invested firms in the zone, including 4 equity joint ventures, 30 contractual joint ventures, 103 foreign companies and 13 representative offices of foreign companies. Tourism by Chinese operators and small-scale border trade were blooming and business people from Yanbian autonomous Korean Prefecture in China could even enter the zone in their own cars. At the same time, the zone exported workers to the nearby Chinese cities of Hunchun, Yanji and Tumen, where they were sought after as reliable, cheap labor in textile, seafood processing and other companies. The development of the nuclear program and sanctions however, for the time being stopped that development: joint ventures became outlawed, though many seem to have only formally changed ownership, the Russian pier since at least two years ceased to work, though it is theoretically exterritorial and explicitly not covered by sanctions (by Russian or other international firms using it might fear anyway "secondary" sanction by the USA), and since early 2017 even tourism came to a halt. With the thawing of relations between North and South from 2018 tourism and small-scale border trade rebounded, but this was short-lived due to the Covid-19 pandemic. Moreover, all kind of larger-scale investment is still illegal. Where there were once several Chinese banks, including subsidiaries of Chinese giants like the China Construction Bank, only one local bank, Golden Triangle bank, survived. The ban on labor exports also severely hampered ideas to build a large-scale industrial complex in Hunchun, where 3.000 North Korean workers were supposed to work for South Korean and Chinese companies.

Is there still a chance for making bilateral and trilateral cooperation viable? Rason did not remain the only special economic zone in North Korea. Besides two zones of a more political nature at the South Korean border, the Kumgangsan tourism zone and the Kaesong Industrial Complex, another zone in Yalu river (Hwanggumpyhong) was planned for Chinese investment, and at least 24 new economic development zones inside the country cover various sectors from agriculture to tourism to high-tech. All these zones, however, are not only not operating due to the Covid-19 crisis and sanctions virtually forbidding any investment in them but are also besides difficult to imagine as magnets for foreign investment. What makes these zones different from the rest of the country? While the first SEZ obviously tried to create controlled, closed islands of economic trial areas strongly disconnected from the rest of the country (in border areas fenced off from the rest of the country and only to be accessed with difficulty from inside the country or on islands in the river), the new economic development zones under Kim Jong-Un seem to be quite equally spread around the country. Ironically, until today they had almost zero success, mostly due to the sanctions, the lack of appropriate infrastructure and tangible economic benefits from investing in these zones (Seliger 2019). Tragically, beside that flexibility North Korea direly lacks a track record of successful foreign investment in SEZ or elsewhere. Instead, all larger investment projects – like Pyongwha Motors built by the "Unification church" or Orascom, the Egyptian-owned cell-phone business – ran into economic difficulties, after initial investment was done.

The fact is that North Korea economic development zones do not really offer an attractive deal compared to similar zones in other countries: access is possible (but not free, and not easy), telecommunication and internet connections exist (but are expensive, unreliable and cannot connect directly to local staff, but only to selected officials), there is no financial system available, and political risks (as well from inside the country, like expropriation, as from the UN system and the US) is high. Who should invest then in these zones? Rason is basically the same, but at least Rason has one tangible, and in the future maybe highly profitable, advantage, namely its access to the Pacific. This already now makes it profitable for China to direct bulk shipments like coal from Northern China to Southern China via Rason, and could in the future become a tangible competitive advantage. At the same time, also political risks, though existing for North Korea, are lower than everywhere else in the country. For sure, the fact that at a time dozens of Chinese business people from Yanji region drive through the zone, basically not closely monitored like the rest of foreigners in the country, seems risky. And, certainly, this leads to the inflow of Chinese, and often also South Korea information, music, films etc., the more so, since Yanbian region is ethnically largely Korean. But this is incomparable in effect to the same degree of openness, would it be practiced inside the country. The North Korean solution was to build a fence around Rason Special Zone, making the trip to and from the rest of North Korea to Rason almost equally difficult for North Koreans and foreigners alike as the trip across the country borders. By this, the negative effects of capitalism encroaching on North Korea can be relatively well isolated in Rason.

For China, the attractiveness of Rason has various facets: for the Manchurian region with 88 million consumers and important industrial cities as a whole, Rason offers a unique logistical advantage (access to the Pacific), a limited touristic value (the same, access to seaside resorts), including some culinary highlights, a source of maritime products, in particular fish and seafood, a limited base of processing trade, though that has never been very important, and other services, e.g. in the construction industry etc. It will not be likely to become a larger-scale industrial base, like the Chinese economic zones had been in the 1980s and 1990s. For this, experimentation with the market economy as a whole was necessary, i.e. liberalization of most prices, liberalization of the labor market, easy entry and exit etc. All of this is not given and was never intended (Seliger 2003, 2006). And for Russia? Here the advantages seem to be even more elusive. Certainly, there is a minimum amount of railway traffic in- and outcoming to DPRK via Rason, but for that any substantial investment in Rason is not really necessary. Indeed, many observers were puzzled by the fact that Russia went through with its determination to rent a pier in Rajin harbor, but China not. Speculations are that it is more a geo-political move or that the harbor might in busy times be a cheap anchor place for Russian ships (though it has never really been used as such until now). Business-wise, the investment in Rajin harbor seems to be rather loss-making. And, Vladivostok as an economic center, which took an enormous upswing with the APEC summit in 2012, does not diffuse so far into the neighborhood to affect Rason. There is a certain need for North Korean labor, maybe, in Far Eastern Russia for construction sites, forest labor etc., but there is no viable plan for a joint growth area (Seliger 2017).

As an isolated area with no connection to the hinterland, the success of Rason might be possible, but limited, once sanctions are eased, but it will not have a transforming quality for the North Korean economy as a whole. While fitting into the Chinese BRI, it can really only be the starting point for a truly integrated North Korean economy. And, liberalization, e.g., price liberalization, in the zone has to be seen not as an isolated policy, but as a trial to be extended if it is successful, to make an impact on the North Korean economy as a whole. This cannot be foreseen by now. Rather, special favors are granted to a limited number of companies in a limited geographical area. This falls short of the intentions of the BRI. So, while there is some potential in North Korea's special economic zone policy and in particular in Rason Special Zone, this has yet to come to fruition.

What does that mean for South Korea's hope for closer integration and inter-Korean cooperation? Rason should not be left out of view, but it certainly has a limited value as a potential place for inter-Korean cooperation. Given the political restrictions to special zones in general, and cooperation with South Korea in particular, models like Kaesong Industrial Complex or Kumgangsan Special tourism zone were much more likely to fulfill necessary political standards (of isolation of South Koreans) from the North Korean point of view (Wrobel 2014). Kalma beach resort in Wonsan might be another potential example for that. In the Golden Triangle, for the time being the South Korean influence could just be indirect, as in the planned logistics center and production hub in Hunchun. The influence of South Korean capital is already clearly visible in the Yanbian region, and more so the influence of South Korean lifestyle, through the migration of "*chosonsok*" (ethnic Koreans) to and from South Korea. A more direct influence, namely direct investment in Rason Special Zone, seems not to be likely in the future. South Korea can, however, have a different positive influence, by strengthening viable institutions for exchange, like the NEAR (North East Asian Association of Regions), the GTI (Greater Tumen Initiative) and other regional initiatives. South Korea could also try to ease the way of North Korea, and in particular Rason, into these initiatives. Given the weak existing institutions governing Rason (beside North Korean administration, in particular the joint North Korean-Chinese Investment council), every additional institutional structure aiming at opening Rason could be very helpful.

5. Conclusion: North Korea's No Belt, No Road policy and the future

To understand the North Korean reluctance to accept greater economic integration even in the case of China, its staunchest ally, and even if all the expenses are paid by someone else, namely the Chinese, it is important to see the interplay of economy and politics in North Korea's economic decision making. All analysis only looking at economic benefits fails to grasp the reality of North Korea. This has been the weakness of South Korea's Moon Jae-In administration, and also previous administrations, when they spoke of "co-benefits" or "mutually-beneficial" policy initiatives. While economically, this was true, the political costs for North Korea obviously outweighed the economic benefits. Clearly, there is not an exact mathematical formula for the benefits and costs, but it is dependent on the beliefs and perception of the North Korean leaders. Earlier potential ideological reasons for non-cooperation, which were already rather weak under Kim Jong-Il, became practically obsolete with Kim Jong-Un. There is no belief in economic superiority of socialist trade or centrally-planned economic development, but simply a belief that this is much easier to control politically. But then, still economic benefits have a huge attraction and may in actual policy-making outweigh the concerns on the political impact of such measures.

For example, in the thaw of 2018 between North and South Korea, North Korea held the belief for some time that the pronouncements of President Moon Jae-In of South Korea, that he could broker a disappearance of sanctions, and an era of co-prosperity, was genuine. And only the disappointment, that differently from its own political calculations, furthered by such South Korean promises, the USA would not accept a nuclear North Korea to normalize its economic relations, explains the later furious rejection of any dealings with South Korea. After the failure of direct negotiations with the USA, the Covid-19 pandemic in 2020 and 2021 made any new political strategy futile, but with the end of the pandemic North Korea will have the same strategic dilemma: should it integrate closer with China, improving its economy, but accepting an erosion of political control, should it even go further and embrace more reforms and maybe closer relations with South Korea? As said before, ideological reasons are no obstacle to this: inside the country, at least since 2009, when a botched currency reform had to be reversed, more market practices were accepted. They can partly explain the relatively successful economic development of North Korea in the 2010s, since in particular private service industries grew and made the whole economy more efficient. But such internal growth, if not coupled with external opening, including competitive pressure, but also the possibility of gains from trade, is limited. And during the Covid-19 pandemic, in times of distress, they were even partly revoked, to allow again more direct political control.

For the time being, "no belt, no road" seems to be the North Korean mantra. An increased ideological campaign for self-reliance actually began already in 2019, before Covid-19 induced self-isolation did actual started. In this situation, it might be necessary also to question the role sanctions play in North Korea's strategic thinking. While it is wrong to blame sanctions for the economic distress of North Korea – it is mainly a problem of inefficient institutional arrangements, i.e. the political intervention into markets – nevertheless it is not easy to defend sanctions which were unable to fulfill what they set out to do, namely preventing North Korea from developing nuclear weapons, and at the same time are directly opposed to the goal, the USA and South Korea, and to a lesser degree Japan and the European Union, as the main sponsors of sanctions, pronounced for the North Korea policy: namely, that North Korea should open up its economy and political system. There were points in time, like when North Korea accepted the South-North joint railway inspection, and when North Korea joined the BRI conference in Beijing, when they were obviously willing to go further in cooperation. Maybe, with isolation policies failing, it is time to give opening policies a try, helping North Korea to become again more integrated regionally, and worldwide?

References

Ahn, Se Hyun (2010): "Framing Energy Security Between Russia and South Korea?: Progress, Problems, and Prospects." Asian Survey, vol. 50, no. 3, 2010, pp. 591–614. JSTOR, www.jstor.org/stable/10.1525/as.2010.50.3.591. Accessed 5 Apr. 2021.

Bermudez, Joseph, et al. (2021): "Powering the Korean Peninsula: Economic and Strategic Considerations," Beyond Parallel, Center for Strategic and International Studies. Internet Link: https://beyondparallel.csis.org/powering-the-korean-peninsula-economic-and-strategic-considerations/ (Internet file retrieved 5 April 2021).

Devonshire-Ellis, Chris (2018): "North Korea Re-Connectivity Gradually Opening Up to the Belt and Road," Silk Road Briefing, Dezan Shira & Associates. Internet Link: https://www.silkroadbriefing.com/news/2018/09/20/north-korea-re-connectivity-gradually-opening-belt-road/ (Internet File retrieved 5 April 2021).

Devonshire-Ellis, Chris (2019): "North Korea's Future is with Belt and Road Reconstruction, Not with Washington Requesting Nobel Peace Prizes for President Trumps Ego," Silk road Briefing, Dezan Shira & Associates. Internet Link: https://www.silkroadbriefing.com/news/2019/02/27/north-koreas-future-belt-road-reconstruction-not-washington-requesting-nobel-peace-prizes-preside%E2%80%A6 (Internet File retrieved 5 April 2021).

Djankov, Simeon – Sean Miner (2016): "China's Belt and Road Initiative: Motives, Scope, and Challenges," PIIE Briefing 16–2, Peterson Institute for International Economics.

KCNA (n.d.): Research Results, online: https://kcnawatch.net/?s=belt+and+road.

Kenderdine, Tristan – Péter Bucsky (2020): "Rail Freight Use on China's Iron Silk Road Underdelivers," The Diplomat, Diplomat Media Incorporation. Internet Link: https://thediplomat.com/2020/11/rail-freight-use-on-chinas-iron-silk-road-underdelivers/ (Internet File retrieved 5 April 2021).

Kung, Chan and Yu Pan (2018): "How China's Belt and Road Initiative Went Astray" The Diplomat, Diplomat Media Incorporation. Internet Link: https://thediplomat.com/2020/05/how-chinas-belt-and-road-initiative-went-astray/ (Internet File retrieved 5 April 2021).

Lee, Dong Gyu (2021): "The Belt and Road Initiative after COVID: The Rise of Health and Digital Silk Roads," Foreign Relations/China, The Asan Institute for Policy Studies. Internet Link: http://en.asaninst.org/contents/the-belt-and-road-initiative-after-covid-the-rise-of-health-and-digital-silk-roads/ (Internet File retrieved 5 April 2021).

Lee, Tai Hwan (2016): "One Belt, One Road strategy and Korean-Chinese cooperation," Northeast Asia, IIAS The Newsletter, no. 74, p. 16.

Lee, Yusin (2013): "Potential Risks of the Russia-North Korea-South Korea Gas Pipeline: Is There Any Lesson Seoul Can Learn from the Russia-Ukraine Gas Dispute?" Asian Survey, vol. 53, no. 3, pp. 584–606.

Nobis, Adam (2017): "The New Silk Road, Old Concepts of Globalization, and New Questions." Open Cultural Studies, vol. 1, no. 1, pp. 203–213. Internet file: https://doi.org/10.1515/culture-2017-0019 (Internet file retrieved 5 April 2021).

OECD (2018): "The Belt and Road Initiative in the Global Trade, Investment and Finance Landscape", in OECD Business and Finance Outlook 2018, OECD Publishing, Paris, https://doi.org/10.1787/bus_fin_out-2018-6-en.

Panda, Ankit (2018): "Five Years Later: Reviewing China's Belt and Road Initiative," the Diplomat, Diplomat Media Incorporation. Internet Link: https://thediplomat.com/2018/09/five-years-later-reviewing-chinas-belt-and-road-initiative/ (Internet File retrieved 5 April 2021).

Parameswaran, Prashanth (2017): "The Real Trouble With China's Belt and Road," The Diplomat, Diplomat Media Incorporation. Internet Link: https://thediplomat.com/2017/05/the-real-trouble-with-chinas-belt-and-road/ (Internet File retrieved 5 April 2021).

Rolland, Nadège, et al. (2020): "An Emerging China-Centric Order: China's Vision for a New World Order in Practice," August 2020, NBR Special Report no. 87, The National Bureau of Asian Research.

Römer, Maximilian (2018): "One Belt, One Road, One Korea?" The Diplomat, Diplomat Media Incorporation. Internet Link: https://thediplomat.com/2018/02/one-belt-one-road-one-korea/ (Internet File retrieved 5 April 2021).

Seliger, Bernhard (2003): Die nordkoreanischen Sonderwirtschaftszonen – eine Wiederholung des chinesischen Erfolgsmodells? (North Korean spezial economic zones – a repetition of the Chinese success model?), in: Patrick Köllner (ed.), Korea 2003 – Politik, Wirtschaft, Gesellschaft, Hamburg: Institut für Asienkunde, pp. 262–285 (in German).

Seliger, Bernhard (2006): Towards a North Korea Boom? Special Economic Zones in North Korea and their Effects on the North and South Korean Economies, in: Seliger, Bernhard (mit Oh Yean-Cheon, Lee Dalgon, Park Sung-Jo), The Unification Research and Strategy in Korea and Germany: Affinity and Specificity, Seoul: Graduate School of Public Administration, Seoul National University, S. 93–122.

Seliger, Bernhard (2017): *Keukdonrossijaeui kyongjae* (The Economy of the Russian Far East), in: Segeshimin (The Global Citizen), no. 9, summer 2017, pp. 114–119 (in Korean).

Seliger, Bernhard (2019): Special Economic Zones in North Korea, in: KORUM (Korea Unternehmen Märkte). Journal of the German-Korean Chamber of Commerce and Industry, 2nd Quarter 2019, pp. 30–33.

Seliger, Bernhard (2020): North Korea's political economy: Hybrid economic institutions and the contributions of German order policy (Ordnungspolitik, Discourses in Social Market Economy), no. 2-2020, Ordnungspolitisches Portal, Internet file: http://ordnungspolitisches-portal.com/wp-content/uploads/2020/03/2020-2-SELIGER-Nordkorea.pdf (Internet File retrieved 5 April 2021).

Silberstein, Benjamin (2019): "The North Korean Economy, August 2019: Why China Will Continue to Dominate," 38 North, The Henry L. Stimson Center. Internet Link: https://www.38north.org/2019/09/bkatzeffsilberstein091019/ (Internet File retrieved 5 April 2021).

Song, Min-Geun (2019): "The Characteristics of South Korea's New Northern Policy and Cooperation with Eurasia Countries' Initiatives Focused on China, Mongolia and Russia." Journal of Digital Convergence, vol. 17, no. 7, pp. 1–13.

UN [United Nations] (n.d.): *UN, United Nations, UN Treaties, Treaties*. United Nations. https://treaties.un.org/Pages/ViewDetails.aspx?src=TREATY&mtdsg_no=XI-B-34&chapter=11&clang=_en.

Ward Peter (2018): "How North Korea fits into China's Belt and Road Initiative," NK PRO, Korea Risk Group. Internet Link: https://www.nknews.org/pro/how-north-korea-fits-into-chinas-belt-and-road-initiative/ (Internet File retrieved 5 April 2021).

Wikimedia (2021a): Main linkages of the One Belt, One Road Initiative, https://commons.wikimedia.org/wiki/File:One-belt-oneroad.svg.

Wikimedia (2021b): Main routes of the original silk road, https://commons.wikimedia.org/wiki/File:Seidenstrasse_GMT.jpg.

Wrobel, Ralph (2014): "Ten Years of Kaesong Industrial Complex: A Brief History of the Last Economic Cooperation Project of the Korean Peninsula," Economic and Environmental Studies, Uniwersytet Opolski, Opole: CEFOL, vol. 14, no. 2, pp. 125–147.

Anastasia Barannikova

South Korea, China and the Road and Belt Initiative: Economic and political factors

1. Introduction

Recent incident in the Suetz Canal, which impacted 12 % of global trade and caused trade losses estimated at tens of billions of dollars (Das 2021), highlighted the need to diversify transport and supply chains. Ongoing impacts of COVID-2019 pandemic, disrupting global trade, economics and logistics, have made that need even more urgent. Alternative transportation routes and supply chains are required to ensure reliable and uninterrupted delivery of medicines and equipment. Many countries have proposed new land-, sea- and hybrid routes long ago before pandemic. Among them, for instance, Russian Northern Sea Route, Chinese Polar Silk Route etc. However, the development and use of polar routes is associated with a number of difficulties. These routes are not navigable all year round. Specific conditions create additional risks for ships and crews and increase shipping costs. Moreover, relevant infrastructure has not yet been built along the NSR (Levick 2018). At the same time there are some promising transport and logistic projects – those provided by the One Belt, One Road initiative (OBOR) (sometimes referred to as Belt and Road Initiative (BRI)) proposed and implemented by China since 2013.

OBOR megaproject provides for modernization and use of numerous land and sea transport and economic corridors connecting Asian, European, and African countries. It is focused on investments, mainly in infrastructure projects in Central and Southeast Asia, Africa, and Europe. However, the initiative also provides economic opportunities for the regions in Northeast Asia. Particularly, three northern Chinese provinces – Liaoning, Jilin, and Heilongjiang – are planned to become part of a Northeast Asian economic zone, which could link Russia, Mongolia, and possibly the Korean Peninsula.

The initiative was first mentioned by Xi Jinping during his visits to Kazakhstan in September 2013 and Indonesia in October of the same year. Later it was promoted in Asia and Europe during state visits of Chinese premier Li Keqiang. On 28 March 2015, China's government released "Vision and Actions on Jointly Building Silk Road Economic Belt and 21st-Century Maritime Silk Road", a detailed plan for the OBOR strategy implementation.

The scale of OBOR can be compared with those of other integration megaprojects like European Union and Eurasian Economic Union. EU is the largest economic bloc, the EAEU covers the largest territory in the world, and OBOR involves the biggest share of the world's population (over 60 % of the world's population including China and member countries).

By the moment implementation of OBOR is temporarily slowed down and the project is being adjusted to new realities – global economic recession caused by pandemic and trade war between China and the US. There are also obstacles permanently affecting the implementation of the initiative. 138 countries and 31 international organization signed cooperation documents and joined Chinese initiative as of December 23, 2020 (PRC Ministry of Foreign Affairs 2020). Participation of such a big number of countries is itself a problem. Along with economic diversity, these countries have their own political interests, considerations and goals, different positions on international issues and problems in international relations. All these factors will sooner or later affect their cooperation with China through OBOR. The present paper considers cooperation between China and ROK through OBOR where the influence of these factors is most pronounced.

2. China – ROK economic cooperation

China and ROK have long been trade partners. Since the two countries established formal diplomatic relations in the 1990s, their cooperation in both economics and politics has developed rapidly. Economic cooperation between the two countries invigorated significantly after Xi Jinping was elected president of the PRC and Park Geun-hye, the Saenuri party candidate, won the presidential election in ROK in 2013. The two leaders exchanged multiple visits and reinforced bilateral strategic cooperation and partnership. On June 27, 2013 they released a joint statement on the future vision of China-South Korea relations. This document included directions, principles, and key areas for strengthening bilateral relations and developing strategic partnership (Hwang 2014).

Park Geun-hye outlined her economic vision for the region at the Global Cooperation in the Era of Eurasia conference in October 2013, where she announced the "Eurasia Initiative". This ambitious initiative called for interconnection of transportation, logistics, and energy networks across Europe and Asia, promotion of the "Silk Road Express (SRX) project" and the use of potential of the Arctic Ocean to develop intermodal transport and logistics network in the region (ROK Ministry of Foreign Affairs n.d.). By implementing EAI and involving in Eurasia integration processes ROK expected to save transportation costs and diversify trade markets for energy and mineral resources and agricultural products. Implementation of EAI could give South Korea access to train routes across Eurasia, reducing the logistics costs for its exports to Europe by up to 30 %. This integration was to be followed by the gradual elimination of trade barriers and the creation of an extensive free trade zone. Important role was given to peace building on the Korean Peninsula. In particular, Eurasian Initiative envisaged for "building corridors of trust and peace on the Korean Peninsula" through the Rajin-Khasan logistics project implemented by Russia and the DPRK and more active role of the DPRK (ROK Ministry of Foreign Affairs n.d.).

South Korea expressed interest in China's OBOR, as the New Silk Road was in line with its Eurasia Initiative and could contribute to establishing peace on the Korean Peninsula. The two countries exchanged positive statements on cooperation in this area. Foreign minister of China Wang Yi stressed the synergic effects of the linkage between South Korea's EAI and China's OBOR strategy when he met with Park Geun-hye in Seoul in 2014. Later, when Xi Jinping visited Seoul in July 2014, Park Geun-hye noted that efforts should be made to link the Eurasia Initiative to China's New Silk Road plan (Kim 2015). Chinese side, in its turn, put forward a number of tangible and practical suggestions for merging the two initiatives. Two countries reached bilateral free trade agreement (FTA) by 2015. FTA among other things was tasked to provide institutional foundation and internal motivation for two countries' initiatives strategic synergy.

EAI proposed by Korean government had many points of possible cooperation with China under the OBOR initiative, including creation of Northeast Asian economic zone. So, it was not surprising that both sides were interested to find the ways of cooperation through their two initiatives. Chinese "Vision and Actions" plan envisages the development of three northeastern provinces – Liaoning, Jilin, and Heilongjiang – and making them sea-land "windows" linking Russia, Mongolia, and other areas in the Far East. One of the key projects of the Eurasia Initiative was the construction of the Silk Road Express with Trans-Korean railway and transcontinental railroads as its main axes (State Council of the PRC 2017). China was already implementing business projects related to transportation infrastructure in North Korea. Progress has also been made in implementation of Trans-Korean railway project of Russia. Renovation of the railway from Russia's Khasan to Rajin port in North Korea was completed by 2014 by a joint venture between Russian Railways and North Korea (TASS 2017).

ROK expressed interest and was expected to become the third party to the project. However, due to strained relations between South and North Korea, ROK could not join either of two (China's and Russia's) projects and implement its own Silk Road Express.

Moon Jae-in who came to power in ROK in 2017 put forward New Northern Policy providing for more active cooperation with countries situated north of the Korean Peninsula (including Russia, Mongolia and Central Asian stated) and building so-called «nine bridges» connecting transportation, logistics, and energy infrastructure of the Korean Peninsula to the rest of the Eurasian landmass. The Vision of new initiative provided, among other things, for implementing Trans-Korean projects of economic cooperation (with participation of Russia, DPRK and ROK). Moon Jae-in's initiative also has many points of cooperation with China's OBOR. Particularly, it provides for «pushing ahead with projects in connection with «One Belt, One Road» and multilateral cooperation projects involving the three Northeastern provinces of China; developing and promoting projects in connection with the China-Mongolia-Russia Economic Corridor initiative using AIIB and GTI (reviewing the possibility of resuming suspended projects, such as the development of an international logistics complex in Hunchun); increasing the use of the Trans-China Railway (TCR) and Trans-Mongolian Railway (TMGR) and ultimately re-connecting ROK and North Korean railways» (Presidential Committee 2017). In December 2017, Xi Jinping and Moon Jae-in jointly announced to launch the second phase of the China-ROK FTA negotiations. Since the assumption of power by Moon Jae-in was marked by Inter-Korean rapprochement, the hopes for the implementation of Trans-Korean Railway project revived as well. However, despite stressing a need for cooperation between OBOR and New Northern Policy there are still divergences between the two countries' political positions.

Despite the ambitions and intentions of president Moon to improve relations with the North and involve in Trans-Korean projects, the South Koreans even did not join the Khasan-Rajin logistics project – part of the Trans-Korean Railway, which was excluded from the UNSC sanctions against the DPRK. South Korean businesses seem reluctant to join the projects involving participation of North Korea (even through the mediatorship of Russia and China), fearing possible unilateral US sanctions (Do 2020). Neither ROK government could obtain sanctions relief and guarantees for South Korean businesses against legal harassment by the US in the case of their participation in such cooperation. The stalemate in the US-DPRK dialog and renewed Inter-Korean tensions have added to the obstacles to this cooperation.

3. Problems

3.1. Political factors

The main problem of implementing Eurasian Initiative was its excessive politicizing. The title of the Initiative – "Opening and Denuclearization of North Korea through the Peaceful Prosperity of Eurasia" – clearly indicates ultimate goals and expectations of the ROK associated with cooperation with China and other countries through this initiative. The policy goals in connection with the project were further made clear by Hyun Kyung-dae, executive vice-chairperson of the National Unification Advisory Council: "the main purpose of the mega project is the creation of "a giant wave" of peace and prosperity in Eurasian societies, which will arise in Europe, Southwest Asia and the Middle East as a reason for the restructuring, opening up and renunciation of nuclear weapons by North Korea as well as the improvement of human rights in the North. We can use the Eurasian countries as a lever to persuade North Korea" (Hyun 2013).

Moon Jae-in's New Northern policy rhetoric is much less assertive and is focused on engagement of North Korea rather than pressure. At the same time North Korea still seems to be the key reason behind the New Northern Policy, while the unresolved nuclear issue of the Korean Peninsula remains its main obstacle.

On the one hand, the main goal of the projects promoted and supported by ROK is cooperation on the Korean Peninsula, which would help stabilize the situation in the region. On the other hand, ROK, in fact, makes its participation in the Chinese OBOR project (as well as in other Eurasian integration initiatives) dependent on the improvement of inter-Korean relations (Khabar 2019). Given the fact that inter-Korean relations, in turn, are made by ROK government dependent on the denuclearization of the DPRK, this condition seems impossible: the failed US policy and the current level of the DPRK nuclear and missile program make any talks on its unilateral disarmament meaningless. Mentioning inter-Korean relations in connection with the OBOR may well be another attempt to make China press on the DPRK and resolve notorious «nuclear issue». However, relations with the DPRK are no less valuable for China than relations with the ROK. China has certain leverage but it would press on the DPRK only to achieve its own goals, not those of ROK or any other country. And it would demonstrate its position on the DPRK through different signals like famous speech by Xi Jinping to mark the anniversary of China's entry into the Korean War (Ser 2020).

It should be noted that the period of revival of China's relations with ROK after new leaders assumed power in both countries coincided with temporary cooling of its relations with the DPRK after the execution of Jang Sung Taek (who was considered an agent of influence of China in North Korea) and course of Kim Jong Un on self-reliance and balancing China. This can explain why Xi Jinping visited Seoul first instead of Pyongyang in July 2014. At the same time, this was perceived by ROK as a shift in priorities in China's policy on the Korean Peninsula and could give false hopes for its government to achieve political goals through cooperation with China. However, the fourth nuclear test conducted by the DPRK in 2016 and ROK's decision on deployment of the THAAD systems, negatively perceived by China, revealed discrepancies in the policy priorities of the two countries.

As long as two countries are in opposing camps in terms of politics, making economic cooperation (through Chinese megaproject or regional initiatives) dependent on political factors is a miscalculation for ROK government. This approach only hinders economic cooperation and even implementation of country's own projects such as Eurasian Initiative and the New Northern Policy.

At the same time, OBOR cannot be unambiguously characterized as an economic project, too. Experts point that despite prioritizing economic component and denying geopolitical motives, OBOR is aimed not only at promoting economic cooperation, but also at increasing China's cultural and political influence. OBOR initiative itself can be perceived as a grand strategy of China (Cheng Guo 2019). These characteristics of Chinese megaproject create additional challenges for ROK participation, given that ROK is bound by allied commitments to the United States, China's geopolitical rival.

3.2. US-China rivalry

ROK relations with the United States will continue to influence its willingness and readiness to cooperate with China through the OBOR project. The United States has already demonstrated its negative attitude towards the Chinese initiative. American media and think tanks are carrying out information campaigns to discredit OBOR, pointing out threats to the sovereignty of countries cooperating with China through the initiative, the lack of transparency of Chinese projects, corruption, etc. The US military sees the Belt and Road as an instrument of strategic expansion, and suspects that cargo ports involved in the project will become the bases of the Chinese Navy in future (Bespalov 2019). It is clear that another "China threat" inflation is just a part of information warfare in the context of growing rivalry between the United States and China. However, the allies of the United States, especially ROK, having ties with China, may face a difficult choice as a result of big powers struggle. The ROK does not have an unambiguous opinion either about the alliance with the United States, or about relations with China and a vision of how these relations should develop. Some experts hint that the United States should thwart Beijing's attempts aimed at decoupling Seoul from Washington, for example, by bringing US-ROK economic cooperation to a level that would weaken ROK's economic dependence on China. It is also recommended to revise the existing military-political alliance and/or strengthen in with an economic component. At the same time, there are also different opinions in ROK, such as calls for strengthening own military forces, weakening dependence on the United States and, as a consequence, more freedom in relations with China (in fact, closer relations with it) (Kwon 2021). Nevertheless, since the US-ROK alliance remains in force, and new US administration has declared "revitalization" of the alliance as one of its priorities (Ferrier 2021), the ROK will presumably continue to take an uncertain position on participation in China's megaproject.

Some observers argue that Beijing wants to weaken Washington's military-political alliance with Seoul and Tokyo, viewing the real goal of that alliance as to "contain China", rather than to deter the DPRK (Boc 2017). In order to weaken the alliance, China can both maintain tension in the region and exert influence on the ROK. Being South Korea's largest foreign trading partner, Beijing has the required leverage to apply economic pressure, particularly given how export-dependent the ROK economy is. Opinion polls show that South Koreans regard China as the most powerful country in the region, and that its influence will continue to grow further.

3.3. China economic growth concerns

China's economic influence growth cannot but cause concerns in ROK. By gaining new accesses to the Eurasian market through implementation of its own initiatives, South Korea hopes to become less dependent on trade with China. It is sufficient to recall that South Korean government announced its Eurasian Initiative soon after China outlined its OBOR. ROK may consider Chinese megaproject prospective and economically beneficial but at the same time it is interested in maintaining independence and the status of an equal partner of China while cooperating through OBOR or any other initiative.

On the one hand, the economic cooperation has always been the most important element in China-ROK relations (Fig. 1: Economically important countries, as viewed from the ROK. Source: Genron 2017, 2018, 2019.). Even during the

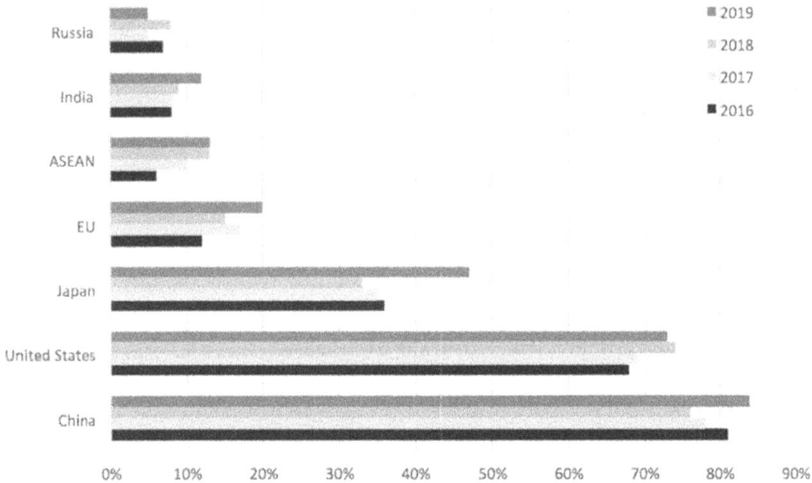

Fig. 1: Economically important countries, as viewed from the ROK. Source: Genron 2017, 2018, 2019.

periods of temporary cooling between two countries their bilateral relations could be characterized as «cold politics and hot economics».

On the other hand, experts use the term "asymmetrical interdependence" to describe China-ROK economic relations, which means that though two countries are interdependent and have been important trading partners for each other, South Korea depends much more deeply on China than China does on South Korea (Ren 2016).

ROK already could feel the consequences of this asymmetrical interdependence after making decision to accept THAAD systems deployment in 2016 (Fig. 2: South Korea exports to China. Source: Trading Economics n.d.; Fig. 3: South Korea imports from China. Source: Trading Economics n.d.). Soon after that decision China started economic pressure on ROK by imposing informal sanctions against its firms, cultural products and introducing ban on tourism. The sanctions over THAAD cost South Korea billions of dollars (Panda 2017). Importantly, that case has demonstrated how prepared China is to use economic leverage for political purposes. As the trade war between the US and China is going on, similar negative scenario for South Korea may repeat. From this point ROK may fear even greater involvement in Chinese projects, which would inevitably lead to increased dependence on China.

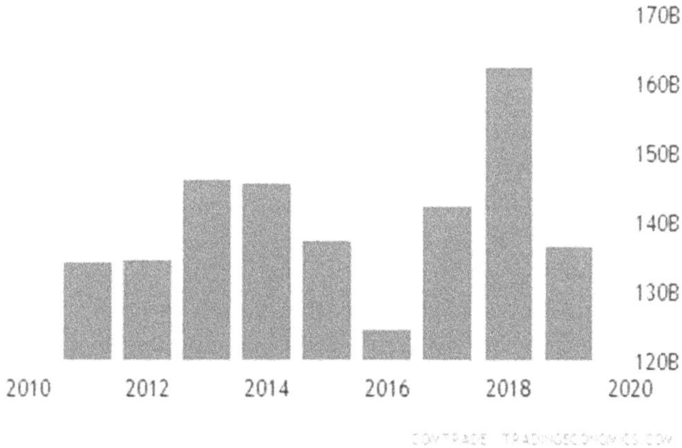

Fig. 2: South Korea exports to China. Source: Trading Economics n.d.

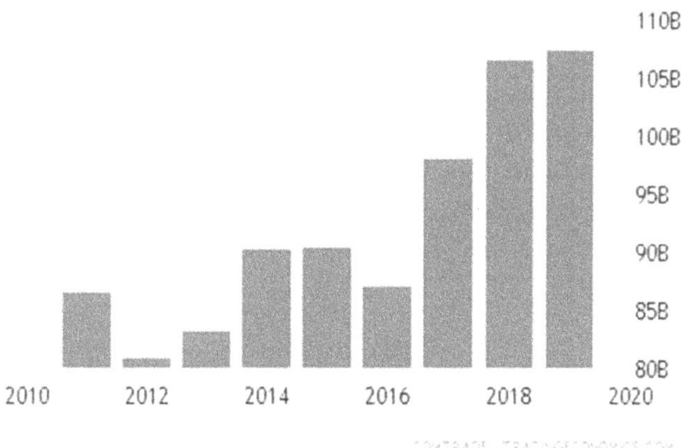

Fig. 3: South Korea imports from China. Source: Trading Economics n.d.

3.4. China's «divide and control» strategy on the Korean Peninsula

While both the OBOR and EAI or New Northern policy could be compatible with each other in terms of economic integration and cooperation, each country's vision for national and regional security are conflicting. The same are the goals pursued by countries in connection with implementation of their strategic projects. Thus, when speaking about the EAI, and then about the New Northern Policy,

South Korean officials consistently emphasized the role the initiatives would play in bringing peace and prosperity to the Korean Peninsula. The underlying goal of the EAI was to develop cooperation on the Korean Peninsula in order to create a more stable security environment and help ROK promote its interests. OBOR pursues broader objectives and excludes any remarks about the development of the Korean Peninsula, partly because it is not so important for China as for ROK. Another reason may be the interests of the Chinese government on the Korean Peninsula and the desire to maintain *status quo* of a divided Korea.

The Korean peninsula is a strategically important region that China has always tried to control. Tensions on the peninsula are in interest of Beijing as long as it keeps these tensions under its control. Escalating tensions would give China an opportunity to mediate between the DPRK on one side and the US and ROK on the other, being the only power that maintains close relations with Pyongyang. Such a position would offer China certain advantages during negotiations with the United States on other matters.

China's influence on the DPRK has drastically increased after the adoption of the UNSC Resolution 2375 in September 2017. As a result, China has monopolized trade relations with the DPRK and has become the only power that can exert pressure on both the DPRK and the United States: Beijing can increase the pressure of sanctions on Pyongyang to make its leadership more pliable, or it can ease that pressure in order to gain concessions from Washington (Lankov 2018).

China's top priorities are maintaining security in the region, preventing a military conflict, averting instability, and generally keeping situation under control. For the sake of stability and predictability, China may even be ready to sacrifice North Korea's nuclear disarmament. That explains why China refrains from active support of any measures that would seriously hurt the North Korean economy.

China's rhetoric and attitude toward nuclear status of the DPRK also changed for recent years. Some remarks by Chinese experts have indicated that China may be willing to reconcile itself to a nuclear-armed DPRK (Sherwell 2017). It therefore cannot be ruled out that the Chinese leadership hopes to preserve and increase its influence on Pyongyang in future. In such a case, a DPRK armed with a small nuclear arsenal will not represent a threat to China. Beijing can also turn a "blind eye" to North Korean nuclear program because it is an obstacle to inter-Korean rapprochement, which would not serve China's interests. Since China regards the entire Korean peninsula as the sphere of its strategic interests, it tries to keep the South under control as well as. At the same time, it monitors closely inter-Korean relations and interfere when the countries' ties become, in Beijing opinion, too close.

China's interests on the Korean Peninsula and its «divide and control» strategy run counter to Seoul's official rhetoric and goals of denuclearization and unification and thus may become another serious obstacle to ROK's participation in OBOR projects or merging two countries economic initiatives.

4. Prospects

If the US fail to revitalize the alliance (which already has multiple problems such as relations between ROK and Japan, doubts in readiness of the US to protect allies in the case of conflict, etc.) or propose adequate alternative to China's economic cooperation, it cannot be ruled out that pro-Chinese sentiments will return in ROK. In the Roh Moo-hyun era, South Koreans embraced a pro-China policy. As a result, the younger generation believed that China was more important than the US in the long term and supported closer ties with China to balance the influence of the US. Similar sentiments arose beginning in 2013 (Ren 2016).

Also, as ROK is being decoupled from the United States (by China or its own will), it may gradually shift from the West-oriented concept of a unipolar world and adopt a new concept of multipolarity, promoted by China, Russia and a number of other countries. It is this concept that projects for the integration of Greater Eurasia, including China's OBOR, are based on. As long as ROK will politicize economic cooperation projects and make economic cooperation with China dependent on its relations with the United States, policy towards the DPRK and KPNI, security issues, especially those concerning North Korea, will hamper the development of China-ROK bilateral relations. At the same time there is a chance that ROK, driven by the same political considerations, will not join unconditionally US-led projects.

The pandemic has made adjustments not only in the development of the economy, transport and supply chains. It provided China with an opportunity to expand and modernize its Belt and Road cooperation agenda. One of the most interesting ideas is Health Silk Road Initiative. China's opponents consider this initiative as plan to supply of vaccines to other countries in order to gain a strategic advantage in competing with the United States for global leadership. However, this initiative has much broader meaning and goes far beyond just providing vaccines and medicines. We are talking about cooperation in different spheres in the post-covid period, which implies that OBOR will be aimed at combating the economic consequences of the pandemic and restoring the global economy.

Despite all the difficulties and obstacles OBOR proved to be viable project even during pandemic. Trade between China and its OBOR partners rose from

$ 1.04 to $ 1.34 trillion from 2013 to 2019. In 2020 it showed 1.5 % growth. Over the 7 years of the initiative's implementation, trade between China and countries that joined OBOR has exceeded $ 7.8 trillion.

Even in conditions of a large-scale suspension and disruption of logistic chains from January to April of 2020 the number of container trains and the volume of cargo turnover between China and Europe not only did not fall, but increased by 24 % and 27 %, respectively, compared to the same period of 2019. The route was used to deliver tons of anti-epidemic cargo (Zhang 2021).

In the post-virus period, the need for economic development and cooperation in the sphere of public health is expected to increase. In this connection China works on involving its OBOR partners in projects to implement Health Silk Road, Digital Silk Road and other initiatives that are aimed at restoring global economy. For example, since it is impossible to hold large-scale events including those devoted to OBOR and other global projects offline, China proposes to use the "Digital Silk Road" and "information corridor" (PRC Ministry of Foreign Affairs 2021).

China, which was the first to take control of the epidemic and restart its economy, has high chances to head and lead the process of recovering global economic system. Its OBOR megaproject, if updated to meet new challenges, will be efficient and promising and ROK in one way or another will look for the ways to participate in it. At the same time, Chinese initiative will likely be implemented in any case, with or without ROK participation. OBOR provides for multiple transport corridors outside the Korean Peninsula (for example, through Russia, Mongolia or Central Asia). However, it should not be ruled out that attempts to attract ROK to the project will intensify in the case of imbalance within the China – ROK – US triangle in favor of the latter. In this case China may start involving ROK more actively in order to put it closer to China's orbit.

To conclude, the main problems of interaction between China and ROK through the OBOR project lie in the political sphere, or rather, in the divergence of political interests and goals of the countries in connection with the project. OBOR undoubtedly has geopolitical significance. This is recognized not only by Western and Russian scholars, but also by Chinese experts. From this point, the project is intended to strengthen regional security and stability, as well as meet China's interests in deepening trade and economic ties with its neighbors. From the point of foreign policy, China views the initiative as a comprehensive plan to promote its interests globally. Interest of ROK to the project, along with natural desire to develop new transport and logistics routes, is also determined by political goals, but these goals are limited to establishing peace and security on the Korean Peninsula. China's interest in ROK's participation in its megaproject is largely determined by economic considerations. From a political point of view, China can consider the project and ROK's participation in it as an additional lever of influence on the ROK. China, which considers Korean Peninsula as its sphere of influence, is not interested in increasing the role and influence of other countries, including ROK. OBOR is based on existing mechanisms of China's bilateral relations with foreign countries and from this point China prefers to develop relations with the DPRK and ROK separately. It is also in line with Chinese "divide and control" strategy. Rapprochement of the countries of the Korean Peninsula and diversification of their trade partners would decrease the role of China and boost integration processes on the peninsula, which is not in interests of China.

Another problem is relations of ROK with the US and current US-China rivalry. By implementing OBOR projects China creates the belt of friendly states, including Russia, Central Asian and some North and South East Asian states. It will give China necessary resources and support in competition for global leadership. Therefore, the US will not only oppose Chinese megaprojects and counter them with their own initiatives but also discourage its allies, especially ROK, from joining China's initiatives. Cooperation of China and ROK through the OBOR project thus will be determined not only by US-China relations but also by ability of the ROK leadership to balance between the two big powers.

References

Bespalov, Anton (2019) *Global China and the fears of its neighbors.* Valdai Discussion Club. January 7, 2019. https://ru.valdaiclub.com/a/highlights/globalnyy-kitay-i-strakhi-ego-sosedey/

Boc, Anny (2017) *For Beijing, the greatest threat to China's national security is not the Kim regime: it is the US.* The Conversation. December 1, 2017. http://theconversation.com/for-beijing-the-greatest-threat-to-chinas-national-security-is-not-the-kim-regime-it-is-the-us-88271

Cheng Guo, Chen Lu, Degterev Denis Andreevich, and Zhao Jielin (2019) *Implications of "One Belt, One Road" strategy for China and Eurasia.* RUDN: Forein Relations. 2019. №1. URL: https://cyberleninka.ru/article/n/implications-of-one-belt-one-road-strategy-for-china-and-eurasia

Das, Koustav (2021) *Explained: How much did Suez Canal blockage cost world trade.* India Today. March 30, 2021. https://www.indiatoday.in/business/story/explained-how-much-did-suez-canal-blockage-cost-world-trade-1785062-2021-03-30

Do Je-hae (2020) *Moon's New Northern Policy gaining spotlight.* The Korea Times. February 21, 2020. http://www.koreatimes.co.kr/www/nation/2020/02/356_283818.html

Ferrier, Kyle (2021) *Biden Takes the Right First Steps With South Korea, But a Long Road Lies Ahead.* The Diplomat. March 12, 2021. https://thediplomat.com/2021/03/biden-takes-the-right-first-steps-with-south-korea-but-a-long-road-lies-ahead/

Genron NPO and East Asia Institute (2017) *The 5th Japan-South Korea Joint Public Opinion Poll: Analysis Report on Comparative Data* (Tokyo: Genron NPO and East Asia Institute, 2017), http://www.genron-npo.net/en/opinion_polls/archives/5363.html

Genron NPO and East Asia Institute (2018) *The 6th Japan-South Korea Joint Public Opinion Poll: Analysis Report on Comparative Data* (Tokyo: Genron NPO and East Asia Institute, 2018), http://www.genron-npo.net/en/180618.pdf

Genron NPO and East Asia Institute (2019) *The 7th Japan-South Korea Joint Public Opinion Poll:Analysis Report on Comparative Data* (Tokyo: Genron NPO and East Asia Institute, 2019), https://www.genron-npo.net/en/7th-Japan-South%20KoreaJointOpinionPoll.pdf

Hwang, Jaeho (2014) *The ROK's China Policy under Park Geun-Hye: a New Model of ROK-PRC Relations.* The Brookings Institution Center for East Asia Policy Studies. 2014. https://www.brookings.edu/wp-content/uploads/2016/06/south-korea-china-policy-hwang-working-paper.pdf

Hyun, Kyung-Dae (2013) *President Park Geun-hye's 'Eurasia Initiative'.* National Unification Advisory Council. October 24, 2013. https://www.nuac.go.kr/ntcnBbs/detail.do

Khabar (2019) *Korea has not joined the Chinese "One Belt, One Road" project.* 24. December 31, 2019. https://www.zakon.kz/video/v/205319.html

Kwon, Peter (2021) SUNY Albany. *South Korea's ongoing quest for security indepenence.* East Asia Forum. January 20, 2021. https://www.eastasiaforum.org/2021/01/20/south-koreas-ongoing-quest-for-security-independence/

Lankov, Andrey (2018) *Third participant. What role does China play in the negotiations between Kim and Trump?* Carnegie Moscow Center. June 13, 2018. https://carnegie.ru/commentary/76582

Levick, Ewen (2018) *The drawbacks of Arctic shipping.* Global Risks Insights. February 8, 2018. https://globalriskinsights.com/2018/02/risks-limits-northern-sea-route/

Panda, Ankit (2017) *China and South Korea: Examining the Resolution of the THAAD Impasse.* The Diplomat. November 13, 2017. https://thediplomat.com/2017/11/china-and-south-korea-examining-the-resolution-of-the-thaad-impasse/

PRC Ministry of Foreign Affairs (2020) Questions and Answers by Member of State Council, Minister of Foreign Affairs Wang Yi at a press conference on China's foreign policy and international relations, May 24, 2020, Ministry of Foreign Affairs of the People's Republic of China official web-site, https://www.fmprc.gov.cn/rus/wjdt/zyjh/t1782419.shtml

PRC Ministry of Foreign Affairs (2021) Questions and Answers by Member of State Council, Minister of Foreign Affairs Wang Yi at a press conference on China's foreign policy and international relations, March 8, 2021, Ministry of Foreign Affairs of the People's Republic of China official web-site, https://www.fmprc.gov.cn/rus/wjdt/zyjh/t1859896.shtml

Presidential Committee (2017) Vision. Strategy. The Presidential Committee on Northern Economic Co-operation. 2017. https://www.bukbang.go.kr/bukbang_en/vision_policy/strategy/

Ren, Yuanzhe, Yu Tiejun, and Wang Junsheng (2016) *Chinese Perspectives: Towards the Korean Peninsula in the Aftermath of North Korea's Fourth Nuclear Test.* Report. Stimson Center. 2016. http://www.jstor.org/stable/resrep10996.7

ROK Ministry of Foreign Affairs n.d., www.mofa.go.kr

Ser, Myo-Ja (2020) *Xi takes digs at U.S. in Korean War speech.* Korea JoongAng Daily. October 23, 2020. https://koreajoongangdaily.joins.com/2020/10/23/national/politics/Xi-Jinping-North-Korea-Korean-War/20201023174100386.html

Sherwell, Peter (2017) *China accepts nuclear North Korea and thinks US must do so too.* The Times. December 3, 2017. https://www.thetimes.co.uk/article/china-accepts-nuclear-north-and-thinks-us-must-do-so-too-qw59p5v2t

South Korea Exports to China. Trading Economics n.d. https://tradingeconomics.com/south-korea/exports-to-china

South Korea Imports from China. Trading Economics n.d. https://tradingeconomics.com/south-korea/imports-from-china

Taehwan, Kim (2015) *Beyond Geopolitics: South Korea's Eurasia Initiative as a New Nordpolitik.* The Asan Institute for Policy Studies. February 16, 2015. http://www.theasanforum.org/beyond-geopolitics-south-koreas-eurasia-initiative-as-a-new-nordpolitik/

TASS (2017) *Republic of Korea eyeing return to Khasan-Rajin railway project.* TASS. November 8, 2017. https://tass.com/economy/974495

The State Council of the People's Republic of China (2017) Full text of the Vision for aritime Cooperation under the Belt and Road Initiative June 20, 2017. http://english.www.gov.cn/archive/publications/2017/06/20/content_281475691873460.htm#:~:text=In%202015%2C%20China%20issued%20The,bonds%2C%20adhering%20to%20the%20principle

Zhang, Hanhui (2021) *"One Belt, One Road": to open the way for mutual benefit.* Embassy of People's Republic of China in Russian Federation. January 16, 2021. http://ru.china-embassy.org/rus/sghd/t1846717.htm

Part III: Destinations of the Belt and Road Initiative

Werner Pascha

Duisburg and its port, endpoint of China's Silk Road – Opportunities and risks

1. Introduction: Interesting times

In 2020, China was again, for the fifth time in a row, Germany´s most important trading partner. Despite the Corona pandemic and its economic effects, the bilateral trade volume actually has increased by 3 % compared to 2019 (Statistisches Bundesamt 2021). At the same time, the political relations between the EU and China and also between Germany and China have worsened considerably in recent months. While China and the EU reached a well-publicized draft accord for a bilateral Comprehensive Investment Agreement in late 2020, the ratification was recently put at risk, after Chinese sanctions against European legislators, academics and institutions that followed earlier, considerably more limited European sanctions against a number of Chinese citizens based on human rights issues, the first such sanctions since the Tianmen Incident of 1989. The atmosphere has become quite tense, with important voices like the London-based Economist getting concerned about what they consider China´s and its Communist Party´s "aggressive diplomacy" (Economist, 3 April 2021). In late March 2021, Günther Oettinger contributed an article to the Berlin-based newspaper "Der Tagesspiegel" with the title "How China is hijacking Europe´s ports and container ships" (Oettinger 2021; translated by WP). This is a remarkably assertive wording for someone who has served as premier of one of Germany´s major states and later as EU Commissioner for Energy and for Budget.

The question, to what extent the EU, Germany, its states or individual localities can and should cooperate with China has thus gained an unimagined urgency in recent months. For a city like Duisburg, located within the state of North Rhine-Westphalia (NRW) along the rivers Rhine and Ruhr and part of the Ruhr area, this has become particularly acute. It has enjoyed an almost global reputation as the "western terminus of the new silk road", with newspapers like the Washington Post, the Guardian or the NZZ (Neue Zürcher Zeitung) picking up such terminology. The mayor of Duisburg, Mr. Sören Link, has famously proclaimed that Duisburg wants to become the "China city of Germany" ("China-Stadt", e.g. Michel 2019), but one wonders whether in economic and in political terms that is still a feasible option.

The following paper will deal with this open question. In the first part, the economic situation of Duisburg will be outlined and put into perspective. It will turn out that Duisburg has not recovered from the decline of coal and steel industries yet and that profiting from the Chinese interest in its logistics network is one of the few options to regain some economic strength. In the following part, the relationship between Duisburg´s economy and the China rail link will be explored. Our main conclusions are that the majority of beneficial effects has probably already been realized and that positive linkage effects with other regional industries seem rather limited. Finally, we will look at the political dimension of the cooperative relationship, including political risks. The tentative conclusion is that for a city like Duisburg as part of an affluent, democratic and rule-based country like Germany, there are several layers of checks and balances, so the risks seem manageable, but have led to a slow-down of cooperative activities. The paper will close with a number of conclusions.

2. The framework: Duisburg's difficult local economy

The city of Duisburg has profited from its geographical location since the Middle Ages. Located on the banks of the river Rhine, close to a ford, it was the starting point (or end point) of the Westphalian "Hellweg", a major salt road leading to the east. At some stage, a royal settlement developed into an imperial castle ("Kaiserpfalz"). When the Rhine shifted somewhat westward, the city began to decline, but with the onset of the industrial age, Duisburg's geography proved lucky again. A huge deposit of coal was identified close to the surface of the landscape, roughly parallel to the Ruhr, a small river that flows into the Rhine in, or at least close to, Duisburg. Duisburg thus proved to be an ideal place to disembark iron ore from elsewhere and to produce steel with the coke made from the coal found nearby. Incidentally, only some 30 km away there is one of the largest limestone deposits of Europe around Wülfrath, lime being an important raw material for producing steel. The steel could be processed into other products or sent elsewhere directly, by loading it on ships and sending it upstream to central and southwest Germany or downstream to Holland. Already in the 1840s, Duisburg became part of the emerging rail networks and thus had a head start of being able to reach out to the whole west European region. Major companies were founded in or near Duisburg, like Haniel, Thyssen and Stinnes, all of them related to steel, coal or transport. The Ruhr area, including a string of cities from – roughly – Duisburg in the west to Essen, Bochum and Dortmund in the east, became one of the prime global heartlands of heavy industry and a growth pole of the industrialization age.

The postwar period offered the coal- and steel-producing Ruhr area at first a bonanza for regional growth through the successful reconstruction drive. A recessionary downturn in 1958 pointed out the limits of this growth model. An enquete commission argued in 1960 that the emerging problems of the coal industry were of a structural nature, but only after the parliamentary elections of 1965 did the government acknowledge that Germany and the Ruhr area were to face a persistent reduction of coal mining (Horn 1977). As for Duisburg, the city responded rather late to these upcoming challenges. The mid-1970s were characterized by protests against the closure of a major steelwork. Moreover, the city government was preoccupied by political trouble about the integration of some smaller neighboring localities (Walsum, Homberg and Rheinhausen) into its jurisdiction. In 1987, the longest labor dispute in West German history started in Rheinhausen, now a part of Duisburg. The incident entered the collective memory of Germans and became part of the image of Duisburg as a prime example for a somewhat grimy rust belt city. Only in 1988 were the city authorities ready to set up "sSTEP Duisburg 2000", a somewhat bold strategy for local redevelopment looking beyond the traditional industrial set-up (Zimmermann et al. 2017: 442–446).

What was the outcome of such plans and aspirations? In 2019, the German Economic Institute (IW) has published a report on the future of the regions in Germany, which received wide publicity in the media, as it offered a sober – and sobering – view on the opportunities and challenges. The collaborating scholars developed a methodology to create an index that identifies structurally weak regions. The indicators used cover the three fields of the economy, demography and infrastructure. The economic strength variable, for instance, is made up of the sub-indicators of the unemployment rate, the GDP per capita, purchasing power and overindebtedness of private households. The study distinguishes 96 regions in Germany and finds that for the economic indicator, Duisburg/Essen belongs to the three most vulnerable regions in Germany (Tab. 1). Among the top 10 regions, actually four belong to the Ruhr area, with Emscher-Lippe, immediately north of Duisburg/Essen, sharing the most negative score. Duisburg/Essen's problematic rating is particularly due to its high unemployment rate. In a convergence analysis, the authors find that also from the perspective of how the unemployment rate changed in recent years, Duisburg/Essen gives cause for concern: Duisburg/Essen and Emscher-Lippe stand out as the two regions that started out with particularly high unemployment rates in 2011 *and* a conspicuously low reduction during the following years, from 2011 to 2017 (Oberst, Kempermann and Schröder 2019: 95). In 2020, the unemployment rate in Duisburg was 12.1 %, which was one of the

Tab. 1: The top 10 economically vulnerable regions in Germany

Region	Index (max. 4)
Duisburg/Essen	1.50
Emscher-Lippe	1.50
Bremerhaven	1.50
Altmark	0.75
Dortmund	0.75
Bremen	0.50
Schleswig-Holstein Ost	0.50
Bonn	0.50
Saar	0.50
Bochum/Hagen	0.50

Source: Oberst, Kempermann and Schröder 2019: 99

highest values in NRW with its rate of 7.5 %, and compared to 6.5 % for whole Federal Republic.

If one takes note of all three indicators together, namely the economy, demography and infrastructure, Duisburg/Essen ranks no. 4 in Germany with respect to vulnerability, a little better than neighboring Emscher-Lippe, which occupies the no. 3 slot. While the infrastructure is considered quite week for Duisburg-Essen as well, particular due to the high indebtedness of the city government, in terms of demography many regions in the east of Germany do much worse than the Ruhr area. With respect to the economic indicator, the report concludes rather mercilessly: potentially left behind ("Potentiell abgehängt", Oberst, Kempermann and Schröder 2019: 99).

When looking for the reasons for such a dismal development, it is tempting to start by examining the only partially successful efforts to attract young and dynamic entrepreneurs to the Duisburg area (We had the chance to do a number of interviews in 2018–19, on which the following remarks are based, accompanying a group of Korean economists and business scholars with whom we have collaborated). While there is a start-up scene in the Ruhr area and, more narrowly, in Duisburg, several interview partners suggested it is not particularly lively. In 2017, the Port of Duisburg established a startup accelerator, with a focus on innovation in logistics and supply chain. For such topics, Duisburg does offer some attractiveness for would-be entrepreneurs. There are 550 square meters of co-working spaces, meeting and presentation rooms, no permanent office spaces though. A team of experts is on hand. The idea of a digi(tal)hub, however, did not really take off, while it worked quite well in neighboring Düsseldorf. There are also regional efforts like ruhr:hub, a coworking space funded by the NRW state government and six cities in the Ruhr area. It focusses on digitization (big data, e-commerce, data security, etc.), includes consulting and pitching and has an accelerator program. Despite such and similar examples, often associated with shiny names, the dynamism seems stronger in places like Düsseldorf or Cologne, and some observers talk about the heritage of an "employee-mentality" in the Ruhr region, of people still having a mentality of feeling like working for big companies, not the mind-set of alert entrepreneurs. It is difficult to substantiate such impressions, and some of this may be exaggerated.

Nevertheless, it is reasonable to conclude that there are some, not negligible aspects of local or regional culture that can either work in favor or against developing a lively entrepreneurial setting. The earlier literature has often focused on the more "technical" relationships between regional industries – upstream and downstream linkages of production processes, character of the local labor market, etc. – in order to identify successful "clusters" (or the lack of them). The somewhat more recent and current literature on so-called "entrepreneurial eco-systems", however, points to a multitude of important attributes, which can be summarized as material, social and, indeed, cultural attributes (Spigel 2017). While the material endowments at least in principle can change quite fast, this is much more difficult for social and even more so for cultural characteristics. In a number of empirical investigations, the character of EEs has been shown to remain surprisingly sticky, due to strong path dependencies (e.g., Andersson and Kostery 2011). Fritsch and Wyrwich (2013), for instance, were able to show that the differences with respect to entrepreneurial activities between eastern and western Germany, despite the decades-long (intermediate) experience of the German Democratic Republic, remained surprisingly stable between 1925 and 2015.

Such arguments notwithstanding, it would be too easy to ascribe all of the current problems to a continuity of local culture that is unfavorable for dynamic entrepreneurialism. After all, the entrepreneurial ecosystems approach argues that the trajectory of the local economic ecosystem is shaped by the complex interplay of cultural *and* material as well as social attributes. From this perspective, it is interesting to compare two cities of the Ruhr area, which started with a similar background of coal and steel, but have developed quite differently in recent years, particularly after the global recession of 2008/2009 (the following is based on Zimmermann et al. 2017). One is Duisburg in the western part of the Ruhr area, and the other is Dortmund in the eastern part of the Ruhr area, which has a reputation of having done better than many other cities in the Ruhr area. The two "dissimilar cases" (on this concept, Gerring 2007) thus promise interesting insights into the role of peculiar conditions that differ between them. As for city planning, Duisburg's redevelopment strategy of "sSTEP Duisburg 2000" originates from 1988, as already mentioned, while Dortmund had already started with a cooperative "Dortmunder Konsens" (i.e. consensus) in 1982. A technology center and "park" was founded as early as 1983, and again, Duisburg followed several years later.

One question suggesting itself is why Duisburg was lagging Dortmund in moving away from the industrial mono-structure. The municipal restructuring of the mid 1980s was one issue that preoccupied local politicians, another the particularly antagonistic industrial relation troubles that took place in Duisburg. One problem to keep in mind is that on the background of the rather similar structures of the Ruhr cities, already a tiny time advantage of restructuring can lead to considerable differences under the intense competition of localities. By 2008, Dortmund was already much less characterized by heavy industry than Duisburg. Its share of services was 60 %, Duisburg's 52 %. With respect to knowledge-intensive services, in relative terms the gap was even wider: 24 % versus 17 %. Based on a somewhat more sophisticated methodology for the "related variety" and the "unrelated variety" of the local economic structures, these differences can be confirmed (Zimmermann et al. 2017: 448).

One sector for which rather small initial advantages can turn into significant gaps later on is retailing. Duisburg was rather late in rebuilding its inner city to make it attractive for strollers and shoppers. Thus, the city centers of the somewhat posh neighboring cities of Düsseldorf in the south, the state capital, and even of Essen, another big industrial-era city somewhat east of Duisburg, plus a large outlet area on the outskirts of Oberhausen somewhat north of Duisburg ("CentrO") were able to redirect significant spending power away from Duisburg. To some extent, bad luck may have played a role as well: in 2010, the city tried to organize a party event for several hundreds of thousands of youths close to the main station. However, things went terribly wrong, and 21 young people died during the ensuing panic, as was reported all over Germany and beyond. The following search of who had committed the decisive mistakes slowed down proactive city planning for several years.

3. The economic interaction: Duisburg and China's new silk road

3.1. The role of the Belt and Road Initiative

Regular train services between China and Duisburg were started by China Rail in mid-2011 (on the following, Xinhua 2011). It took 13 days to reach Duisburg from Chongqing, a major city in central China, one of only five independent metropolitan cities in China, with an urban agglomeration of some 13 million inhabitants, although the jurisdictional entity is even bigger. In the very beginning, there were only few trains per month, but this has increased to some 50–60 per week from different locations in China to Duisburg currently. One major reason to start regular train services from Chongqing was to deliver consumer electronics from the region to Europe. Foxconn, Acer and Hewlett-Packard had already been in place producing laptops, so it seemed sensible to avoid shipping the goods to the coast first and then by ship to European destinations.

The timing – 2011 – is conspicuous for two reasons. First, the rail connection to Duisburg already existed some ten years before the regular rail service was started. The problem was rather to reduce the bureaucratic hurdles along the track. It is said that before 2011 it took more than 30 days to reach Duisburg from Chongqing by train. One important piece of the jigsaw puzzle in this context was the signing in 2010 of a strategic agreement of China with Russia and Kazakhstan on the use of the rail tracks to open the traffic with Europe. Chongqing itself has a good connectivity to other places in central China, so the direct train link with Europe can be seen as a policy measure to open up China's central and western regions to the dynamic effects of economically opening up beyond the western border. The opening up of China had so far been concentrated on the already prospering coastal regions with their adjoining overseas ports.

The second reason, why the year 2011 is conspicuous, is that the rail line opened actually two years *before* the official start of the Belt and Road Initiative (BRI) in 2013. At this stage, it is meaningful to provide a rough sketch of the highly publicized BRI initiative of the Chinese government, although this is not the place to discuss it in detail (for recent overviews: Fang and Nolan eds. 2019, Li and Taube eds. 2020; the following arguments are based on Pascha 2020a, b). The basic concept was introduced to the world with two speeches of China's President Xi Jinping in 2013, with the core idea of developing a so-called "belt" across Eurasia with three routes and a maritime "road" with two routes. Originally, 58 countries were identified for primarily bilateral cooperation with China. Memoranda of Understanding (MoU), phrased by China in a standard format, were the instrument of choice to initiate concrete cooperation, which were then to lead to concrete contracts between specific partners and Chinese policy banks, companies, local development agencies, etc. While the initial focus was clearly on infrastructure, four other links were also referred to, namely policies, trade, finance, and people. Cooperation was to be based on five principles, in line with the UN Charta: "mutual respect for each other´s sovereignty and territorial integrity", non-aggression, non-interference, equality, mutual benefit and peaceful coexistence, according to the principal 2015 document outlining BRI (National Development and Reform Commission 2015). Several finance mechanisms were put in place, both domestic and multilateral schemes. They include the Silk Road Fund, with 40 billion USD from foreign exchange resources, the Chinese sovereign wealth funds and the newly founded multilateral Asian Infrastructure and Investment Bank (AIIB), a Chinese initiative with a capital stock of 100 billion USD.

So far, the experiences made with BRI are mixed. The image of BRI in international public opinion has deteriorated considerably, even before the most recent tensions between China and the West (Garcia-Herrero and Xu 2019). Compared with the expected size of about 1–2 trillion USD, actual disbursement is still much lower. Unfair contracts, favoring the Chinese partners, became a concern, so did questions about the technical quality of project execution by Chinese contractors. Some problems have surfaced for partner countries, among them fears of a debt overburden for borrowing countries (e.g., Herskovitz and Marlow 2019). The AIIB acted much more prudently than some had feared. On the flipside, the size of AIIB lending so far was much smaller than expected. Much criticism is based on the fact that the BRI pursues an entangled mix of geostrategic and economic motives. Being engaged or controlling ports is one case where such an entanglement of interests is not unlikely. According to Oettinger (2021), China now owns, has its own terminals or has shares in 14 European ports, including Piraeus, Rotterdam, Antwerp, Le Havre, Bilbao, Valencia, Marseille and Malta.

When evaluating the role and development of BRI, two points should be kept in mind. First, the initiative is a flexible instrument that serves public relation purposes, namely the bold positioning of China as an aspiring international power, but it lacks a clear and uniform organizational structure; there is, for instance, neither a headquarters nor a consolidated budget (Öztürk 2019; Taube 2020). When, further below, we look at the role of Duisburg in these dynamics more closely, it is therefore meaningful not to relate this to the concept of BRI in a narrow sense only, but to the wider Chinese engagement with Duisburg. We might call this more encompassing context the "new silk road", thus acknowledging the somewhat fuzzy nature of the interaction.

A second point to be noted is that the idea of BRI and the scope of new silk road-related projects is constantly changing and dynamic. To some extent, this is owed to learning processes within China, but also and possibly more so to the severe competition for international infrastructure projects with Japanese, American and European interests also making an impact (Pascha 2020a). A notable development is the Second Belt and Road Forum of April 2019, in which Xi Jinping took up the challenge to redefine the Chinese approach. The Joint Communique speaks of aiming for "high-quality, reliable, resilient and sustainable infrastructure" (Leaders' Roundtable 2019), thus reacting to the international critique that emerged after 2013 quite explicitly.

When asking what these evolving dynamics of BRI and the new silk road means for Duisburg, one should start with elaborating why the rail connection between the German city and China has become so attractive in recent years.

3.2. The economics of the rail link between Duisburg and China

The main point about the attractiveness of rail transport in comparison to sea or air freight between China and Europe is that it is faster than sea transport, but cheaper than air freight, while of course being slower. It thus offers a niche segment for goods that are not quite urgent enough to justify the expensive air lift, but should be faster than being shipped beyond the Indian Ocean and through the Suez Canal or even around Africa. According to DSV global logistics provider, a 40-foot container to be sent by train from China to Europe can be expected to cost around USD 8,000, while by sea it would cost around USD 4,000 and by air USD 32,000. The company estimates that door-to-door rail travel will take some 15 and 18 days, roughly half the time compared to ocean shipping (DSV undated). Sending goods by air may take three to five days (TopShipping undated). Obviously, such calculations only offer rough guidance. For instance, it makes a big difference whether one calculates with port-to-port costs and durations or whether one takes a door-to-door view, i.e. from the location of production to the final destination. From that perspective, a convenient "port" in Europe is most important for solving the logistical challenge. Duisburg can conveniently be reached via a southern rail route through Kazakhstan and southern Russia or via a northern route through Siberia and passing through Moscow. The southern route is most suited for freight to and from central China, for instance from Chongqing, whereas the northern route can best serve locations like Beijing and Dalian (DSV undated). From Belarus into Poland (Warsaw) and onwards to Germany (Berlin), the major rail connections basically follow one route. In line with this, Lodz near Warsaw, for instance, has also developed into a logistics hub for rail transport with China. The first service between Lodz and China, namely with Chengdu, started operation in late 2012, and like in the case of Duisburg *before* the official announcement of the BRI (pg/st 2018). Different locations within Europe thus compete for the position as a preferred stop for Chinese freight trains, and Duisburg's advantages as an early mover mainly depend on three factors: its convenient location, which is a permanent strength, the efficiency of its logistical services, like efficient intermodal services, and the capacity of its facilities. Arguably, a fourth factor might come into play, namely "soft" factors like a China-friendly environment, more on which later.

The economic efficiency of the rail connection between China and Europe as such or, more specifically, between China and Duisburg is thus influenced by a number of important factors. One important issue is the duration of the train journey, for instance between Duisburg and China. According to the CEO of Duisburg's port, Mr. Erich Staake, trains as of 2018 took on average six days to travel the 1,300 km from the Polish-Belarusian border to Duisburg, but only as little as 5.5 days for the 10,000 km from Chongqing to the border station (Oltermann 2018). The red tape on the European side is obviously still significant. One more impediment that slows down the rail journey is that the wheel spacing of trains has to be laboriously changed twice during the trip, as the Russian gauge is wider. Another consideration is that the containers that return from Europe to China are often not fully loaded, which makes the connection less economical than it could be.

Looking into capacity issues, it is important to realize that a large container ship like the "Ever Given", which recently got stuck in the Suez Canal, has a capacity of some 20,000 20-feet-containers. A typical train carries only up to 100 20-feet-containers (TBN undated). It thus takes 200 trains from China to Europe to carry the same amount of goods as by a single journey of the Ever Given. it is understandable that rail transport still makes up only 1–2 % of total China-Europe trade volume, while more than 95 % are still transported along the sea route (Taube 2020). In 2018, on average some 120 trains either left Duisburg or came from China per week according to Chinese data, and since then the number is said to have increased further, despite "a period of less departures due to Chinese restrictions on empty containers" (van Leijen 2019). Duisburg seems to be nearing its capacity limit, and it is said that some trains already had to be redirected elsewhere. Accordingly, the number of train destinations or intermediate stops in Europe has increased considerably in recent years, without taking effective business away from Duisburg due to the surplus demand, though. Duisburg is still involved in some 30 % of all China-related freight rail.

Duisport is planning a new "Duisburg Gateway Terminal", which is to become Europe's biggest inland container facility. It will involve an investment of about 100 million Euro, on an area of 240,000 square meters (including storage areas) within the port. The final processing capacity will be 850,000 20-feet-containers yearly or 100 trains to China per week. Partners in this venture will be Cosco Shipping Logistics from China, Hupac SA from Switzerland and HTS Group from the Netherlands (Duisport 2019).

Taube (2020) adds the important point that so far the connection is heavily subsidized by the Chinese side, with an amount of several billion US dollars per year; While there were plans to cut this amount significantly in 2020, it is doubtful whether under the condition of Covid-19 this was actually realized. Nevertheless, it is quite conceivable that the Chinese provinces will somewhat reduce their subsidies, which are handed out to promote the regions of inner China, in the future (Giustolisi and Terstriep 2020). This would obviously impede the attractiveness of some connections.

3.3. Duisburg's attractiveness as a China-related business hub

Duisburg has made considerable efforts in recent years to increase its attractiveness as a logistics hub. At the core of such activities is the redevelopment of the port of Duisburg, which has a 300-years history, as a game-changing multimodal logistics hub with a strong focus on containers. Since 2000, the port, with the official name Duisburger Hafen AG, uses the term Duisport for its activities. It is co-owned by the state of NRW (2/3) and by the City of Duisburg (1/3). Already from 1998, the port used the concept of "logport", with a trimodal involvement of ship, rail and road, to utilize unused areas for huge logistics and storage facilities. Today, there are six logports, also beyond the city borders. The first of its kind was a 265 ha area, equivalent to 371 soccer fields, that is located on the former site of the Krupp-steel plant in Duisburg-Rheinhausen, the one that had caused so much public unrest in the 1980s (Duisport undated). Today, Duisport is the biggest container terminal in the world with a handling of some 40 million 20-feet-containers per year and a maximum capacity of 50 million. The Port is engaged in a number of other activities; an innovation platform "startport" was opened in 2017, for example. The already mentioned Duisburg Gateway Terminal will be another major cooperation project with China. A 100 million Euro investment obviously involves some business risks, but Duisport is a profitable enterprise, so the risks will be manageable and if the huge project can be development speedily and reliably, it will be an important signal to China and other international partners that Duisburg is a location that can deliver.

Duisport has also moved beyond beyond its own region, actively promoting strategic alliances with relevant Chinese partners, supported by the state government of NRW and by its related agencies. With respect to activities along the new silk road, Duisport owns a 0.67 % stake in the "Great Stone" industrial park near Minsk in Belarus, involving a rail terminal and a logistics area (Taube 2020); among others, the China Merchants Group is a partner in this project. Arguably, so far too few German and European players have made a sincere effort to participate in the economic potential of the new silk road. In this respect, Duisport is a welcome frontrunner, although the engagement is relatively small and although opportunities of course also imply potential risks. China is, like in Duisport's case, one potential partner, while the recent 2018 EU infrastructure initiative "Connecting Europe and Asia: Building Blocks for an EU Strategy" and the 2019 agreement between the EU and Japan "Partnership on Sustainable Connectivity and Quality Infrastructure between the European Union and Japan" will hopefully open further options (Pascha 2020a, b). More competition in this field can be expected to lead to innovative ideas and to more efficient solutions, also in the sense of counteracting potential risks.

When considering the local attractiveness, one should not overlook soft factors that can support or impede closer relations. Duisburg enjoys the oldest twin city agreement with the People´s Republic of China in former West Germany, namely with Wuhan, also a former "steel city", which started in 1982. Bilateral relations go back to 1978, when a group of Duisburg companies started to build a cold rolling mill in Wuhan. Giustolisi and Terstriep (2020: 9–10) mention the foundation of contemporary Asian studies at Duisburg University in the 1990s (now Duisburg-Essen University) and of a Confucius Institute in 2009 as relevant developments. From a German perspective, Duisburg is surprisingly well-known in China. The University now hosts more than 2,000 students from China, the largest group among German universities. Also, during the current pandemic, amicable relations have been nursed further; according to Prof. Dr. Yuan Li of Shandong University, "Duisburg and Wuhan … timely took actions to help each other. The high school students in Duisburg-Essen sang a song in Chinese to show their support and encouragement to Wuhan, which was broadcast all over China" (personal communication, 24 March 2021).

3.4. Regional economic effects

Economic effects for Duisburg and the wider region can be sought on different levels. Here, we first discuss growth and employment effects in general and then turn to the attraction of foreign direct investment from China (Of course, the effect of such investments from abroad constitutes a part of the general economic effects).

With respect to the growth and employment effects for Duisburg, positive effects through the growth of logistics activities in the port area and of Chinese investments are noticeable. With respect to employment, in 2018 it was estimated that employment related to Duisport, including indirect effects on subcontractors etc., had soared from 19,000 to 50,000 (Oltermann 2018). This is sizable, but it still has to been in perspective. Between the mid-1970s and mid-2000s, Duisburg lost more than 30 % of its jobs (counted as employment with social insurance contributions). From a level of about 600,000 inhabitants, after the municipal restructuring of the mid 1970s, the number of citizens dropped to around 500,000 currently. From a level of about 160,000 jobs around 2010, this number has risen to 177,000 in 2018, the highest number since the 1990s (Bundesagentur für Arbeit 2019). It seems fair to assume that the positive development of Duisport played a considerable part. The planned "Duisburg Gateway Terminal" will add to the capacity significantly, when realized, but will not be a game changer. The unemployment rate is still far higher than in the rest of the country, and there is no evidence that Duisburg will be able to rebuild the economic strength it possessed during the earlier postwar period any time soon.

Kleimann, Li and Schmerer (2020) have undertaken a more analytical approach to identify employment effects for Duisburg. They use the so-called synthetic control approach to analyze whether a certain intervention has an impact (here: on employment) compared to other cases where this intervention was not realized. The authors choose the commencement of regular freight train services between China and Duisburg in 2011 as the relevant intervention point. Eventually, they cannot identify a positive employment effect from their econometric analysis, although based on their qualitative analysis, they still expect there to be one.

When considering such growth and employment effects, one aspect that deserves closer attention is whether the region and Duisburg in particular can attract foreign direct investment (FDI) from China. Taking the whole state of North Rhine-Westphalia as a point of departure, new FDI cases from abroad have stagnated somewhat in recent years, with most investors still originating from Europe and the share of Asian FDI cases somewhat declining. While there were 72 new cases from Greater China in 2018, the number declined to 65 in 2019, while in terms of employment, Chinese FDI created 564 new jobs in 2018, but almost twice as much, 1,097, in 2019 (NRW Invest 2019). NRW is by far the most important location for Chinese FDI in Germany, and among the total of more than 1,200 Chinese investments from Greater China in NRW, about half have chosen Düsseldorf (Landeshauptstadt Düsseldorf 2021). While the hype about Duisburg and the new silk road has attracted wide attention, it is noteworthy that the neighboring city of Düsseldorf has attracted by far the highest number of Chinese FDI in the wider region of NRW and has developed into the most popular center for Chinese business activities in Germany (Knieps 2019).

The Ruhr area as a major part of NRW, attracted 74 new cases of FDI in 2019, the second-highest number in NRW, while the region of and around the state capital of Düsseldorf registered 174 new investors. Giustolisi and Terstriep (2020: 9), using their own data search, counted 200 cases of Greater Chinese FDI for the Ruhr area between 2003 and 2020. The highest number (75) was registered for Duisburg, while 43 cases were counted for Essen. Dortmund, discussed earlier, in the Eastern part of the Ruhr area has only 14 cases. Looking at this data in perspective, it is conspicuous that Duisburg could attract a rather high share of Chinese investment. One reason is indeed its status as a logistics hub that is interesting for Chinese producers who want to tap the huge west European market. This is clear when looking at the 75 companies more closely: At least 29 of them are related to wholesale and retail, 9 related to logistics, including forwarding agents, and 7 related to technical and other cases of consulting (ibid.: 10).

The rail connection with China certainly plays a role in this, but it is also Duisburg's geographical attractiveness as a logistics hub as such. An important and well reported event was, for example, that China Rail Container Transport, which belongs to the China State Railway Group, established its European subsidiary in Duisburg in 2019 (van Leijen 2019). As for another example, a Chinese retailer that specializes on Asian food came in 2016 and uses storage space close to the port for distributing its merchandise directly all over Europe. Interestingly, the food does not arrive by rail, but by ship, so the retailer was attracted by Duisburg's position as a logistics hub and by cheap rents (Giustolisi and Terstriep 2020: 10).

Another factor that can be expected to have an impact on Duisburg's attractiveness for Chinese investors is its vicinity to Düsseldorf. It is highly likely that the combination of the international business hub of Düsseldorf and the logistics hub of Duisburg create positive synergies for the region. For instance, it is conspicuous that there are far less Chinese investment cases the further one moves to the eastern side of the Ruhr area. Of course, there could be some competition between Duisburg and Düsseldorf. For instance, TP Link in 2020 started a European logistics center for distributing routers in Düsseldorf, not in Duisburg (Landeshauptstadt Düsseldorf 2021). At the same time, however, rents in Duisburg are much lower than in Düsseldorf, so quite a number of cases have been identified in which Chinese investors preferred the western Ruhr area to settling in the center of Düsseldorf, but remaining close to it (Giustolisi and Terstriep 2020: 8). Eventually, it is probably a win-win situation for both cities, although in terms of economic promotion efforts, they usually do not work closely together. Düsseldorf rather views itself in the context of Cologne and Bonn, sometimes also Aachen, which share a reputation for more contemporary and future-oriented industries compared to the image of Duisburg and the Ruhr area.

4. Political influences: Risks and challenges

So far, the upside of continuing and profitable relations with business partners in China was discussed. However, there are also downside risks, most of them related to potentially deteriorating political relations.

A first level of such risks is related to a possibly overly optimistic expectation of future business opportunities with China, which could lead to an over-investment and problematic performance of the local economy, if such risks materialize. Interestingly the Business Report of Duisport in its chapter on chances and risks only speaks about the upside potential with respect to China (Duisport 2020). As the capacity utilization of Duisport is already high and because according to reports some traffic already had to be diverted away in the recent past, it is not likely that Duisport and the local economy are currently overexposed to business with China. There is other business that Duisburg could attract, as it has successfully established itself as a leading multimodal logistics center with a still reasonable price level for necessary inputs.

At the same time, it seems to be a fact of life that not all plans with a thriving and dynamic business partner like China (and its companies) move forward as planned. This can also happen to Duisburg, and one can indeed already point to some major example. In 2017, the establishment of a major business park, named "China Trade Center Europe" was announced for the western part of the city, between Rheinhausen and Homberg. The Chinese investor planned to create 60,000 square meters of office space, including an office tower with 13 stories. In early 2021, it has turned out that the plan has been abandoned, actually already a while ago (Cnotka 2021). An investment volume of 260 million Euro with 1,000 to 2,000 jobs to be created will not be realized. The ground is said to have been problematic for buildings of that size, neighbors were worried about the additional traffic, and the business case was at least doubtful, as one third of the area of the Businesspark Niederrhein, which started 30 years ago in that very area, is still unused.

A second level of risk concerns the question whether China will develop an undue influence over Duisburg and its economy, which could be contrary to Duisburg's narrower, but even to Germany's and the EU's wider interests. Already in 2018, an article was published on the website of T-Online with the suggestive title "What helps Duisburg can harm the world" (Schaible 2018). No explicit case was made against a particular event or business deal related to Duisburg or against any of the organizations or decision-makers involved. This also holds for other publications that voice some diffuse concern about Duisburg's engagement with China (e.g., Investigate Europe 2019). The obvious worry and the context that are addressed in the rather general arguments are the problematic developments in other parts of the world that have been associated with BRI and the new silk road. Negative experiences with Chinese FDI in Germany and elsewhere, related to the exploitation of technological knowledge and other problems, also support such negative evaluations (for a critical study from IW, the German Economic Institute, see for example Matthes 2020). We cannot do justice to such concerns in detail here. As for Duisburg, the risks under discussion seem to be relatively limited, however.

First, Duisburg's port is not in an unfavorable business situation that would make it easy for outsiders to gain undue influence. The port earned a net profit of 13 million Euro in 2019 and could actually raise it further in the corona-year 2020. This is quite different from a port like Piraeus in Greece that had to be privatized in the midst of the European financial crisis and was bought by Chinese investors. The profitable Duisport is co-owned by the state of NRW and by the City, so there is little basis for serious concerns.

Second, the business environment in which Chinese actors may be interested in Duisburg is not the high-tech sector. Retailing and wholesale, storage spaces and related services are not particularly worrisome in terms of technological leakage. Such a rather unproblematic pattern of engagement is also confirmed when looking at regional Chinese FDI in recent years, as discussed above.

There is one more complex issue, however. In late 2017, the City of Duisburg and Huawei signed an agreement according to which they will cooperate in turning Duisburg into a "smart city". Key words in this context are "smart government, smart port logistics, smart education, smart infrastructure, 5G and broadband, smart homes, and urban IoT" (Huawei 2018). In June 2018, Huawei and the Duisburg public utilities company (DVV) signed a "Framework Agreement on the ´Rhine Cloud´ – the brand name of a smart city and public service cloud platform – and Smart City services" (ibid.). The idea of the cooperation is to supply Duisburg with expertise and sell Huawei's technological solutions for 5G, Wi-Fi, IoT (Internet of Things) platforms and else. The cooperation had a rather difficult start, as the city government initially refused to publicize the Memorandum of Understanding. In the meantime, the MoU has become available on the internet (Duisburg and Huawei 2017). Indeed, Article 3.2 of the MoU had only allowed the partners to make public the existence and a summary of the agreement. Apart from that, the MoU seems fairly inconspicuous, particularly as it states explicitly that it does not create any obligations, but only summarizes the "current vision" (Article 2.1). Nevertheless, the agreement and the secrecy surrounding it raised concerns that Chinese actors would gain access to and structural information about highly sensitive and important urban infrastructure, possibly also data about individuals and organizations (like companies), which would not be compatible with data security and could, in the worst case, be misused by Chinese state or business actors (e.g., Merten 2020).

Helping Duisburg to build a "digital benchmark city" (Huawei 2018) is not an isolated action for the city at the end of the new silk road, but it fits a more general Chinese strategy followed since 2015 that has been dubbed the "Digital Silk Road". The idea is to strengthen internet infrastructure and cloud computing, to work on common standards etc. with like-minded partners. A leading Chinese technology firm like Huawei is a central part of such efforts. The International Cyber Policy Center has counted 47 cities all over the world that are related to "Huawei´s smart-city and 5G footprint", including Duisburg – and the city of Gelsenkirchen, also a part of the Ruhr area (based on: Economist Corporate Network 2019: 11). From a more academic perspective, it has been argued that the strategic support of certain cities is a core component of the "dream of a future order in which China occupies a central position", namely by creating "urban corridors and smart surveillance cities" (Curtis and Mayer 2020: 1). On a more mundane level, there is political concern in the US, but also in the EU and Germany, among others, that it would be dangerous for competition and for security to rely on Huawei's 5G technology (only) (We cannot do justice to this complex debate here. For the nuanced EU position, see for instance: European Commission 2020).

The Duisburg-Huawei MoU has a duration of five years, i.e. until late 2022. Recently, there seems to be very little momentum left to push the agenda forward (for similar view: Verfürden 2021). Why have the actors become more hesitant? I would argue that the various layers of checks and balances in a democratic and rule-based political economy like Germany make sure that a significant deviation from a rather benevolent and safe course of action will be unlikely. First, on the city level there is also the opposition and concerned civil society that carefully watches developments. For instance the left-wing party "Die Linke" kicked of a question in the City Council about the MoU, relating it to freedom of information-rights, and the website "FragdenStaat" ("Ask the State") offered templates for citizens who wanted to make use of their individual freedom of information-rights (the website is currently still open: https://fragdenstaat.de/anfrage/informationsfreiheit-smart-city-abmachung-mit-huawei/). Second, there is the state level. For example, NRW owns two thirds of the Duisport group, as already mentioned. Third, there is the federal level, and fourth, the EU-level. Moreover, there are the media, and even a rather ordinary municipality like Duisburg can and will be covered by the Washington Post or CNN, for example, in case of political relevance.

5. Conclusions

On the background of the recent rise of political tension between the EU and China, the question to what extent the EU, Germany, its states or individual localities can and should cooperate with China has gained considerable urgency.

A city like Duisburg promised to be a particularly interesting case study in this context. On the one hand, its location is ideal as the "western terminus of the new silk road", so considerable economic benefits from closer cooperation can be expected. On the other hand, the precarious economic situation as a former city of steel and coal make it vulnerable to economic and political risks.

The paper has identified relevant pro and con factors and evaluated the available evidence. The economic heritage and current situation of Duisburg has indeed been found difficult. Profiting from the Chinese interest in its strength as a logistics hub was and is one of the few options to regain economic strength. Duisburg has noticeably profited from the Chinese interest, but the impetus is not significant enough to fully recover from the decline of coal and steel industries. A large share of the potential benefits has probably already been realized, while plans to increase the container capacity of the port further should nevertheless be duly acknowledged. Positive linkage effects with other industries, beyond rail and logistics, still seem rather limited. With respect to the political dimension of the relationship, the typical risks associated with BRI are somewhat limited in Duisburg's case, because Duisburg, as a part of prosperous Germany is not in a particularly dire situation, despite its difficulties, so the potential leverage of Chinese actors is limited, and because Duisburg is not the home of many high-tech companies that might be attractive targets. In the case of the Duisburg-Huawei cooperation, which does indeed involve some political risks, the momentum for the more problematic endeavors has recently declined, due to the various checks and balances that have been in place, while the win-win projects of the agenda will hopefully still be realized. While some players (including parts of the media) have indulged in the idea of an economic bonanza beckoning on the horizon and others have dramatized the looming political risks, the hype in both directions seems to have been exaggerated during the past few years.

Currently, the city seems to be reconsidering its future options and possible trajectories with respect to China. A research project, financed by various regional and local actors, has just started, based on the initiative of the energetic Mr. Johannes Pflug, the City's special representative for China and a former member of the federal parliament, and executed by members of the Institute of East Asian Studies of Duisburg-Essen University (N. N. 2021).

References

(All internet sources mentioned were last accessed in April 2021).

Andersson, Martin and Kostery, Sierdjan (2011): Sources of persistence in regional start-up rates – Evidence from Sweden, Journal of Economic Geography, Vol. 11, 2011, pp. 179–201

Bundesagentur für Arbeit (2019): Neue Zahlen zur Beschäftigung in Duisburg – Beschäftigung steigt weiter, Presseinfo Nr. 15, 12 April 2019, https://www.arbeitsagentur.de/vor-ort/duisburg/content/1533722442681

Cnotka, Daniel: China Center (2021): Am Ende der Seidenstraße in Duisburg, Neue Ruhr Zeitung (NRZ), 1 April 2021, https://www.nrz.de/staedte/duisburg/china-center-am-ende-der-seidenstrasse-in-duisburg-id231949143.html

Curtis, Simon and Mayer, Maximilian (2020): Belt and road cities begin to find their form, CIDOB opinion 630, Barcelona, July 2020

DSV Global Transport and Logistics (n.d.): Rail freight transport between China and Europe, undated, https://www.dsv.com/en/insights/expert-opinions/rail-freight-between-europe-and-china

Duisburg and Huawei (2017): Absichtserklärung, 23 October 2017, available from: https://www.duisburg.de/microsites/smartcityduisburg/partner/partner-huawei.php

Duisport: Duisburger Hafen bekommt größtes Hinterland-Terminal in Europa (2019) Webpage Internationales Verkehrswesen, 23 October 2019, https://www.internationales-verkehrswesen.de/duisburger-hafen-bekommt-groesstes-hinterland-terminal-in-europa/

Duisport (2019): Geschäftsbericht 2019. Wir sind das Netzwerk, Duisburg 2020

Duisport (n.d.): Webpage, undated, https://www.duisport.de/

Economist Corporate Network: BRI Beyond 2020, 2019, available from: https://www.bakermckenzie.com/-/media/files/insight/publications/2019/china/bribeyond2020-v2.pdf?la=en

Economist (2021): The: China sees its moment. The Communist Party's aggressive diplomacy is a bet that the West is in irreversible decline, Chaguan column, 3 April 2021, p. 48

European Commission (2020): Shaping Europe's digital future. International Cooperation on 5G, last updated 29 September 2020, https://ec.europa.eu/digital-single-market/en/5G-international-cooperation

Fang Cai and Nolan Peter (eds) (2019): Routledge Handbook of the Belt and Road. London: Routledge, 2019

Fritsch, Michael and Wyrwich, Michael (2013): The Long Persistence of Regional Levels of Entrepreneurship: Germany 1925–2005, Regional Studies, Vol. 48, Issue 6, 2013, pp. 955–973

Garcia-Herrero Alicia and Xu Jianwei (2019): The next step of Belt and Road Initiative: Multilateralisation with Chinese characteristics. Bruegel Blog Post. 18 April 2019. https://bruegel.org/2019/04/the-next-step-of-the-belt-and-road-initiative-multilateralisation-with-chinese-characteristics/

Gerring, John (2007): Case Study Research. Principles and Practices, Cambridge et al.: Cambridge University Press, 2007

Giustolisi, Alessio and Terstriep, Judith (2020): Chinesische Investitionen im Ruhrgebiet. Eine Chance für den Strukturwandel?, Forschung Aktuell 09/2020, Institut für Arbeit und Technik, Gelsenkirchen

Herskovitz Jon, Marlow Iain (2019): China Faces New Competition as Japan. India Eye Sri Lanka Port. Bloomberg News, 21 May 2019. https://www.bloomberg.com/news/articles/2019-05-21/japan-india-in-deal-at-belt-and-road-colombo-port-nikkei

Horn, Manfred (1977): Die Energiepolitik der Bundesregierung von 1958 bis 1972, Berlin: Duncker & Humblot, 1977

Huawei (2018): Huawei Deepens Cooperation with Duisburg to Transform Germany's Industrial Heartland into a Smart City, Huawei website, 3 September 2018, https://www.huawei.com/en/news/2018/9/huawei-duisburg-germany-smartcity

Investigate Europe (journalist team) (2019): China: Der gefürchtete Partner, Der Tagesspiegel, 16 September 2019, https://interaktiv.tagesspiegel.de/lab/china-der-gefuerchtete-partner/

Kleimann, Martin, Li, Yuan and Schmerer, Hans-Jörg (2020): Estimating Causal Effects of BRI Infrastructure Projects Based on the Synthetic Control Method, ADBI Working Paper Series No. 1180, September 2020

Knieps, Stephan (2019): Wie Düsseldorf zum beliebtesten deutschen China-Standort wurde, WirtschaftsWoche, 20 November 2019, https://www.wiwo.de/my/unternehmen/it/chinesische-investitionen-wie-duesseldorf-zum-beliebtesten-deutschen-china-standort-wurde/25245998.html?ticket=ST-525837-22hrrZoV9jgyDZ9t2tcx-ap6

Landeshauptstadt Düsseldorf: Nordrhein-Westfalen und Düsseldorf bleiben trotz Pandemie Top-Standorte für chinesische Direktinvestitionen, February 2021, https://www.duesseldorf.de/techguide/uebersicht/3-seitentemplates/32-newsuebersichtsseite/detail/newsdetail/nordrhein-westfalen-und-duesseldorf-bleiben-trotz-pandemie-top-standorte-fuer-chinesische-direktinvest.html

Leaders' Roundtable (2019): Joint Communique of the Leaders' Roundtable of the 2nd Belt and Road Forum for International Cooperation. Beijing, 27 April 2019

Li, Yuan and Taube, Markus (Eds.) (2020) How China's Silk Road Initiative is Changing the Global Economic Landscape, London and New York: Routledge, 2020

Matthes, Jürgen (2020): Unternehmensübernahmen und Technologietransfer durch China – Gefahrenpotenziale und Gegenmaßnahmen, IW-Report 34/ 2020, https://www.iwkoeln.de/fileadmin/user_upload/Studien/Report/PDF/ 2020/IW-Report_2020_Unternehmensuebernahmen_China.pdf

Merten, Milena (2020): Wie sehr kann eine Stadt dem Konzern Huawei trauen?, Handelsblatt and Ada-Magazin, 1 September 2020, https://www.handelsblatt.com/technik/digitale-revolution/ada-magazin-wie-sehr-kann-eine-stadt-dem-konzern-huawei-trauen/25592874.html

Michel, Mike (2019): Duisburg will China-Stadt bleiben, Rheinische Post online, 30 August 2019, https://rp-online.de/nrw/staedte/duisburg/duisburg-plant-neue-china-strategie_aid-45358749

National Development and Reform Commission (2015): Vision and Actions on Jointly Building Silk Road Economic Belt and 21st-Century Maritime Silk Road, 2015

N. N. (2021): Duisburger China-Studie über die Neue Seidenstraße, Rundschau Duisburg, 26 March 2021, https://www.rundschau-duisburg.de/2021/03/26/ duisburger-china-studie-ueber-die-neue-seidenstrasse/

NRW Invest (2019): Foreign Direct Investment (FDI) in NRW Ergebnisse 2019, https://www.nrwinvest.com/fileadmin/Redaktion/downloads/FACTSHEET_ FDI_Reporting_2019.pdf

Oberst, Christian, Kempermann, Hanno and Schröder, Christoph (2019): Räumliche Entwicklung in Deutschland, in: Michael Hüther et al. (eds.): die Zukunft der Regionen in Deutschland: Zwischen Vielfalt und Gleichwertigkeit, IW Studien, Cologne 2019, pp. 88–114, 2019

Oettinger, Günther (2021): Wie China Europas Häfen und Containerschiffe kapert, Der Tagesspiegel, 31 March 2021, https://www.tagesspiegel.de/wirtschaft/schluss-mit-der-blauaeugigkeit-wie-china-europas-haefen-und-containerschiffe-kapert/27054840.html?utm_source= pocket-newtab-global-de-DE

Oltermann, Philip (2018): Germany's 'China City': how Duisburg became Xi Jinping's gateway to Europe, The Guardian, 1 August 2018, https:// www.theguardian.com/cities/2018/aug/01/germanys-china-city-duisburg-became-xi-jinping-gateway-europe

Öztürk, Ibrahim (2019): The Belt and Road Initiative as a Hybrid International Public Good, Working Papers on East Asian Studies, No. 125/2019

Pascha, Werner (2020a): The quest for infrastructure development from a "market creation" perspective: China's "Belt and Road", Japan's "Quality Infrastructure" and the EU's "Connecting Europe and Asia", in: International Economics and Economic Policy, Vol. 17, Issue 3, 2020, pp. 687–704

Pascha, Werner (2020b): Belts, Roads, and Regions: The Dynamics of Chinese and Japanese Infrastructure Connectivity Initiatives and Europe's Responses, Asian Development Bank Institute (ADBI) Working Paper No. 1114, Tokyo, April 2020

Pg/st (2018): China-Poland freight trains boost economic development in Łódź, Poland In website, 27 August 2018, https://polandin.com/38677429/chinapoland-freight-trains-boost-economic-development-in-lodz

Schaible, Jonas (2018): Was Duisburg hilft, kann der Welt schaden, t-online Website, 23 May 2018, https://www.t-online.de/nachrichten/ausland/internationale-politik/id_83813870/angela-merkels-besuch-in-china-was-duisburg-hilft-kann-der-welt-schaden.html

Spigel, Ben (2017): The Relational Organization of Entrepreneurial Ecosystems, Entrepreneurship Theory and Practice, January 2017, pp. 49–72

Statistisches Bundesamt (2021): China 2020 im fünften Jahr in Folge Deutschlands wichtigster Handelspartner, Pressemitteilung Nr. 077, 22 February 2021, https://www.destatis.de/DE/Presse/Pressemitteilungen/2021/02/PD21_077_51.html

Taube, Markus (2020): The Global Economic Regime at a Critical Juncture – The "Belt & Road Initiative" as a Means to Leverage Chinese Interests, in: Nele Noesselt (ed.): China's New Silk Road Dreams, Berliner China-Hefte No. 52, Zurich 2020: Lit Verlag, pp. 7–20

TBN Logistic and Trade GmbH (n.d.): Cost-Efficient Alternative to Air and Sea Transport, undated, https://tbngroup.de/en/international-forwarding-hamburg/rail-fraight-from-china-to-europe/

TopShipping Global Freight Company (n.d.): Shipping from China to Europe, undated, https://topshipping.cn/shipping-china-europe/#Germany

van Leijen, Majorie (2019): China Railway strikes down in Duisburg, RailFreight.com website, 6 December 2019, https://www.railfreight.com/beltandroad/2019/12/06/china-railway-strikes-down-in-duisburg/?gdpr=accept

Verfürden, Michael (2021): Duisburg will "Deutschlands China-Stadt" sein – doch Jobs fehlen und die Zeit läuft ab, Handelsblatt, 9 February 2021, https://www.handelsblatt.com/unternehmen/handel-konsumgueter/partnerschaft-mit-china-duisburg-will-deutschlands-china-stadt-sein-doch-jobs-fehlen-und-die-zeit-laeuft-ab/26866194.html

Xinhua (News Agency) (2011): Rail linking Europe to open up China's West, 2 July 2011, http://www.chinadaily.com.cn/bizchina/2011-07/02/content_12823190.htm

Zimmermann, Karsten, Christian Hundt, Christian Jütte und Carolin Pofalla (2017): Dortmund, Duisburg und die Rezession von 2008/2009 – Warum zwei Städte derselben Region ökonomisch unterschiedlich resilient sind, Raumforschung und Raumordnung, Volume 75, 2017, pp. 439–453

Joachim Ahrens and Katja Kalkschmied

China in Africa: Competitor of the EU?

1. Introduction: Beyond the forgotten continent

For many years, Africa, especially Sub-Saharan Africa (SSA), had been viewed as the forgotten continent with several lost decades in terms of economic growth, political stability, and inclusive people-centered development. Particularly Western countries, most notably the USA and European countries, have a long tradition to fight poverty and support marginalized African nations with traditional approaches of development aid and cooperation, while private sector engagement such as trade and investment have remained at very low levels compared to other world regions. Especially Official Development Assistance (ODA) payments and other financial transfers brought only partial success or even failed in the long run to support the emergence and creation of self-sustaining economic, social, and political structures in recipient countries (Easterly, 2006; Moyo, 2009). The overall economic situation started to change at the beginning of the 2000s. Economic growth rates began to increase and per-capita incomes began to grow in many African countries, leading to a nascent but in some cases steady process of growth and development. Yet, many problems have persisted. Africa is still the continent with widespread poverty and misery, poor governance, the lowest living standards, unequal income and asset distribution, political instabilities, and the lowest levels of human development measured by health, educational, and income indicators (UNDP, 2021; World Bank 2021).

The changes in the economic situation since 2000 have been accompanied by a fast-growing presence of China in Africa. It was China which reminded the world of the forgotten continent with its new interest for partnerships with African countries and its novel approach to design development aid and cooperation presumably at eye level and in a pragmatic manner. China developed a serious approach to engage numerous African states in its so-called belt-and-road initiative (BRI) and invested large sums of money in numerous long-term infrastructure projects. Better infrastructure reduces trade costs and allows African countries to develop domestic industries and markets and to integrate into world markets. This opens new development and trade opportunities for Africa, China and the rest of the world. Better infrastructure reduces trade costs and allows African countries to develop industries and markets and to integrate into world markets. This opens new development and trade opportunities for Africa, China and the rest of the world but also new threats that have to be taken care of.

Even in Europe a serious new interest in Africa has evolved. This has been mainly driven by growing concerns over migration and refugee flows from Africa to Europe. As a reaction, the European Union (EU) and its member countries seek to reduce and prevent the inflow of people and aim at stabilizing the economies and polities in selected African countries to decrease the incentives for migration and the causes for flight. This new policy priority, together with general concerns over underdevelopment and poverty, brought authorities in Europe and the EU itself to rethink and redesign traditional approaches to development cooperation and aid payments. New political strategies across Europe formally call for genuine partnerships among equals and negotiating about development support at eye level. They also request the cooperation of the development community including international organizations and traditional bilateral donors and partner countries. Most multilateral and bilateral agencies of development cooperation officially conclude that it takes the cooperation and coordination of the international community to support African countries to achieve self-sustaining trajectories of development. In fact, the African Union and the Organization for Economic Development and Co-operation (OECD) jointly request: "New development strategies are necessary" (African Union/OECD, 2018).

However: Reality has proven to be different. Notwithstanding visible and partially effective approaches to cooperation and coordination, e.g., among European countries, between Europeans and the US, within the G20, or between international organizations and bilateral donors, the current activities of third countries' governments, companies, and non-governmental organizations resembles rather a competition for political influence, access to markets and natural resources, and determining the directions of development. Some observers already diagnose a "new scramble for Africa" (The Economist, 9th March 2019, and Carmody, 2016).

Being the addressees of this competition: How will African countries react? What are the alternatives and what should they do? Should African countries jump on the developmental bandwagon of the BRI? Should they accept the cooperation offers of the EU and its members? Or should they follow distinct own initiatives, either in their region or inter-regionally? These questions guide this essay. They are being discussed in three steps. First China's growing role in Africa is being described in Chapter 2. It appears to challenge the traditional and novel approaches to development cooperation, European- or Western-style, which are addressed in Chapter 3. Chapter 4 contrasts the Chinese and the European initiatives, strategies, and models of development. Chapter 5 concludes.

2. China in Africa

Within the last 20 years, China has massively expanded its footprint in Africa. It made enormous coordinated efforts to build economic relations with African countries. These efforts paid off. China is among the top four bilateral partners for Africa in trade, investment (both loans and foreign direct investment (FDI)), and aid. Yet, the Chinese way of building alliances depends on far more than the flows in goods, services and capital. The economic partnership is built on, accompanied by and complemented by Chinese officials' efforts to build political partnerships, business networks and individual relationships between African and Chinese people. The goods, services and capital flows are directed in strategic areas. They come together with the building of infrastructure, the adoption of new technologies, the creation of social networks and social capital, and the transfer of knowledge and skills from person to person alongside with the transfer of persons from continent to continent. *Guanxi* is the Chinese word that describes the relationship-based cooperation approach that is distinctively different from the transaction-based approach of Western countries.

When Sino-African relations started to intensify at the turn of the millennium, African countries were not perceived as attractive economic partners due to serious deficiencies in infrastructure, political instabilities, high corruption, a lack in rule of law, missing or malfunctioning legal property rights and contracting institutions. Yet, China started to invest heavily in building infrastructure. Most analyses on what lies behind China's encompassing endeavors with and in African countries identify two primary motives: First, to secure access to raw materials and energy. For domestic production, China relies heavily on coal, oil, and raw material imports. Natural resource and energy shortages had slowed down production and consequently economic growth in China. The second motive is to build new markets for Chinese goods. It is the world's number one provider of low-value manufactured goods. Global demand for low-value manufactured goods slows down as developed countries' markets are increasingly saturated (Zhao, 2017). China's recently announced five-year plan for the 2021–25 period includes a 'dual circulation strategy' that intends to invest in the development of domestic markets in order to decrease the dependence of China's economic growth on export markets (Cheng, 2020). Still, a switch in the economic growth model is unlikely to happen in a short period in time. It is much more likely that China remains dependent on world markets in the future.

Cooperation with African economies can refuel Chinese economic growth by solving both issues. Africa is abundant of natural resources, oil, precious metals and coal. Also, African markets are only about to develop. Many African economies have experienced sustained, above world average growth rates throughout the last two decades (Zamfir, 2016). China, African, Asian, and Latin American developing economies are the world's growth engines. Since China and Africa will host about 40 % of the world's population already in 2050 (Marafa, 2009), Chinese and African consumer markets are of increasing importance in future. Investing in African countries now, China can critically influence the direction of the structural and economic development in African countries in a way to make it fit to China's present and future political and economic interests.

That the design of a country's foreign policies and cooperation strategies is driven by its economic interests is standard theory of international relations. What is new or particular of the Chinese approach is the *guanxi* way taken to pursue its interests. It centers on the narrative of a brotherly South-South cooperation for mutual benefits. The philosophy of guanxi shines through China's 2021 *White Paper on International Development Cooperation*, in which China casts its duty as a responsible member of the global community, emphasizing "*humanware* over hardware, highlighting capacity building, livelihood initiatives, volunteerism, and people-to-people connectivity" (Mulakala and Hongbo, 2021) to alleviate poverty in the world. Chinese officials communicate to target a cooperation between developing countries in which the parties meet at eye level and do not interfere in internal affairs, in which each party pursues its own endeavors and, in doing that in a cooperative way, win-win situations are created (World Foresight Forum, 2011). The speeches given by the Chinese foreign minister, Wang Yi, during his five-country trip to Nigeria, the Democratic Republic of Congo, Botswana, Tanzania and the Seychelles in January 2021 were all about *guanxi*. Wang laid out a seven-point plan to upgrade China-Africa cooperation for 2021, and pledged that China will provide substantial finance to bolster health, agricultural, digital, environmental, military and security cooperation, regional connectivity and free trade as well as industrial capacity in Africa (Mulakala and Hongbo, 2021).

Another reason why China was able to grab a foothold in African countries within such a short period of time lies in the pragmatism of the Chinese approach (Jing, 2017). China is exceptionally fast in making decisions and letting actions follow, whether this concerns providing finance, implementing infrastructure projects, negotiating and agreeing on trade conditions, setting up businesses, sending Chinese experts and workers as well as providing military support, support in educational or medical matters.

The foundation of the Forum on China-Africa Cooperation (FOCAC) in 2001 marks the beginning of increased Chinese efforts to cooperate with African countries. In the FOCAC framework, Chinese and African senior officials meet every three years to refresh their "brotherly ties", deliberate, plan future cooperation actions and reevaluate past ones. At the 2018 FOCAC Beijing summit, Chinese and African leaders agreed to build a stronger Sino-African community with a shared future. As mechanisms to foster friendship between the Chinese and African people, the Think Tank Forum, The People's Forum, the Press Center and the Youth Festival were implemented. By 2021, China has provided some 120,000 government scholarships, and opened 61 Confucius Institutes and 44 Confucius Classrooms in 46 African countries. As many as 21,000 Chinese medical personnel have worked in 48 African countries, providing treatment to around 220 million African people. The shared common future entails building a Sino-African community of development with support in enhancing infrastructure, advancing industrialization and building up capacity for independent development (speech by Wang Yi, Chinese Minister of Foreign Affairs, on 12. November 2020). Chinese trade and development cooperation with Africa go hand in hand. Bilateral trade agreements reduce non-physical trade barriers, infrastructure and industry building projects reduce physical trade barriers.

The Belt and Road Initiative (BRI), launched in 2013, is the central mechanism for the realization of infrastructure and industry building projects. 42 out of 54 African countries have already signed an agreement to take part in the BRI. China began many of its investment activities in the East Africa region, given its access to ports and need for rails and roads, but initiatives have since branched out to numerous projects across the continent. Major road infrastructure projects stretch to Southern and Northern Africa, such as Mozambique's Maputo–Katembe bridge and Algeria's Cherchell Ring Expressway Project (Dong et al., 2018). The success in fostering Sino-African trade and development cooperation within the last 20 years can be seen in the increase of trade flows, provision of loans, provision of aid, FDI flows, the number of Chinese-owned enterprises and the number of Chinese workers in Africa.

China is Africa's largest bilateral trader. In 2019, it was the largest export market for 16 African countries and the largest source of imports for 35 African countries. According to the Johns Hopkins China-Africa Research Initiative (SAIS-CARI) which draws on UNComtrade data, trade between Africa and China has been growing at approximately 20 % per year from US$ 14.71 billion in 2000 to US$ 191.73 billion in 2019. The value of exports to China in 2019 was US$ 78.68 billion. The largest exporter was Angola followed by South Africa and the Republic of Congo. Exports predominately consisted of resources such as oil and minerals as well as semi-processed raw materials including copper, base metals, wood and articles thereof. The value of imports from China was US$ 113.05 billion in 2019. The largest importers were Nigeria, South Africa and Egypt. Imports predominately consisted of manufactured goods including electrical machinery, other machinery, vehicles, articles of iron or steel and plastics and articles thereof (The Africa Report, 2019). To boost free trade, eight special economic zones were installed; two in Algeria and one in Egypt, Sudan, Nigeria, Zambia, Malawi and Mauritius. Mauritius became the first African country to sign a free trade agreement with China in 2019 (The Economist Intelligence Unit, 2021).

No other country provides as many loans to Africa as China does. Between 2000 and 2019, SAIS-CARI estimated that Chinese financiers signed 1,141 loan commitments worth 153US$bn with African governments and their state-owned enterprises. By far the most loans went to Angola followed by Zambia, Sudan, Ethiopia, Cameroon and Kenya. Loans worth 46.6US$bn went to transportation projects, US$ 38.0 billion to power projects and US$ 18.4 billion to mining projects. Loan finance is varied. Chinese loans constitute export credits, suppliers' credits and commercial loans that are not concessional in nature. Some government loans qualify as ODA and are concessional for infrastructure and export credits. According to the State Council Information Office of the People's Republic of China (2021), 44.65 % of Chinese foreign aid expenditures between 2013 and 2018 went to Africa. At the 2018 FOCAC summit in Beijing, Chinese President XI Jinping pledged another US$ 60 billion of finance for African growth: US$ 20 billion for credit lines, US$ 15 billion for grants, interest-free loans and concessional loans, US$ 10 billion as special fund for development finance, US$ 5 billion as special fund for financing imports from Africa and US$ 10billion for other investment over three years. Funds will flow into eight major initiatives: industrial development, infrastructure connectivity, trade facilitation, green development, capacity building, health care, people-to-people exchanges, peace and security (The Africa Report, 2019).

FDI complements loans as another channel of China's financial involvement in Africa. Though there is a primacy of loans over FDI, the gap narrows. Starting from nearly zero in 2000, the Chinese FDI stock in China has grown faster than trade to US$ 49 billion in 2016 with an average annual growth rate of 40 % (McKinsey, 2017). Chinese largest FDI stocks are in South Africa, followed by Nigeria, Zambia, Angola, Ethiopia, Kenya and Tanzania. The FDI sectors vary greatly across these countries. FDI has been targeted and differentiated. In resource rich countries like South Africa, Nigeria and Zambia, FDI has been directed towards transport, power, extractives, and telecoms sectors. In Ethiopia,

Kenya, Tanzania and also Nigeria, FDI went into transport and industrial sector projects. With respect to ownership, Chinese state-owned enterprises have played and still play a critical role in the natural resources sector. In other sectors such as manufacturing or services, there is a rapid rise of privately-owned Chinese companies which invest mainly their own money. According to a 2016–2017 McKinsey field study, only about 15 % of enterprises were linked to the Chinese government. The private Chinese firms do well. In 2015, nearly one-third of them reported profit margins of more than 20 %. Most Chinese firms in Africa operate in manufacturing (31 %), services (25 %) and construction and real estate (15 %) sectors. An increasing number diversifies into new high-growth-potential industries: agriculture and food production, banking and insurance, housing, information communications technology and telecommunications, and transport and logistics. McKinsey reports that 89 % of the employees were African. Yet, only 44 % of the managers were African. An extrapolation across the continent suggests that there are more than 10,000 Chinese-owned firms operating in Africa today. Together with Chinese state-owned firms, they hired about 200,000 Chinese workers.

The Chinese endeavors in and with Africa seem to bite. Chinese investments in Africa over the last two decades have successfully improved infrastructure and increased industrial capacity, they have created jobs – the 10,000 private Chinese enterprises surveyed by McKinsey together already hired 300,000 African workers – and they have certainly contributed to the above world average growth rates of African countries. This is the winning part for African countries. The winning part for China lies in increased imports of natural resources from African countries, increased exports of manufacturing goods to African countries and the high profitability of private Chinese firms in African countries (McKinsey, 2017).

Yet, not all is gold. On the financial side, experts are increasingly concerned that African countries will default on their debts. Several countries such as Zambia are bumping up against their debt ceilings, failing to make repayments to China and other lenders. The Covid-19 pandemic has aggravated the situation (Acker et al., 2021). On the business side, there are concerns regarding employment conditions and regulations. Many Chinese firms operate with insufficient regards for the health and safety of workers, taking advantage of the few regulatory constraints in many African countries. Many Chinese workers who moved to Africa live in very decent conditions and are hardly integrated into local communities (Asongu and Ssozi, 2015). On the environmental side, the concerns lie in failing to jump on the track of sustainable development. Instead, the extraction of non-renewable resources is continued and currently viewed as an important pillar of China-Africa trade and development cooperation, which drives growth in China and Africa. Although the Chinese 2021 White Paper puts emphasis on strengthening efforts for a green development, few actions have been taken in that direction so far. On the development side, little is known about the long-run prospects of the Sino-African cooperation. Not everybody won so far. The most obvious losers are the African manufacturers that have come under pressure from both imported manufacturing products from China and products of Chinese-owned manufacturing sites in Africa. There are concerns that China is not Africa's biggest development partner but Africa's biggest development competitor, whose explosive growth and insatiable quest for resources and global markets threatens Africa's industrialization and competitiveness (Zeleza, 2014). These concerns are not only among economists. In the wake of the 2006 FOCAC summit in Beijing, Thabo Mbeki, president of South Africa at that time, was quoted as declaring:

> "(…) if Africa just exported raw materials to China while importing Chinese manufactured goods, the African continent could be 'condemned to underdevelopment'. He [Thabo Mbeki] said that this would simply mean 'a replication' of Africa's historical relationship with its former colonial powers." (BBC News, 2006)

3. Europe's approach to development cooperation, trade, and investment

Despite the growing trade and development cooperation between China and Africa, the EU has been and still is (even after Brexit) the largest donor of ODA, investor, and trading partner of Africa. African-European cooperation initiatives have been traditionally driven by the desire to fight poverty and misery and to overcome underdevelopment especially in Sub-Saharan Africa (SSA). Due to their colonial past, European countries have assumed particular responsibilities as donors to African countries. Due to persistent bonds from the colonial period, some European countries, especially France and the United Kingdom, maintained special political and economic relations with distinct countries (i.e., the francophone African countries in the French case).

More recently, overarching problems such as growing migration from Africa to Europe, political instabilities and international terrorism, the need to find global solutions for the challenges of climate change, and environmental degradation strengthened further motives for European engagement for and with Africa. The perceived need to limit, control, and eventually prevent labor migration led to numerous European involvements with countries of origin of migration as well as with typical transit countries to physically stop people from migrating, to stabilize economies and governments. The pursuit to reduce migration also found its way into more recent updates of European development strategies for Africa as did measures to cooperate with African countries in matters of climate and environmental protection. The EU is seeking partners in Africa who are willing and prepared to join the EU on the way towards a so-called green transition and limiting climate change. Eventually, European authorities also see economic prospects and business opportunities: access to natural resources in Africa, low-cost production locations, and steadily growing markets.

New global challenges such as flight, labor migration, climate change, and international security issues as well as sobering experiences and failed development cooperation approaches in the past led European authorities (i.e., the European Commission, the European Parliament, and the European Council) to rethink and revise African-European relations recently. Key problems with traditional donor-recipient relations were the lack of ownership, credibility, and acceptance of aid-cum-reform packages on the one hand and the lack of absorptive capacities, capabilities, as well as inappropriate incentives systems on the other hand. Especially development aid through money transfers frequently induced dependencies on donors, cemented persisting conditions, promoted corruption, possibly financed violent conflicts, and destroyed incentives for doing business (Easterly 2006; Jakupec 2018; Moyo, 2009). A novel European development approach with Africa was elaborated by the European Commission and the High Representative of the Union for Foreign Affairs and Security Policy (2020) in the *Comprehensive Strategy with Africa*. This strategy will become the new foundation for a long-term sustained strategic partnership with the African Union (AU) along various dimensions including inter alia fighting poverty, promoting political dialog, fostering private-sector development, trade as well as inclusive growth-cum-development, technical and financial cooperation, virtually all Sustainable Development Goals (SDGs) as well as more modern topics such as digitalization, cybersecurity, data protection, preventing labor migration and refugee flows, drugs, environment protection, slowing climate change, and fostering the green transition (Boidin, 2020). The *Comprehensive Strategy with Africa* is complemented by other multilateral and bilateral approaches. The EU prepares the ratification process of a treaty to replace the so-called Cotonou agreement (Boidin, 2020; Yotova, 2021). In Germany, the government has introduced its Marshall Plan *with* Africa in 2017 and, in the same year under its G20 Presidency, initiated the *G20 Compact with Africa* (Federal Ministry for Economic Cooperation and Development, 2021; G20, 2021).

As regards economic relations between the EU and Africa, the Cotonou Agreement is the most important document. It is a partnership agreement between the EU and African, Caribbean and Pacific (ACP) countries. Especially, it covers trade and aid, but also relates to human rights and good governance. The Cotonou Agreement had replaced the unilateral trade preferences under the Lomé Convention with so-called Economic Partnership Agreements (EPAs). These include open-ended, interest-driven, reciprocal trade relations, i.e., free access to each partner's domestic market (Boidin, 2020). However, EPAs are often seen as mechanisms which predominantly seek to promote opportunities for European businesses and eventually adversely affect production and trade in Africa (Tadesse Abebe and Maalim, 2020).

In terms of international trade, the EU received 31 % of all African exports (China: 11 %, USA: 6 %) and accounted for 29 % of Africa's imports (China 16 %, USA: 5 %). More recently, EU trade relations with Africa as a whole have become more balanced with export and import values accounting for some 150 billion Euro and 140 billion Euro, respectively. However, total trade turnover was unevenly distributed with almost negligible values of some 20 billion Euro for Eastern and Central Africa. The largest European trading partners in absolute terms have been traditionally France, Germany, Spain the Netherlands, Italy, and Belgium. While the EU market has been important for African exports and imports, the opposite is the case from a European standpoint. Exports to Africa account only for 3.8 % of extra-EU trade for Germany and 10.9 % for France (Eurostat, 2021).

Aid payments have been at the forefront of development cooperation and economic relations between Europe and Africa for decades. In 2019, EU institutions disbursed 45.8 % of their total ODA to Africa and 33.4 % to SSA, indicating the importance of strengthening African economies from a European perspective. Germany as the second largest ODA donor (after the US), provided 24.6 % and 17.2 % of its ODA payments to Africa and SSA, respectively. OECD's Development Assistance Committee (DAC) countries offered 28.7 % and 24.8 %. In 2019, all DAC countries disbursed US$ 29.6 billion and US$ 25.6 billion to Africa as a whole and SSA according to merits and needs. Germany as one of the largest bilateral donors spent US$ 4.5 billion and US$ 3.2 billion. The EU Institutions provided US$ 6.8 billion to Africa and US$ 5.0 billion to SSA. While German ODA payments to Africa as well as globally nearly doubled between 2013 and 2019, EU Institutions' contributions hardly changed. DAC countries disbursements to Africa remained stable as well, but increased overall (i.e., to ODA recipients globally) by 10 %. Approximately 60 % of all ODA payments to Africa consistently come from DAC donors, almost 13 % from EU Institutions, and about 40 % from EU institutions plus European DAC members. If *Other Official Flows* (OOFs) and private flows (including direct and portfolio investments) are included, Europe (including EU Institutions and DAC EU members) provided financial means to Africa (SSA, respectively) between US$ 26.8 (17.2) billion and US$ 52.9 (43.6) billion in the period 2013–2019. About two thirds of these flows have been ODA payments (OECD, 2021).

The European private sector had largely neglected Africa, especially SSA. Only recently, some nascent dynamics emerged in terms of expanding trade relations and direct investment projects in a few African countries. Private sector flows from DAC countries including direct and portfolio investments to African countries have been highly volatile (especially portfolio investments). Direct investments to Africa as a whole and to SSA accounted to some US$ 98 billion and US$ 67 billion, respectively, in 2013–2019 (OECD, 2021). This implies that between 4.4 % (−0.6 %) and 18.4 % (26.1 %) of all annual private flows from DAC countries to developing countries went to Africa (SSA). These flows have been typically subject to strong volatility. In addition, these numbers reveal a sobering insight if compared to global private flows. It shows that direct investments to African countries have consistently accounted for less than 4 % of global direct investment and less than 10 % of direct investment to developing countries. Trade and investment data reveal that African economies are still of minor importance for European businesses (OECD 2021; UNCTAD, 2020).

All new European development strategy initiatives view Africa as Europe's direct neighbor who should be engaged through partnerships at eye level with a clear focus on ownership, responsibilities, and rights for self-determined development. This appears to be the condensed message which follows from virtually all official documents, speeches, and emerging strategies of the EU and single European governments. Another common feature of these European, German, French, and other initiatives is the perception that partnerships with African countries need to be guided by clear principles and criteria. In contrast to the proposed G20 Compact with Africa, but similar to the European Commission's strategy, the German Marshall Plan with Africa shows a broad scope. The Marshall Plan with Africa focuses on distinct objectives such as stability, employment, and the rule of law as well as measures to be taken in Germany, the EU, African countries and at international levels. This calls for a multilateral framework and creates a more suitable basis for development than an approach which merely emphasizes private investment, i.e., only one partial aspect of sustained development (Menkhoff and Stöhr, 2019).

Traditional European development strategies with Africa centered on aid transfers. Promising and providing aid in terms of money transfers is simpler and faster than agreeing and implementing a common strategy to restructure and develop a continent. The still existing weakness to coordinate communication, interests, and policies among European actors and between them and African governments and other stakeholders constitutes a bottleneck to the implementation and enforcement of European development cooperation with Africa. This particularly holds for the lack in effective communication with (potential) African partners, and this also relates to a neglect to ask for needs, priorities, and strategies which African governments and nations may favor (Tadesse Abebe and Maalim, 2020).

Effective development cooperation between European and African partners also suffers from the EU's and single European countries' heavy bureaucratic setup that produces numerous texts with many, at times, overlapping or even conflicting priorities (Boidin, 2020). The post-Cotonou agreement concluded between the EU and the ACP countries in December 2020 still needs to be ratified, which is expected to take up to three years. Disagreements among EU members threaten to undermine or at least delay the ratification process, so that Yotova (2021) warns that the momentum may be lost and a renewed strategic partnership between the two continents becomes increasingly more unlikely so that the agreement may amount to not much more than political rhetoric in the end.

Finance is another issue. The new European approaches lack sufficient financial resources, focus on a small number of so-called reform partnerships, and disregard failed or failing states (Menkhoff and Stöhr, 2019). Financial support may become less predictable as the EU merged the European Development Fund in the general EU budget. The programming of aid flows as well as management rules are no longer subject to joint deliberation, but can now be altered at the EU's will. Another problem is the lack of pooling resources and expertise to gain more leverage and developmental momentum. Boidin (2020, p. 6) concludes that "the new system of financial cooperation (…) will be much less 'partenarial' than before". At present, European financial commitments reach a similar level as the Chinese payments do. Yet, Europe lacks an authoritatively coordinated development cooperation policy or an initiative to pool forces to address the causes for flight. That is being further aggravated as EU countries pursue different political interests (Menkhoff and Stöhr, 2019).

The need for replacing the old with a new European development strategy is urgent. Yet, the planned AU-EU summit to negotiate the new strategic partnership had been delayed to 2021. Yotova (2021) argues that the AU-EU summit could be further postponed to 2022 as the next FOCAC meeting had been already scheduled to take place in 2021. Some Members of European Parliament feel time pressure and fear that the EU may lose further ground vis-à-vis China on the African continent the longer the summit will be postponed.

However, the new European development strategy as well as the novel bilateral approaches will hardly have groundbreaking effects. All novel approaches emphasizing and seeking genuine partnerships with African countries are still characterized by traditional, old traits of yesterday's donor-recipient relations. Partnerships are advertised, but documents still convey (explicitly or between the lines) the expectation that only those African countries qualify as partners which share certain (European) values, norms, and cooperation objectives and fulfill distinct (European) standards of governance, democracy and the rule of law, market capitalism, and social development. Hence, European approaches still reflect donors' aims, preferences and self-interests. They neither account for the actual situation in African countries, nor for priorities which African people would need. They do not take account of African governments and elites which would possibly need to act against their own interests if they actually pursued the advertised (new) European development strategies (Booth and Golooba-Mutebi, 2011; Köhler, 2017).

In sum: The European approach to development cooperation, trade, and investment has changed recently. Yet, bureaucratic hurdles, lack of finance and conflicting interests among European authorities continue to be controversial issues. Moreover, the new approaches continue to show essential traits of the paternalistic donor-recipient relationships which had brought about numerous disappointments with the traditional approaches. Therefore, one may still agree with Booth and Golooba-Mutebi (2011: 1–2), who argued ten years ago:

> "Despite the frequently reported death of the Washington Consensus, international policy prescriptions for low-income Africa remain ideological, unimaginative and out of touch with reality. The intellectual capital and financial leverage Western donors and concessional lenders still exercise is dissipated on the promotion of a standard package of institutional 'best practices' which includes sound macroeconomic management, transparent public finances, free and fair elections, the rule of law, well-defined property rights and an arm's length relationship between private enterprise and the state. (…) With the exception of sound macroeconomic management, the standard list of best practices owes very little to the actual experience of those poor developing countries which have reduced mass poverty and enabled the attainment of basic human rights in any part of the world, in recent decades (..). It does not correspond closely even to the earlier history of the countries that now take the lead in advocating free markets, multiparty politics and the rule of law around the world."

4. European *developmental paternalism* vs. Chinese *smartness*

Disappointments relating to traditional European approaches to development aid and cooperation with the typical donor-recipient relations as well as the

Tab. 1: Comparison of the European and Chinese development and cooperation approaches

Washington Consensus **and the European approach**	***Beijing Consensus*** **and the Chinese approach**
Universality: One model of development based on economic liberalization, democratization, and Western values and experiences	Particularity: Model(s) of independent, country-specific development allowing heterodox approaches
Primary role of state: ensure market institutions work, promoting an open social, ecological market economy	Strong states making strategic interventions, semi-free markets, illiberal political systems possible
Adherence to specific values and norms as precondition for cooperation: human rights, democracy, rule of law in Western-style interpretation	Principle of non-interference in internal affairs and self-determination, presumed unconditionality of loans/aid
Developmental paternalism: no genuine partnership of equals, lack of ownership, credibility and acceptance of (imposed) reforms	Chinese smartness: pragmatic South-South partnerships at eye level for mutual benefits, clearer ownership, relative high credibility, and acceptance of policies
Problem of simultaneousness, focus on holistic development. Implementation: slow	Focus on gradual one-step-at-a-time development. Implementation: fast

Source: Authors' compilation.

missing success of (post)Washington Consensus policy reforms prescribed by the World Bank and the International Monetary Fund – which often were prerequisites for ODA flows from Europe and the US – entailed growing dissatisfaction in African countries and beyond. This opened room for new cooperation "offers". One offer emerged at the beginning of the 2000s, when China proposed the so-called *Beijing Consensus* as an alternative model of development. The Chinese development approach may not be restricted to China. It relies on principles and shows characteristics which could be attractive for governments of less developed countries eager to catch up economically. If so, the Beijing Consensus would seriously challenge the *Washington Consensus* approach which had guided European-African cooperation for a long time.

The two models of development and their inherent development-cooperation approaches differ significantly from each other. Tab. 1 contrasts them in five aspects to better understand why Chinese involvement has been welcomed in African countries and gained so much importance within the last twenty years, while Europe's influence decreased.

First, proponents of the Washington Consensus and its successor strategies claim universality. Respective policy and institutional reforms are normative and propose essentially the same strict reform packages to nearly all developing countries irrespective of their heterogeneous economic, political, cultural, and environmental structures. Internal and external economic liberalization and stabilization need to go hand in hand with democratization. This development model does not only declare macroeconomic stability, deregulation, and secure private property rights as development goals but also prescribes the ways to reach these goals. These approaches are based on European experiences, norms and values as much as on European interests such as preventing migration and adapting to the EU's so-called *Green Deal*. China instead acknowledges the need for idiosyncratic approaches to meet country-specific challenges. Therefore, it gives pragmatism priority over ideals in its development cooperation with African countries. The Chinese approach allows independent, country-specific development under heterodox approaches and does not dictate distinct policy measures to those who seek development (Ramo, 2004). Whatever approach a country takes, China approves it as long as it is compatible with Chinese interests, i.e., having access to natural resources, export markets and profitable business opportunities.

Second, the two development models differ regarding the role of the state. The Washington Consensus sees the primary role of the state to ensure that market institutions work. The principles of liberalization, privatization, and deregulation are closely associated with the neoliberal school of thought (Turin, 2010). In a European tradition, this approach combines the development of functioning markets with building democratic governance structures, ensuring social cohesion and addressing ecological concerns. The Beijing Consensus suggests an almost diametrically opposed approach (Serra and Stiglitz, 2008). It recognizes the need for flexibility and pragmatism in solving multifarious problems and underlines the role of the state in macroeconomic planning and strategic market interventions. Semi-free markets and industrial policies are not only allowed but advised, even required, when market or coordination failures persist. This approach also acknowledges that development requires effective governance. Yet, it argues that effective governance is possible in non-democratic regimes (Ahrens and Stark, 2015; Ramo, 2004). The Beijing Consensus is based on a state-capitalist regime. China does not seek to impose its own model on African countries, but it clearly communicates its presumably positive developmental characteristics and highlights its focus on innovation, equitable development, and self-determination. The Chinese development model is especially attractive to African countries under authoritarian leaderships for its non-requirement of political change and its opportunity to legitimize illiberal leadership through economic success.

The third aspect considers the conditionality of cooperation. Europe expects the adherence to and implementation of human rights, democracy and rule of law in its Western interpretation as political preconditions for partnerships. This requires some African authorities and elites to act against their (personal) interests in order to meet specific European institutional standards, expectations, and conditions. The allocation of aid, trade arrangements, and technical support from Europe to African countries is subject to conditionalities. African partners are expected to agree with policy and development priorities set by their European partners. These priorities include peace and governance, migration and mobility, green transition and energy access, digital transformation, sustainable growth and jobs (European Commission and the High Representative of the Union for Foreign Affairs and Security Policy, 2020). The priorities mainly reflect their European interests and European perception of what would be good solutions to African problems. China does not require good governance or the adherence to human rights, labor rights, and climate-friendly production conditions for cooperation. Chinese authorities appear to adhere to the principles of non-interference and self-determination. Whatever countries do is their business as long as it does not interfere with the Chinese business model. African leaders frequently welcome the provision of expertise, the favorable terms of trade, aid and loans which China offers while promising to keep hands off internal affairs (Gresh, 2008).

Fourth, for its strict prescription of distinct reforms, development priorities, and objectives as well as for the attached conditionality of development cooperation African actors may perceive the European approach as illegitimate developmental paternalism. African-European cooperation cannot be seen as a partnership of equals as long as genuine African interests and needs are disregarded and African voices remain unheard. As a result, the European approach cannot easily bring about African ownership of reform programs and development strategies. This eventually undermines the acceptance of presumably imposed aid-cum-reform packages in African countries. Due to conflicting national interests among different European governments and inconsistencies in its implementation, the European approach also lacks credibility. The German Marshall Plan *with* Africa, e.g., aims at correcting these insufficiencies of the traditional donor-recipient development cooperation approach. It seeks to offer an approach of "genuine partnerships", putting African development goals into the center of cooperation endeavors and giving responsibilities for development into the hands of African authorities. Still, little has changed in the practical design of African-European partnerships yet. There is still no common European voice and development strategy with African countries. China instead acts in a smart way to get African countries into a cooperation that meets its interests. China uses smart power (Nye, 2009), a combination of hard and soft power, to lure African countries into cooperation which benefits China and seemingly African countries, too, at least in the short run and with respect to accelerated economic growth. The narrative of a South-South partnership at eye level for individual and mutual benefits under the principle of self-determination and under country-specific economic development trajectories has enhanced credibility and acceptance in African countries.

Fifth, the Western development-cooperation model appears to be a holistic development approach that requires changes in economic, political and social spheres all at once. The all-encompassing plan for broad societal change is hard to achieve. It usually is politically impractical, especially if not adapted to country-specific challenges and interests. Also, it may be prohibitively costly, overcharge existing institutional capacities, and possibly require ruling elites to act against their interests (Yao, 2011). Numerous comprehensive structural adjustment programs in the 1980s and 1990s that had been imposed on African countries by international organizations – at times in concert with bilateral European donors – failed. This has certainly negatively affected the acceptance of Western policy advice and ODA and slowed down African-European development cooperation. The Chinese approach is again smarter. Changes are piecemeal, but pragmatic, gradual rather than shock-therapy like. Where changes and reforms go easy, they are prioritized and build the foundation for further steps to follow. The one-step-at-a-time strategy combined with pragmatism, self-interest and short-time orientation allows a faster implementation with continuous success experiences.

5. Conclusion: Whither Africa?

Now, can we say that there is a competition for Africa between Europe and China? The answer is clearly a "Yes". But competition for what? It is a competition in several dimensions: a competition for natural resources and markets in the economic dimension, a competition for political influence and geopolitical power (including winning African countries to take Chinese side in UN matters and securing transportation ways) in the political dimension, and a competition for a suitable development model in a normative view of development.

What may be the implications of this intensifying competition? The gradual shift in African countries' development and trade cooperation away from Europe towards China is a driver as much as an outcome of a reallocation of political and economic power and influence at the expense of the Western nations and in favor of China. This power reallocation holds opportunities as much as threats for Africa and the world in general.

China's growing presence in Africa also offers opportunities for African countries. On the economic side, it helps to increase Africa's intra- and interregional connectivity, develop industries and markets. On the political side, it necessitates Europe and the West in general to rethink their developmental partnership approach. In that sense, competition between China and Europe increases Africa's bargaining position for it may seemingly have a choice among alternative trade and development partners as well as models. Yet, China's success with and in African countries may imply serious problems and risks. In the short run, we already see human rights violations and the legitimization of illiberal politics, labor rights violations, natural resource exploitation driving climate change, and manufactured goods imports blocking domestic industries to evolve. In the medium and long run, one may expect debt defaults and intensifying dependencies on China. At some later point, African countries may find themselves in a severe lock-in situation, in which Sino-African cooperation may turn to become harmful for African countries, but lock-in effects prevent African governments to reduce cooperation.

China's success in and with African countries may serve as a wake-up call for European authorities and governments. They may find it beneficial and necessary to pool resources, to seriously rethink their development cooperation strategies, and eventually to explicitly account for African interests and needs and to actively involve African stakeholders in development cooperation. The actual and conceivable risks and threats of Sino-African relations might, in addition, strengthen the momentum of such a reset and new start of African-European relations. When China is becoming a major geopolitical power in Africa, a multilateral development alliance including African, European, American, and possibly Asian powers (such as India) might be a true alternative to Chinese pragmatism and short-term economic and financial lures. The Covid-19 pandemic may actually represent an opportunity for Europeans and their allies to regain trust if they agree to pragmatically provide large aid packages, vaccines, and medical support without any strings attached.

Moreover, and in more general terms, it is necessary for European authorities to accept that African actors need to be in the driver's seat. Horst Köhler, former Federal President of Germany and former IMF Managing Director, stated that

African transformation will only succeed with African actors and their own priorities. Köhler (2017) requests that several European actors need to give up their "Allmachtsfantasien" (fantasies of omnipotence), and he adds that African transformation will only emerge from itself and not from donors' sense of mission nor from European defensive reflexes. This implies a clear warning not to misuse policies of development cooperation as obvious instruments for steering and controlling migration.

As long as the Europeans do not really act in a coordinated manner and do not speak with one voice in the realms of foreign policy and development cooperation, the EU, its member states, and their governance structure will appear to be weak, even fragile, not being able to credibly commit to genuine partnerships with African countries. If the EU manages to supra-nationalize foreign policy and development cooperation, if European development agencies focus on distinct projects based on African needs, suggestions from African governments and stakeholders and embedded into the institutional framework of the African Union, if Europeans apply a more inclusive, people-centered, pragmatic, less paternalistic approach, if they refrain from normative holistic development approaches, and if they successfully engage in effective multilateral development coalitions – then Europe and its partners may be able to generate an alternative offer to African nations which may appear to be more attractive than development cooperation, Chinese-style. In such a scenario, African governments and actors may have a real choice and be able to choose a self-determined path of development.

China has come to Africa to stay and to seek benefits; possibly at the expense of others. Without any doubt, China's presence in Africa will shape the development of millions of people on the previously forgotten continent. European governments have to accept this competition and badly need to bring about a more attractive offer for African partners – this will be in the interests of all neighbors in Africa and Europe.

References

Acker, Kevin; Brautigam, Deborah; Huang, Yufan (26.02.2021): The pandemic has worsened Africa's debt crisis. China and other countries are stepping in, The Washington Post; available at https://www.washingtonpost.com/politics/2021/02/26/pandemic-has-worsened-africas-debt-crisis-china-other-countries-are-stepping/ (accessed 30 April 2021)

African Union/OECD (African Union Commission/Organisation for Economic Co-operation and Development) (2018): Africa's Development Dynamics

2018. Growth, Jobs and Inequalities, Addis Ababa: AUC/Paris: OECD Publishing.

Ahrens, Joachim and Stark, Manuel (2015): Independent Organizations in Authoritarian Regimes: Contradiction in Terms or an Effective Instrument of Developmental States? In: B. Seliger, J. Sepp, R. Wrobel (eds.), East Asia and Eastern Europe in a Globalized Perspective. Lessons from Korea and Estonia. Frankfurt am Main: Peter Lang, pp. 163–197.

Asongu, S. A. and Ssozi, J. (2015): Sino-African relations: some solutions and strategies to the policy syndromes, African Governance and Development Institute, Working Paper.

Boidin, Jean-Claude (2020): "ACP-EU relations. The end of preferences? A personal assessment of the post-Cotonou agreement", ecdpm Discussion Paper No. 289OACPS-EU; available at https://ecdpm.org/wp-content/uploads/ACP-EU-Relations-End-Preferences-Personal-Assessment-Post-Cotonou-Agreement-ECDPM-Discussion-Paper-289-2020.pdf (accessed 29 April 2021)

Booth, David and Golooba-Mutebi, Frederick (2011): "Developmental patrimonialism? The case of Rwanda", Working Paper 16, Overseas Development Institute, London; available at https://www.researchgate.net/publication/270777957_Developmental_Patrimonialism_The_Case_of_Rwanda (accessed 29 April 2021)

Carmody, Padráig R. (2016): The New Scramble for Africa (2nd ed.). Cambridge, UK: Polity Press.

Cheng, Evelyn (31.08.2020): How China is preparing its economy for a future where the U.S. isn't the center of global demand; available at https://www.cnbc.com/2020/09/01/dual-circulation-how-china-is-preparing-for-a-new-role-in-international-trade.html (accessed 29 April 2021)

Dong, Carolyn; Davis, Matthew; Yu, Simin (5.11.2018): China's One Belt One Road: Opportunities in Africa. Africa Connected: Doing Business in Africa (1). DLA piper; available at https://www.dlapiper.com/en/southafrica/insights/publications/2018/11/africa-connected-doing-business-in-africa/chinas-one-belt-one-road-opportunities-in-africa/ (accessed 29 April 2021)

Easterly, W. (2006): The White Man's Burden: Why the West's Efforts to Aid the Rest Have Done So Much Ill and So Little Good. Oxford: Oxford University Press.

European Commission and the High Representative of the Union for Foreign Affairs and Security Policy (2020): Joint Communication to the European Parliament and the Council. Towards a comprehensive Strategy with Africa. Brussels; available at: https://ec.europa.eu/international-partnerships/system/files/communication-eu-africa-strategy-join-2020-4-final_en.pdf (accessed 29 April 2021)

Eurostat (2021): Africa-EU – International trade in goods statistics; available at https://ec.europa.eu/eurostat/statistics-explained/pdfscache/71514.pdf (accessed 29 April 2021)

Federal Ministry for Cooperation and Development (2021): A New Partnership for Development, Peace and a Better Future. A Marshall Plan with Africa; available at https://www.bmz.de/en/countries/marshall-plan-with-africa (accessed 29 April 2021)

G20 (2021): About the Compact with Africa; available at https://www.compactwithafrica.org/content/compactwithafrica/home.html (accessed 29 April 2021)

Gresh, Alain (03.11.2008): Le Monde Diplomatique; available at https://mondediplo.com/2008/11/03beijingconsensus (accessed 29 April 2021)

Jakupec, Viktor (2018): A Critique of the Development Aid Discourse, in: V. Jakupec (ed.), Development Aid – Populism and the End of the Neoliberal Agenda. Cham: Springer, pp. 37–52.

Jing, Yijia, (2017): The transformation of Chinese governance: Pragmatism and incremental adaption, Governance: An International Journal of Policy, Administration, and Institutions, Vol. 30(1), pp. 37–43.

Köhler, Horst (2017): "Welt im Umbruch, Afrika im Aufbruch – passt unsere Entwicklungspolitik noch ins 21. Jahrhundert?" Rede von Bundespräsident a.D. Prof. Dr. Horst Köhler beim Zukunftsforum "Globalisierung gerecht gestalten" Bundesministerium für Wirtschaftliche Zusammenarbeit und Entwicklung Berlin, 15. Februar 2017; available at https://www.horstkoehler.de/wp-content/uploads/2017/02/3.-Zukunftsforum-Welt-im-Umbruch-Afrika-im-Aufbruch-Horst-K%C3%B6hler-2017.pdf (accessed 29 April 2021)

Marafa, L. M. (2009): African's Business and Development Relationship with China, Nordiska Afrikainstitute, Uppsala. Discussion Paper 44.

McKinsey Study (2017): Dance of the lions and the dragons: How are Africa and China engaging and how will partnership evolve?

Menkhoff, Lukas, and Stöhr, Tobias (2019): "Europe must work together to alleviate migratory pressure from Africa", DIW-Weekly Report, 16+17+18/2019, pp. 164–166.

Moyo, Dambisa (2009): Dead Aid. Why aid is not working and how there is another way for Africa. London: Allen Lane.

Mulakala, Anthea and Hongbo Ji (25.01.2021): Development Policy Center, Insights on China's 2021 white paper on international development cooperation; available at https://devpolicy.org/insights-on-chinas-2021-white-paper-on-international-development-cooperation-20210125-2/ (accessed 29 April 2021)

Nye, Joseph S. Jr. (2009), Get Smart: Combining Hard and Soft Power, Foreign Affairs, Vol. 88, No. 4, pp. 160–163.

OECD (2021): Geographical Distribution of Financial Flows to Developing Countries 2021. Disbursements, Commitments, Country Indicators. Paris: OECD Publishing; available at https://read.oecd-ilibrary.org/development/geographical-distribution-of-financial-flows-to-developing-countries-2021_a50961e5-en-fr#page1 (accessed 29 April 2021)

Ramo, Joshua Cooper (2004): The Beijing Consensus. *The Foreign Policy Centre.*

Serra, Narcis and Stiglitz, Joseph (2008): The Washington consensus reconsidered: Towards a new global governance. Oxford: Oxford University Press.

Tadesse Abebe, Tsion and Maalim, Hafsa (2020): "Relations between Africa and Europe: mapping Africa's priorities", Institute for Security Studies, Africa Report 25; available at https://issafrica.org/research/africa-report/relations-between-africa-and-europe-mapping-africas-priorities (accessed 29 April 2021)

The Africa Report (19.09.2019): China's growing reach in Africa: are we seeing a fair trade?; available at https://www.theafricareport.com/17380/chinas-growing-reach-in-africa-are-we-seeing-a-fair-trade/.# (accessed 29 April 2021)

The Economist Intelligence Unit (2021): Africa-China relations: Taming the dragon: new frontiers of co-operation?

Turin, Dustin (2010): The Beijing Consensus: China's Alternative Development Model, Inquiries Journal, Vol. 2(01), pp. 1–2.

UNCTAD (2020): World Investment Report 2020. International Production Beyond the Pandemic, Geneva: United Nations; available at https://unctad.org/system/files/official-document/wir2020_en.pdf (accessed 29 April 2021)

UNDP (2021): Human Development Index (HDI); available at http://hdr.undp.org/en/content/human-development-index-hdi (accessed 30 April 2021)

Wang Yi, Chinese Minister of Foreign Affairs (12. November 2020): Speech: Build on Twenty Years of Proud Achievements and Open Up a New Chapter in China-Africa Relations; available at Build on Twenty Years of Proud Achievements and Open Up a New Chapter in China-Africa Relations (fmprc.gov.cn) (accessed 29 April 2021)

World Bank (2021): World Development Indicators; available at https://databank.worldbank.org/source/world-development-indicators (accessed 30 April 2021)

World Foresight Forum (2011): The Beijing Consensus: An alternative approach to development, Issue Brief No. 02.

Yotova, Denica (2021): "After Cotonou: How Europe can forge new relations with Africa in 2021"; available at https://ecfr.eu/article/after-cotonou-how-europe-can-forge-new-relations-with-africa-in-2021/ (accessed 29 April 2021)

Zamfir, Ionel (2016): Africa's economic growth: Taking off or slowing down? European Parliamentary Research Service.

Zeleza, Paul (2014): The Africa-China relationship: Challenges and opportunities, Canadian Journal of African Studies, Vol. 48(1), pp.145–169.

Zhao, Suisheng (ed.) (2017): China in Africa: Strategic Motives and Economic Interests. Milton Park: Routledge.

Part IV: Soft power approaches of the Belt and Road Initiative

Tereza Novotná

From connectivity to sanctions and from soft to hard power approaches: How the European Union and South Korea have been responding to the US-China competition

Introduction

> *"...The pandemic has reinforced the sense how connected and interdependent we are in strategic domains. As ever, the key question is: who controls these flows and who will set the rules and standards?... The European approach to connectivity with its emphasis on rules, sustainability and local benefits and ownership matches how many in the [Asian] region want to proceed. But this is a competitive field: some big players are moving in a determined way. There is a battle of standards underway... the EU will need a pro-active approach and to leverage its economic and other assets, working with like-minded partners wherever this makes sense."*
>
> *Josep Borrell, 12 March 2021*

In the quote above from his blog post on the European Union's (EU) strategic approach to the Indo-Pacific (Borrell 2021), the High Representative of the Union for Foreign Affairs and Vice-President of the European Commission (HRVP) Josep Borrell highlights how he sees the link between connectivity and long-term geo-political and geo-economic challenges for the EU in the Indo-Pacific. Although the world is increasingly connected and interdependent, the resulting situation is not more cooperation but more competition – with Indo-Pacific becoming its center-stage, the United States (US) and China the key rivals and connectivity one of the ways in which the competition manifests itself.

Even if an increasing number of Asian countries appreciates the "European approach" and various types of partnerships with the EU across the region have intensified, the fragility of "a more connected, contested and complex world", as Borrell's predecessor, HRVP Federica Mogherini, expressed it in her EU Global Strategy (European Union 2016) has become apparent throughout the global pandemic. Once the Covid19 hit, interdependence and interconnectedness between the two continents showed their limits: not only the Coronavirus has been spreading at a rapid speed but also nationalism which was shutting the open borders and protectionism that was shuttering the global supply chains.

Notwithstanding the immediate reaction to the health crisis, the question how the EU will shape its relationship with China, and whether or not European capitals join forces with Washington and others in contesting Beijing's rise, is the elephant in the room that has been looming behind the turmoil brought about by Covid19. On top of this, the EU has been mulling over which parts of its toolkit to employ in its dealing with China – from soft to hard power approaches and from trade deals up to sanctions. It is however not only Europe which has been confronted with such a tough predicament; South Korea – and many other countries in Asia-Pacific – are in a similar position and face an identical dilemma of "being caught between the US and China". They, too, have been reflecting on what strategy and methods to use.

This chapter therefore examines the ways in which the EU (and South Korea) have been responding to China's geopolitical and economic growth and how their reactions complement, or contradict, the policies pursued by the US, first under the Trump and then under the Biden administrations. Even though Donald Trump has been more vocal in his bid to oppose China, the chapter argues that there might be more continuity with the new administration than anticipated even if Joe Biden liaises more frequently with his partners in Europe and Asia. His accent on the alliances may, paradoxically, give the EU (and South Korea) more hard time to chart their own independent course. As an example, the chapter looks at the first Quad meeting and its implications for both Seoul and Brussels.

The second part of this chapter examines how the EU and South Korea interact with China's policies towards Europe and Asia, including its Belt and Road Initiative (BRI). The chapter explores how BRI has been countered by various forms of connectivity by Brussels and Seoul who view them from different angles, how BRI fits within today's geopolitical landscape and whether and where there is any space for creating synergies between the EU and South Korea but also with others to offset it. Furthermore, the chapter investigates how other types of EU policies from trade to sanctions have shaped the EU's relationship with China and how Beijing responded to these EU initiatives. The chapter argues that a combination of soft- and hard-power approaches which Brussels have put forward may in the end work well for the EU and others, including the US. Throughout the text, where possible, the chapter indicates when and how North Korea could be included into the equation. To conclude, the chapter suggests policy areas where cooperation rather than confrontation between all the actors is possible, proposing the fields of health, international trade, climate action and people-to-people exchanges.

From Trump to Biden: Europe (and South Korea) caught between the US and China

The European view on how the Trump Administration has approached the Covid19 pandemics – and China more broadly – has been, to put it mildly, ambivalent at best. On the one hand, Brussels has shared Washington's concerns about uncertain origins of the Coronavirus and handling of the illness by Beijing, including the lack of transparency by the Chinese authorities at the beginning of the epidemic. Even though the Europeans may have disliked President Trump's rhetoric about "China virus", Beijing didn't endear itself to them by a rather clumsy "mask diplomacy" towards various EU Member States and aggressive statements and steps against any critics condemning the Chinese intransigent approach, both at home and abroad.

On the other hand, the ineffectual response to the dangers of Covid19 by the Trump Administration was compounded by uncoordinated actions, such as the US travel ban on European countries whose leaders did not receive any advance notice. In a similar vein, the American attempt to buy off and monopolize the CureVac, a German company that was at that time the frontrunner for a Covid-19 vaccine (Hernández-Morales 2020), has made the US a dubious leader and ally in the fight against the common enemy – Coronavirus – in the eyes of many Europeans. According to a Pew poll (Gramlich 2020) from late September 2020, a staggering 84 % of the Europeans (and 93 % of the South Koreans) thought that the US had done a bad job dealing with the Coronavirus outbreak, whilst China received an average of 40.3 %[1] for handling Covid-19 well among the surveyed Europeans (but only 20 % among the South Koreans).

These developments induced by the worldwide Covid19 emergency have nonetheless been accompanied by tendencies that could have been observed for some time. The rise of China throughout the preceding decades and its demands to have a seat at the table while suggesting that Beijing is ready to take on greater responsibilities commensurate with its increased weight created tensions over who will set the standards of global trade already under previous US administrations. After all, it was President Barack Obama who proposed the Trans-Pacific (TPP) and Transatlantic (TTIP) trade partnerships in order to

1 Author's own calculations, based on Pew Research (Gramlich, 2020).

reduce the growing Chinese economic clout and to foster open trading rules in tandem with Washington's closest partners, such as the EU (Morin et al. 2015).

In spite of a temporary truce due to the "phase one" deal in early 2020, the Sino-American trade frictions persisted throughout Donald Trump's tenure. Although the Trump Administration was concerned about the issues such as level-playing field, access for American companies to the Chinese market and protection of the intellectual property rights, it put the main emphasis on the bilateral trade deficit. Since President Biden took office in January 2021, despite his determination to distinguish himself from his predecessor as much as possible, the US-China trade war has not been stopped. Although the Biden team may have a more nuanced view of the US priorities when it comes to trade with China – as well as with other counterparts, such as the EU and South Korea – given the economic repercussions of the Covid19 crisis and the predictions of a protracted economic recovery, it is not very likely to end anytime soon.

When we turn from geoeconomics to geopolitics, Biden's overall approach seems not too different. At the time of writing, there is no new US "China Strategy" yet. Nonetheless, there are various indications that, on China, there might be more of continuity between Biden and Trump rather than between Biden and Obama. That despite the fact that a number of nominees who have been chosen to posts at the US Department of State, National Security Council and other US offices have been veterans of the Obama as well as previous Democratic administrations. In fact, in his Address to the Joint Session of Congress in late April 2021 (Biden 2021) which was otherwise prevalently focused on the domestic economic, social and health situation, Joe Biden mentioned China and President Xi seven times, whereas other US adversaries received much less attention: Russia and Vladimir Putin three times, Iran and North Korea once each.

Although Trump's presidency has been clearly marked by a harsh anti-Chinese rhetoric, the Biden-Harris team's policies on China might be based on as much – if not even more – hard power approach than that of their immediate forerunner. However, in contrast to Trump's "America First" policy, and perhaps more in tune with the pre-Obama Democratic Presidents, the Biden Administration has been very vocal in drumming up support for its containment of China among its allies – both in Europe and Asia. Perhaps the clearest sign yet has come from Biden's reinvigoration of the Quad – a quadruple alliance between the US, Japan, Australia and India – which has been quite unequivocally aimed at strengthening the US position in the Indo-Pacific while limiting any space for Chinese economic and political expansion. In fact, even the continued use of the expression "Indo-Pacific" is a signal that it may not only be the terminology which will survive from the Trump to Biden years.

For South Korea, however, any participation in a Quad+ arrangement is difficult, partly because of its apprehension of alienating China and partly because of the prominent position of Japan within the Quad which, for historical reasons, has been Korea's (and particularly its progressive governments') historical archnemesis. To paraphrase Lord Ismay's famous saying about the purpose of NATO, for Seoul to be able to join the Quad as a nucleus of "Asia's NATO", it would have to meet three conditions: to keep North Korea in on the agenda, to keep China out of its main rationale and to keep Japan's influence down as much as possible. Korea's triple wish is nonetheless not very likely to happen as illustrated by the Quad's leaders first statement on "The Spirit of the Quad" from March 2021 (White House 2021). The announcement explicitly refers to "complete denuclearization of North Korea" rather than of the "Korean peninsula" which has been a standard phrase advocated by Seoul and used in various North Korea-related declarations since at least the 1990s, including the April 2018 Moon-Kim Panmunjom Declaration and the June 2018 Trump-Kim Singapore Statement.

Even though terminology has been improved since the US North Korea policy review have been unveiled, should the "denuclearization of North Korea" reappear in the new strategy, any progress with the DPRK on the matter is going to be *a priori* improbable, as words by North Korea's first vice-minister Choe Son Hui about US Secretary Blinken's "lunatic theory" and "groundless rhetoric about complete denuclearization" illustrated (KCNA 2021). Having been aware of such a potentially rocky start for any US-DPRK negotiations, South Korea's foreign minister Chung was at pains to explain that denuclearization of the Korean peninsula is "more correct" at a press briefing after a 2 + 2 meeting, standing next to Secretary of State Blinken who came together with Secretary of Defense Austin for his first overseas trip after having visited Japan.

Apart from this initial linguistic slip of tongue, the Quad statement nevertheless highlights Tokyo's other political priority vis-à-vis the DPRK, i.e. solving the abductee issue. As much as it might be painful for the relatives of those Japanese who were kidnapped by North Korean agents from the 1970s to 1980s, it is a topic that Seoul (and surely Pyongyang) would want to go away rather than playing any substantial role in the US policy towards NE Asia. Similarly to Donald Trump who had a better rapport with his Japanese rather than South Korean counterparts, it seems that the Biden Administration may have the same preferences – to the chagrin of Seoul and despite the fact that both the White and Blue House are occupied by two progressive presidents.

But the Quad statement could also be seen as controversial from the European perspective. Even though the EU has acknowledged how Biden's team rectified the previous mismanaged handling of Covid19 in the US, and European countries have so far been envious of the rapid deployment of vaccinations within Biden's first 100 days, the EU has also advocated an equitable access to Coronavirus shots and their manufacturing by poorer countries around the world through the COVAX mechanism. The US has however banned any export of Covid19 vaccines and raw materials needed for their production before the American population is sufficiently inoculated. Although the Quad Vaccine Partnership promises to "flood" Asia with at least 1 billion vaccines by 2022, it is not clear how quickly, who and how will decide which country will get how many and what jabs. This incites suspicion that there is a political calculation behind the Quad's humanitarian zeal – to outflank China (Heath 2021) in Beijing's own "vaccine diplomacy" – while simultaneously neglecting multilateral solutions such as the WHO-led and EU-backed COVAX.

The Europeans may have been "enchanted" (Pacheco Pardo and Reiterer 2021) by President Biden's promise of America "being back" and "building back better" not only his country at home but also partnerships abroad. Yet his stress on utilizing the alliances selectively to pursue the American interests – in this case, confronting China – may prove to be a bigger challenge for leaders in Seoul, Brussels and elsewhere in Europe and Asia than Trump's outright heavy-handed bullying. After all, it is at times easier to refuse to work with your colleague if you feel coerced into it than if you are asked politely.

From investment and connectivity to sanctions: Europe and (South Korea) caught between China and the US

It is however not only the US which has been putting pressure on the EU as well as others – in Asia and beyond. Since at least the Covid19 outbreak, Chinese Communist Party leaders have clearly become more assertive and not shied away from using combative language particularly on social media, including trolls, propaganda and statements by "wolf warrior" diplomats posted to third country capitals, as well as violence to deliver the same message of strength on the ground. Beijing's attempts to suppress the protests against the extradition and national security laws in Hong Kong, and confrontational words against anyone who stands up for the Hong Kongers, including the UK and other governments, are the cases in point.

Brussels, and particularly the German EU rotating presidency in the second half of 2020, have been trying to restore the balance with Beijing while using the window of opportunity to push China on trade issues. Even though Chancellor Merkel's brainchild, an in-person meeting between President Xi and 27 EU heads of states and governments scheduled for September 2020 in Leipzig, had to be canceled due to sanitary concerns, the EU held, in an unprecedented way, three virtual summits with the Chinese side (one of them as a substitute for the scrapped Leipzig's get-together) within the time-span of about six months. Shortly before the year's end, Beijing and Brussels (with a vehement support of Berlin but also Paris) have eventually agreed in principle on the Comprehensive Agreement on Investment (CAI) that has been in the works for nearly nine years since the decision to launch EU-China negotiations in February 2012 that began later in 2013.

The resulting EU-China investment agreement should ensure improved market access in China for European businesses in areas from automotive industry and manufacturing through financial and telecommunications services up to health and R&D, curb the forced technology transfers and subsidies for Chinese state-owned enterprises and embed sustainable development provisions, including labor and environmental standards. For Chancellor Merkel, CAI would have been the crown jewel of her last EU Presidency, but also of her 16 years at the helm of Germany (and, some would say, of Europe).

Although the final push to conclude CAI undoubtedly came from Berlin, the motivation was not only to help the German (and other European) industries improve their standing on the Chinese market, particularly because of the need for Europe to recover their economies after the Covid19 pandemic. By an equal measure, the investment agreement should put the European businesses on an equivalent footing with what Washington had achieved in creating better conditions for the American companies via the US-China "phase one deal" – before the new Biden administration was about to come in. In other words, the CAI has been "an effort to level the playing field with the United States" (Friedlander 2020) as much as – if not more than – with China.

From the long-term perspective, CAI has been operationalization of one of the streams in the EU's overall three-pronged approach to Beijing that was first announced in the "EU-China Strategic Outlook" in March 2019 (European Commission and EEAS 2019). According to this joint communication, China should simultaneously be looked at as a cooperation and negotiating partner, an economic competitor and a systemic rival. The investment deal falls mainly into the first and second categories of this "EU China Strategy". Its underlying logic, however, corresponds with another preceding EU plan, i.e. the "EU's Connectivity Strategy" (European Commission and EEAS 2018) which, although it pre-dates the China outlook, has been inspired by Beijing's growing economic power and political influence. The EU published its connectivity strategy in 2018 as an implementation of its Global Strategy, partly in response to the China-led

Belt and Road Initiative (BRI) and partly as the EU's own blueprint setting the standards for a values- and rules-based approach to connectivity.

In contrast to BRI which has been blamed for generating "debt traps" for countries along the modern-day Silk Road that are unable to meet their financial obligations (He 2020), the EU's connectivity strategy aims at promoting transparent and sustainable financing of infrastructure investment in the areas of transport, energy, digital and others all across Asia. The EU's extensive experience with comprehensive yet targeted sponsoring of infrastructure projects – whether within the EU through structural funds or in the EU's candidate states via pre-accession assistance (Copsey and Haughton 2009; Novotná 2015) – is the key advantage of the EU's involvement with connectivity. Yet nowadays even the Chinese side seems to be at the verge of reckoning with the consequences of the BRI's framework which produces debt dependency that is untenable both for the creditor and borrower. According to a Boston University database, lending to BRI's "project of the century" by China's banks collapsed a year before the Covid19 hit and Beijing currently finds itself mired in debt renegotiations with a number of countries along the road (Kynge and Wheatley 2020).

The EU's connectivity strategy, on the other hand, chimes well with South Korea. President Moon has been pursuing his own version of it through his New Northern Policy via the DPRK, Russia and Central Asia and, in particular, through his New Southern Policy (NSP) via South East (SE) Asia (Yeo 2020). Especially in its upgraded "Plus" version, the NSP complements well the EU's soft power values-based approach with Korea's focus on openness and inclusivity and areas of public health, trade, digitalization, smart cities, tourism and culture. Similarly to Brussels that has elevated its relationship with ASEAN by naming it its 11th Strategic Partner in December 2020, Seoul has been looking at the ways in which it can work with countries in SE Asia to find like-minded partners and economically decouple from China. South Korea joining the Regional Comprehensive Economic Partnership (RCEP) together with ASEAN, albeit China (as well as Japan) are on board of the RCEP too, could potentially be interpreted in a similar manner (Pacheco Pardo 2020).

Apart from the goal of economic diversification from China by teaming up with others, Seoul has been expanding its outreach to the ASEAN states because most of the SE Asian countries have good diplomatic relations with the DPRK with some exceptions, such as a tense period between North Korea and Malaysia due to the murder of Kim Jong Nam, a half-brother of Pyongyang's leader, at the Kuala Lumpur airport (Fifield 2019) in 2017. Even if a number of the NSP projects must have been provisionally suspended due to Covid19, the NSP Plus might turn into the second most significant legacy of Moon Jae-in's presidency next to his efforts for inter-Korean reconciliation (Hoo 2021), particularly if the NSP helps Seoul achieve the main government's objective of fostering peace on the Korean peninsula. In addition, if South Korea could exert political and economic pressure on the Myanmar's military junta that took power in a coup in February 2021 to alleviate the critical situation in the country, Seoul's soft power approach which encouraged many Korean companies to pursue their business interests in Myanmar can give the NSP a hard-power edge. A South Korean intervention to support a return to democracy in Naypyidaw would surely be welcome both in Brussels and Washington (Kim 2021) but would also highlight the geopolitical importance of connectivity in areas outside of economics.

Even though there is as of now no specific arrangement between Brussels and Seoul to intertwine their respective connectivity strategies, the EU has already concluded a "connectivity partnership" with Japan in 2019, albeit there is no grand joint project yet, and another similar association with India in May 2021. If Seoul and Brussels were to deepen their strategic partnership that celebrated its tenth anniversary in October 2020, adding the connectivity to the mix of free trade and security agreements would be a good ingredient. Such a new additive would be especially appropriate since the EU has since expanded its connectivity strategy to the global level via its Global Gateway plan from December 2021.. Moreover, connectivity has by now become one of the key takeaways (Pejsova 2021) in the EU's Indo-Pacific Strategy – the fourth EU document focused on the power competition within Asia published in September 2021.

Apart from the multifaceted connectivity policy, the EU has also put the third element of its China strategy – the systemic rivalry – into action. Based on its newly minted "European Magnitsky Act" to prosecute human rights violations around the world, in March 2021, the EU member states (Council of the European Union 2021) agreed on targeted sanctions against four Chinese individuals and one entity who were deemed to be directly responsible for mistreatment of the Uyghur population in Xinjiang. China was not the only country to be listed under the EU Global Human Rights Sanctions Regime – there were previous designations against several Russian nationals and, out of Asia, the Myanmar military and three North Korean officials – ministers for state security and social security and the DPRK's public prosecutor – were explicitly named by the Council as those conducting state-sponsored killings, torture and forced labor.

Even though the EU's restrictive measures were carefully calibrated to focus on alleged mid- to high-ranking officials in Xinjiang rather than top-level decision-makers in Beijing and, particularly in the case of the North Koreans, the human rights sanctions have primarily a symbolic value (Zwirko 2021), China reacted with a furor and retaliatory countermeasures of a different degree: it designated several members of the European Parliament (EP), including the chair of its China Delegation and the entire Human Rights Subcommittee, the EU's Political and Security Committee which consists of 27 ambassadors of all member states, several members of national parliaments and Swedish, Danish and German academics and think tanks.

The designated Europeans and their families may not have had any plans to travel or to conduct business in China soon anyway. However, by sanctioning the members of the EP who need to endorse the EU-China investment deal for it to come into force, China has resorted resorted to a highly counterproductive action instead of waging a "resolute" and "swift counterattack" as labeled by the Chinese state-run outlet, the Global Times (Global Times 2021). Indeed, it did not take too long for the EP to react. During the May 2021 plenary session, an overwhelming majority of 599 European lawmakers (with 30 MEPs against and 58 abstentions) decided to suspend any vote on CAI until Beijing lifts its sanctions (European Parliament 2021; Lau 2021). Nonetheless, given the culture of "saving one's face", it will be hard for Beijing to step back from any escalation , as the case of two Canadians who were arbitrarily detained in retaliation for arresting Huawei's CFO Meng Wanzhou demonstrates. After nearly three years and no evidence of their espionage, the "two Michaels" were released in a film-style prisoner swap after Meng admitted to guilt in September 2021 (The Associated Press 2021).

On the other hand, even before Beijing's self-defeating reaction, the approval of CAI in the EP was far from certain due to MEPs' concerns about insufficient guarantees over forced labor in Xinjiang. Here the experience with the EU-Korea FTA may serve as a positive example of the EU's "trade conditionality". Particularly South Korea's conservative governments have been reluctant to ratify four ILO conventions, including those on forced labor, making the EU to invoke a dispute settlement mechanism under the FTA's sustainable development chapter (Novotná 2020). Only after a panel of experts ruled that Seoul is in breach of its commitments under the EU-Korea trade agreement in January 2021, and after the president's progressive party won a crushing victory in national elections several months before that, did the South Korean National Assembly pass three out of four ILO conventions in February 2021 (Yonhap News 2021).

Whether Beijing could be compelled to follow in Seoul's footsteps in case it won't voluntarily commit to these international rules, and whether their ratification would make any difference on the ground even if it did, is currently hard to assess, especially since there have been credible reports about forced labor and abuses of Chinese workers not only in Xinjiang but also along the BRI (Kuo and

Chen 2021). It is however pretty much evident that the EP is unlikely to assent to an investment agreement with China when its members and sub-entities are under Beijing's sanctions as the EP resolution unequivocally shows. No matter whether President Xi has been aware of the intricacies of the EU's decision-making and the role of the EP in it, he should have realized that a deal with Angela Merkel (and Emmanuel Macron) doesn't automatically mean a deal with everyone else in Europe.

Similarly to TTIP that was not officially terminated but did not go anywhere after Donald Trump took office, CAI has as of now ended up being "put in a freezer" as the former EU trade Commissioner formulated it (Malmström 2017). The key difference nonetheless is that the EU could have waited for a new administration in the White House to revive any trade talks with the US; there is not much a chance of any similar alternation happening in Beijing. Above all, however, if President Xi's goal was to force the EU to "distance itself from Washington's extreme policies to contain China" (Global Times 2021), the Chinese hostile overreaction may have achieved just that.

Conclusion: Facing a new Cold War, or working for a hot peace?

Even though there is at the moment of writing only about a year into Joe Biden's Presidency, the danger that an antagonistic relationship between the US and China may turn into a systemic long-term competition and a new Cold War which will define the years to come is definitely there. A rancorous first meeting between American and Chinese foreign affairs envoys in Alaska in March 2021 was a strong hint at that possibility (Nikkei Asia 2021). It is equally likely that China will keep asserting itself more forcefully, both domestically and towards others in its immediate neighborhood, but increasingly so towards anyone across the globe. BRI is only one of its devices; other techniques range from an old-style intelligence (e.g. a suspected spying by a former EU Ambassador to South Korea and his Chinese partner; Chazan 2021) through modern-day assaults on critics of Beijing in the cyberspace (often using Twitter and other social media that are banned back in China) up to tools like weaponization of trade.

In that area, South Korea became one of the first China's trial balloons that felt the heat after the Blue House had allowed deployment of the US-made THAAD anti-ballistic missile system in 2017. Beijing punished South Korea's move with a trade and tourism boycott, costing Seoul billions of dollars in lost revenues (Hemmings 2021). More recently, Canada and Australia suffered a similar fate: Canberra after advocating for a thorough investigation of the Covid19 origins in China, while Ottawa as another price for apprehending Huawei's Meng Wanzhou. If the EU continues to speak up and, even more so, to take actions against any ill-treatments within China and Hong Kong, especially after CAI has been put on ice, the Europeans should be aware that they might be the next in the line. The extreme retaliation against the EU's human rights sanctions was Beijing's explicit warning.

There are other clues though, such as an ire by the Chinese consumers and their shunning of European brands like H&M which refuse to use "Xinjiang cotton" in their supply chains. South Korea can serve again as a good example here. When BTS, the iconic K-Pop boyband, didn't acknowledge the sacrifices by the "Chinese volunteers" during the Korean War who however fought on the other – North Korean – side, Chinese netizens blasted BTS so much that several retail brands withdrew BTS merchandise from their stores on the Chinese mainland. In the end, a Chinese Communist party official had to intervene to prevent the nationalist fervor spilling over into a political spat with Seoul (Novotná 2020).

This chapter therefore explored various ways in which the EU (and South Korea) have so far been navigating the Sino-American rivalry. Such a compound geopolitical situation leaves them – as well as other "middle powers" – in an unappealing predicament of having to chart a course between the two superpowers. Neither Brussels nor Seoul are keen on following a hard-power approach to China as Washington would have liked them – unless they are compelled to do so by circumstances. They both have tried to use more subtle ways, or to combine the two, sometimes with more and sometimes with less success. However, not all is lost and there are still areas where a mutual cooperation is possible if not desirable.

Firstly, instead of running a "vaccine diplomacy" as Beijing was accused of, while hoarding vaccines and raw materials for their production as Washington does, Brussels and Seoul could encourage the two to work together on making sure that everyone comes out of the woods of Covid19 pandemic as soon as possible. To that end, using multilateral solutions such as the COVAX facility as the EU has been pleading for could be the easiest way out. The dire situation in India may help accomplish that, but other countries successful in fighting Covid19 (Park 2021) and COVAX supporters, such as South Korea, could be instrumental in bringing both the US and China into the fold. Moreover, prioritizing COVAX is in the interest of the Blue House not only because of the global power dynamic and its own difficulties with the inoculation stocks, but also because North Korea has applied for its fair share. Participation of the DPRK in an international vaccination mechanism with Washington onboard could help Seoul restart the engagement with Pyongyang (Novotná 2020).

Secondly, as much as there has been complementarity in connectivity strategies between Brussels and Seoul, albeit more synchronization would be helpful, the overlap between the European and Korean Green Deals has been visible, too. By re-joining the Paris Accord and launching his own initiatives, such as the climate package and summit in April 2021, Joe Biden also exhibited a renewed US "green leadership", whereas President Xi has been open to collaboration in this regard. Climate action therefore seems to be the area most prone to a quadri- and multilateral dialog.

Thirdly, despite all the trade frictions, the EU and South Korea are intertwined thanks to their bilateral FTA, but also through the web of other arrangements that they are a part of, especially with their partners in Asia-Pacific. Even though revamping of the international trading system, including the WTO reform and unblocking of the WTO's appellate body would be the best prospect, expanding on inter-regional and plurilateral trade agreements could serve as a fitting substitute. RCEP, CPTTP and possibly EU deals with ASEAN and the US would be a good way forward. If nothing else, the US and China but also the EU and South Korea should be preparing how to stave off any shocks in trade should another disease outbreak happen in the future. Last but not least, for any bilateral relationship to function, an intensive interaction between civil societies is the key. People-to-people exchanges should therefore not be restricted but kept on and further expanded even if political relationships are frosty.

Whether or not the Sino-American rivalry may eventually deescalate will become obvious in the next several months. At this moment, it nonetheless seems that the Biden Administration may be trying to go the "European way" in its approach towards China. In his opening statement at the Alaska meeting with Chinese Foreign Minister Wang, US Secretary of State Blinken appropriated the EU's triad of China being simultaneously "a negotiating partner, economic competitor and systemic rival" when he characterized Washington's relationship with Beijing as "competitive where it should be, collaborative where it can be and adversarial where it must be" (Nikkei Asia 2021). To conclude, this chapter proposed several areas where collaboration rather than competitiveness and adversity between the US and China might be feasible. For the sake of Washington and Beijing but also everyone else, the best prospect would be if, instead of facing a new Cold War, all parties start working for – even if hot – peace.

References

The Associated Press. 2021. Canadians released after Huawei CFO resolved U.S. charges, 25 September. https://www.nbcnews.com/news/world/canadians-released-after-huawei-cfo-resolves-u-s-charges-n1280079

Biden, Joseph. 2021. "Remarks by President Biden in Address to a Joint Session of Congress." Washington: The White House. https://www.whitehouse.gov/briefing-room/speeches-remarks/2021/04/29/remarks-by-president-biden-in-address-to-a-joint-session-of-congress/ (accessed 30/04/2021).

Borrell, Josep. 2021. "The EU Needs a Strategic Approach for the Indo-Pacific." *A Window on the World*, 12 March 2021. https://eeas.europa.eu/headquarters/headquarters-homepage/94898/eu-needs-strategic-approach-indo-pacific_en.

Chazan, Guy. 2021. "Former EU diplomat says reputation 'destroyed' by German spy probe." *Financial Times*, 4 December. https://www.ft.com/content/2e03678b-92f3-4e35-ac4a-930224a459e9 (accessed 05/06/2021).

Copsey, Nathaniel, and Tim Haughton. 2009. "The Choices for Europe: National Preferences in New and Old Member States." *JCMS: Journal of Common Market Studies* 47 (2): 263–286. doi:https://doi.org/10.1111/j.1468-5965.2009.00804.x.

Council of the European Union. 2021. Council Implementing Regulation (EU) 2021/478 of 22 March 2021 Implementing Regulation (EU) 2020/1998 Concerning Restrictive Measures Against Serious Human Rights Violations and Abuses. Brussels.

European Commission, and EEAS. 2018. "Joint Communication to the European Parliament, the Council, the European Economic and Social Committee, the Committee of the Regions and the European Investment Bank: Connecting Europe and Asia - Building Blocks for an EU Strategy." https://eeas.europa.eu/sites/default/files/joint_communication_-_connecting_europe_and_asia_-_building_blocks_for_an_eu_strategy_2018-09-19.pdf (accessed 30/04/2020).

European Commission, and EEAS. 2019. "EU-China – A strategic outlook." https://ec.europa.eu/info/sites/default/files/communication-eu-china-a-strategic-outlook.pdf (accessed 30/04/2021).

European Parliament. 2021. Chinese countersanctions on EU entities and MEPs and MPs. https://www.europarl.europa.eu/doceo/document/TA-9-2021-0255_EN.html (accessed 05/06/2021).

European Union. 2016. "A Global Strategy for the European Union's Foreign and Security Policy - Shared Vision, Common Action: A Stronger Europe." http://www.eeas.europa.eu/archives/docs/top_stories/pdf/eugs_review_web.pdf (accessed 4 April 2017).

Fifield, Anna. 2019. *The Great Successor: The Divinely Perfect Destiny of Brilliant Comrade Kim Jong Un*. New York: Public Affairs.

Friedlander, Julia. 2020. "Furor Over Europe's Investment Agreement with China is Overblown." https://nationalinterest.org/feature/furor-over-europe's-investment-agreement-china-overblown-175397 (accessed 30/04/2021).

Global Times. 2021. China's Sanctions Over EU Officials and Entities Are Justified and Timely: Global Times Editorial. https://www.globaltimes.cn/page/202103/1219143.shtml (accessed 04/05/2021).

Gramlich, John. 2020. Americans Give the U.S. Low Marks for Its Handling of COVID-19, and So Do People in Other Countries. https://www.pewresearch.org/fact-tank/2020/09/21/americans-give-the-u-s-low-marks-for-its-handling-of-covid-19-and-so-do-people-in-other-countries/ (accessed 16/04/2021).

He, Alex. 2020. "The Belt and Road Initiative: Motivations, Financing, Expansion and Challenges of Xi's Ever-Expanding Strategy." 2020:31. doi: https://doi.org/10.24294/jipd.v4i1.1180.

Heath, Ryan. 2021. "U.S. and Pacific partners to flood Asia with vaccines." *Politico Europe*. https://www.politico.com/news/2021/03/12/us-and-pacific-partners-to-flood-asia-with-vaccines-475571 (accessed 30/04/2021).

Hemmings, John. 2021. "South Korea's Growing 5G Dilemma." Washington: CSIS. https://www.csis.org/analysis/south-koreas-growing-5g-dilemma (accessed 05/05/2021).

Hernández-Morales, Aithor. 2020. "Germany Confirms that Trump Tried to Buy Firm Working on Coronavirus Vaccine." *Politico*. https://www.politico.eu/article/germany-confirms-that-donald-trump-tried-to-buy-firm-working-on-coronavirus-vaccine/ (accessed 16/04/2021).

Hoo, Chiew-Ping. 2021. "What's in the New Southern Policy Plus? An ASEAN Perspective on Building Niche-based Pragmatic Cooperation with South Korea." World Economy Brief 21–15, Korea Institute for International Economic Policy.

KCNA. 2021. "Statement of First Vice Minister of the DPRK." *KCNA*, 18 March 2021.

Kim, Sea Young (Sarah). 2021. Why South Korea Matters for Post-Coup Myanmar. https://keia.org/the-peninsula/why-south-korea-matters-for-post-coup-myanmar/ (accessed 01/05/2021).

Kuo, Lily, and Alicia Chen. 2021. "Chinese Workers Allege Forced Labor, Abuses in Xi's 'Belt and Road' Program." *The Washington Post*, 30 April. https://www.washingtonpost.com/world/asia_pacific/china-labor-belt-road-covid/2021/04/30/f110e8de-9cd4-11eb-b2f5-7d2f0182750d_story.html (accessed 04/05/2021).

Kynge, James, and Jonathan Wheatley. 2020. "China Pulls Back from the World: Rethinking Xi's 'project of the century'." 30/04/2021, 11 December. https://www.ft.com/content/d9bd8059-d05c-4e6f-968b-1672241ec1f6.

Lau, Stuart. 2021. "European Parliament Votes to 'freeze' Investment Deal Until China Lifts Sanctions." *Politico*, 20 May. https://www.politico.eu/article/european-parliament-freezes-china-investment-deal-vote/ (accessed 05/06/2021).

Malmström, Cecilia. 2017. "Handle with Care: Safeguarding Trade in the Age of Protectionism." http://trade.ec.europa.eu/doclib/docs/2017/march/tradoc_155448.pdf (accessed 17 April 2017).

Morin, Jean-Frédéric, Tereza Novotná, Frederik Ponjaert, and Mario Telò, eds. 2015. *The Politics of Transatlantic Trade Negotiations: TTIP in a Globalized World*. Farnham: Ashgate.

Nikkei Asia. 2021. "How it happened: Transcript of the US-China opening remarks in Alaska." *Nikkei Asia*. https://asia.nikkei.com/Politics/International-relations/US-China-tensions/How-it-happened-Transcript-of-the-US-China-opening-remarks-in-Alaska (accessed 05/05/2021).

Novotná, Tereza. 2015. *Negotiating the Accession: How Germany Unified and the EU Enlarged*, *New Perspectives in German Political Studies*. Basingstoke: Palgrave Macmillan.

Novotná, Tereza. 2020. "What EU-ROK Partnership within the US-China Conflict?". Paris: Asia Centre Europe. https://centreasia.eu/evenement/eu-korea-convergence-and-partnerships-10-years-after-the-eu-korea-fta-in-the-post-covid-era-and-within-the-us-china-trade-war/ (accessed 17/12/2020).

Pacheco Pardo, Ramon. 2020. South Korea and the RCEP. *Korea Chair Explains*. https://mailchi.mp/cebda5a3b33d/kf-vub-korea-chair-policy-brief-candlelight-moonlight-olympics-korea-in-transition-1335178?e=0f61ca5d68 (accessed 30/04/2021).

Pacheco Pardo, Ramon, and Michael Reiterer. 2021. The EU and the US in Search of Common Ground: Extending the Transatlantic to an Indo-Pacific Partnership? *CSDS Policy Brief* 4. https://brussels-school.be/sites/default/files/CSDS%20Policy%20brief_2104_0.pdf (accessed 30/04/2021).

Park, June. 2021. "Institutitons Matter in Fighting Covid-19: Public Health, Social Policies, and the Control Tower in South Korea." In *Coronavirus Politics: The Comparative Politics and Policy of COVID-19*, edited by Scott L. Greer, Elizabeth J. King, Elize Massard da Fonseca and André Peralta-Santos, 105–126. Ann Arbor: University of Michigan Press.

Pejsova, Eva. 2021. The EU's Indo-Pacific Strategy in 10 Points. *The Diplomat*. https://thediplomat.com/2021/04/the-eus-indo-pacific-strategy-in-10-points/ (accessed 01/05/2021).

White House. 2021. "Quad Leaders' Joint Statement: 'The Spirit of the Quad.'" https://www.whitehouse.gov/briefing-room/statements-releases/2021/03/12/quad-leaders-joint-statement-the-spirit-of-the-quad/ (accessed 30/04/2021).

Yeo, Andrew. 2020. South Korea's New Southern Policy and ASEAN-ROK Relations. What Role Does Southeast Asia Play in Moon's Foreign Policy? *The Diplomat*. https://thediplomat.com/2020/07/south-koreas-new-southern-pol icy-and-asean-rok-relations/ (accessed 30/04/2021).

Yonhap News. 2021. "S. Korea Ratifies key U.N. Labor Conventions." *Yonhap News*, 26 February. https://en.yna.co.kr/view/AEN20210226006551315 (accessed 03/05/2021).

Zwirko, Colin. 2021. "EU Hits North Korea with Human-Rights Related Sanctions for the First Time." Seoul: NK News. https://www.nknews.org/2021/03/eu-hits-north-korea-with-human-rights-related-sanctions-for-the-first-time/ (accessed 01/05/2021).

Joohyun Go

The prospects of cultural exchange to foster the economic relationship between the EU and Korea

1. Introduction

2021 marks the 10th anniversary of the Korea-EU FTA. Despite the controversy over Korea-EU FTA trade gains, there was an absolute increase in total trade volume as well as an expansion of exchanges that stretch beyond the economic sector.

In addition, there are various measures proposed to enhance the effectiveness of FTA between the two regions. As a result, the importance of cultural recognition and image management/enhancement through cultural exchanges also increased. Cultural exchange contributes to mutual understanding and interests and further increases mutual recognition, ultimately increasing inter-regional trust. This brings positive influence to the image of the other country and increases accessibility to the other country's products. Cultural exchange may also facilitate private sector participation in international affairs, which then provides clues to any possible disputes between countries (Feigenbaum 2001: 30).

More than anything, cultural industry's share of the national economy is increasing significantly. In particular, there was an institutional foundation for revitalizing economic exchanges between the two regions. Therefore, efforts to enhance each country's cultural industry and image are of utmost importance. To that end, cultural exchange is considered as an essential goal and means to achieve such goals.

Cultural exchange is linked to enhancing the image of the country, which is also directly linked to its industrial interests in the perfect competition market. Enhancing the image of a country through cultural exchange raises people's interest in that country. At the same time, it can also increase trust in other countries as a whole. Then, this eventually leads to an increase in the purchasing power. Following this line of logic, cultural exchange can be a mechanism for creating added value to that country's products.

European fans that consume Korean cultural content want to follow the story behind certain cultural products. For example, BTS "ARMY" fans associate Korean culture with the content they consume. Thus, purchasing decisions for related Korean products will be easier for them. In other words, potential consumers' attraction toward Korean culture can lead to actual consumption of the products.

As such, exchanges in the cultural sector deepen mutual understanding and eventually leave a positive impact on trade. With that in mind, this paper will examine the current status of cultural exchanges between Korea and the EU. In particular, it explores the current status of cultural exchanges between the regions. Then, it proposes measures to expand exchanges. Then, it further suggests means for revitalizing economic relations between the two regions.

2. Discussion on the concept of cultural exchanges

Defining concepts about similar terminology is necessary when it comes to studying cultural exchanges. Every country uses different terms regarding cultural exchange. Reference to international cultural exchange varies from each country such as international cultural relationship, international cultural exchange, external cultural exchange and so on. Although there are differences in the nuances, these terms share similar traits.

Mulcahy saw the value of cultural exchange as enabling a greater understanding of perceptions of other national history (Mulcahy 1982: 295). In other words, he argues that cultural exchanges will make a better world. He said that cultural exchange cannot be a sufficient condition for national security, but it is essential to establishing a stable world order (ibid: 298; Khademi 1999: 48).

Hye-In Kim (2015) and Jung-Sook Jeong (2012) attempted to define the concepts of the international cultural exchange and systematically classify these concepts. Jung-Sook Jeong (2012) argues that international cultural exchange is a natural activity in which various actors cross national boundaries and engage in cultural activities. These activities began even before the national policy framework was put in practice. The author also points out that arriving at the definition of such concept has been reserved since international cultural exchanges have virtually been an area of practical activities. On that note, the concept of international cultural exchange is presented as shown in Tab. 1. These are based on the cultural concepts presented by the UNESCO Declaration on Cultural Diversity. In addition, the consultative concept of international cultural exchange is explained as "considering the implications and external factors of international cultural exchange activities, and the public sector of international cultural exchange being achieved through public support" (Jung-Sook Jeong 2012:14; Ministry Culture, Sports and Tourism 2017:48). On top of that, these

Tab. 1: Conceptual definition of international cultural exchange

Activity centered	Postulated as a policy concept of exchange. Suggests practical usage of policy building.
Performance & goal oriented	Activities that contribute to the continuation and spread of cultural diversity at international level by all actors in the cultural sector, gaining understanding and serving as a stimulant at individual level, and sending and accepting cultural arts and cultural industries.

Source: Jung-Sook Jeong, 2012; Sports and Tourism. 2017:48

concepts, in accordance with the purpose and performance of international cultural exchanges, are postulated as policy concepts of international cultural exchanges. It also suggests that it can be of a practical use in policy-making.

Cultural exchanges in this article focuses on activities that revitalize economic. In a way, we must approach this from a cultural and diplomatic point of view that aims to capture the hearts of the other country's public. Cultural Diplomacy is conceptually associated with public diplomacy and the soft power suggested by Nye (2008). In simpler words, it is an activity that builds a positive national image, gains trust, and promotes cooperation in the public of the other country by attracting a wide range of culture. Unlike traditional foreign policies that pursue short-term goals, cultural diplomacy (Cull 2008), considered as a sub-region of public diplomacy, expects long-term results. However, it has attributes that directly affect changes in the perception of people in other countries. Thus, international community has been competitively developing cultural and diplomatic strategies to enhance its national status.

Heart of cultural diplomacy lies in pursuing national interest in the realm of international political order. The government plays a major role as a key player because most cultural and diplomatic projects are backed by public funds. However, in the case of cultural diplomacy through art, the government's capabilities alone are not merely enough. Such diplomacy requires us to form a horizontal and cooperative relationship with the arts sector, which is the primary agent in producing contents. This would also mean that there is a need for a cooperative system that exerts mutual influence through the principle of supplementation which ultimately compensates for each other's shortcomings. This is why there needs to be policy discussions that wrap together the above factors.

As the agents of cultural diplomacy includes not only the government but also non-state actors, it shows that there are changes in forms and contents of cultural diplomacy. However, by nature, cultural diplomacy is inextricably linked to the national interest. Therefore, it is highly likely that government actors will participate in the process of promoting and conducting cultural diplomacy. Even if the targets of cultural diplomacy projects or programs are ordinary citizens or the general public in other countries, they are still planned and funded by the government. Even NGOs and civilians, which can be major actors of cultural diplomacy, also operate in partnership with the government. Taken together, cultural diplomacy is defined as a series of cultural activities conducted by certain organizations that are supported by the government with the goal of realizing their own interests abroad. Therefore, cultural exchange can be seen as a key component of cultural diplomacy.

This suggests that the ultimate goal of this study is to examine the current status of cultural diplomacy exchanges between Korea and the EU. It first looks at how much cultural exchanges between the two regions have grown since the adoption of the Protocol on Korea-EU cultural cooperation. It then examines if there are any constraints and if so, what are the ways to improve exchanges in the future.

To this end, we will look at two types of cultural exchange support policies at government level. Among them, we must first pay attention to an agreement on the co-production of audiovisual materials between Korea and Europe stipulated by the "Cultural Cooperation Protocol," which was adopted as an annex to the Korea-EU FTA. Based on this, the article focuses on the current status of cooperation between the two regions. Cultural industries such as movies and media are flocking to exchange projects aimed at overseas expansion and export. Exchange activities with this purpose include exporting Korean cultural content and importing foreign content. It also includes the distribution of profits related to foreign capital funding and copyrights. There are also co-planning and co-production activities. On that note, the International Join Film Festival is an area where two-way cooperation is possible based on mutual cultural understanding. Co-production may sometimes take place separately from bilateral agreements. However, films that have been recognized as national films by mutual countries can benefit from receiving production support. This can then facilitate overseas cooperation further.

Next, I will review the current status of cultural exchanges of arts industry. Public and private organizations in the field of culture and arts are carrying out various exchange projects on their own. Among them, we will look at programs involving government agencies. In particular, we focus on the projects that establish networks and strengthen the expertise of culture and arts-related personnel.

3. Current status of cultural exchange between Korea and the EU

South Korea has established and operated a cultural cooperation committee in accordance with the Protocol on Cultural Cooperation, an annex to the Free Trade Agreement with the EU. This consultative body aims to promote exchanges of cultural activities, products, and services, including audiovisual products. Since the first meeting held on December 2013, there has been an annual meeting between the two regions to discuss cooperative agendas.

The 2013 "EU-South Korea: Current Trends of Cultural Exchange and Future Perspective" was published as part of the implementation of the Protocol on Cultural Cooperation. The report describes the status of exchanges between the two regions, focusing mainly on five areas related to cultural exchanges (Marie Le Sourd et al. 2013). Even when the report was published, Europe was not a strategic priority area for Korean cultural organizations and sponsors. This phenomenon was especially noticeable in the audiovisual field. The number of movies co-produced by Korea and the EU was very limited. Of the total 60 co-produced films at the time, only five were collaborated with partners in the EU. Starting with the Netherlands in 2006, there have been only four cases of cooperation with France.

Eight years have passed since the above report was published. Fast-forward to 2021, Korea and the EU is now celebrating the 10th anniversary of the FTA. Therefore, it is now necessary to reassess the performance of the cooperation. The above report looked at five areas related to cultural exchanges between Korea and the EU, including publishing, performing arts and audiovisual contents. This study particularly focuses on co-production of films and performing arts. Among them, it goes deeper into the government's support mechanism and evaluation of actual participants. I also examine how much the Korea-EU Cultural Cooperation Protocol has achieved. Furthermore, I also review the areas of cooperation with Europe according to the comprehensive plan for promoting international cultural exchanges announced in 2020.

1) Co-production of films between Korea and Europe

According to the Korea Film Council, a total of 328 international co-production films supports took place between 2009 and 2020. China (149), Japan (72) and the United States (47) had the largest number of cooperation, followed by Europe (46) (Fig. 1). Among them, France had the largest number of cooperation (41) and the rest were with Italy, Germany, Belgium and Spain. However,

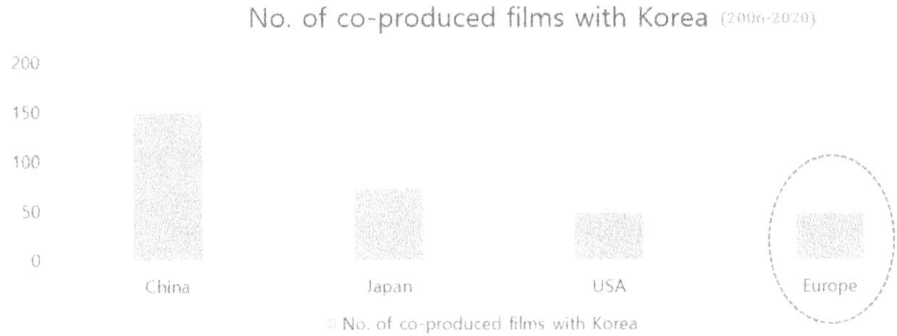

Fig. 1: Film co-production between Korea and EU
Source: Author's own calculation based on data obtained from Korean Film Council.

although not supported by the Film Council, there are 11 additional films that fall into the category of co-production. Taken together, the total number of co-production between Korea and Europe (2006–2020) was 57. This is because the criteria recognized as co-produced film and the criteria supported by the Film Council are different(Korean Film Council).

France (2006) was the first country to sign an agreement with South Korea on co-production of international films. Afterwards, Korea signed international co-production agreements with New Zealand in 2008, Australia in 2014, and China and India in 2015. So far, a total of five countries have signed a bilateral co-production agreement with Korea. Since 2008, the Film Council started supporting co-production in strategic areas, including France. As a result, various co-production projects received planning and development support with. Such support includes scenario translation, mentoring, and local investment meetings. The reason why co-production with France is highlighted is that films made with France involving more than a certain percentage of contribution by countries other than France can also be recognized as French films according to the audio-visual industry support policy within the EU. Therefore, other European countries may participate in films co-produced between Korea and France. This allows Korean cultural products to penetrate other European countries (Han Sun-Hee et al. 2019).

For example, let's look at the benefits of the co-production agreement between Korea and France. First of all, South Korea is entitled to apply for production support from the Film Council. It will also be subject to mandatory screening of Korean films at theaters (73 days per year) made possible through investment by the Korea Film Investment Association. In the meantime, France will be able to secure the cost of producing the next film under the automatic support system. It is also eligible for support for production and distribution through the selective support system. Coly produced films are subject to pre-purchase by French broadcasters and investment by SOFICAs, a professional film investment association.eur

What is noteworthy here is that despite the audio-visual co-production agreement under the cultural cooperation protocol, there is virtually not much cooperation with European countries except for France. This may be seen as a relatively small amount of cooperation with countries that have developed film industry in Europe. There is also the Creative Europe-Media Sub-program, an audiovisual support program among European Union member states. It helps launch projects or foster new technologies. If it is a co-production involving Korea under the leadership of the one of the European entity, Korean producers can also support the development of the project. This is guaranteed under the European Agreement on Co-Production of Films. In order to be recognized for the status of co-production, at least three co-producers must participate in the work. These co-producers must be based in three different countries. Co-producers that are not based on this agreement (for example, Korea) can participate but their total contribution cannot exceed 30 % of the total production cost. Co-produced works must also meet the definition and standards of European Cinematographic Work set forth in Appendix II of the Agreement. If these conditions are met, a coly produced film is deemed to have obtained nationality when it is pre-approved by the competent authority (Korea Film Council in case of Korea or CNC in case of France, etc). In other words, co-produced films will be eligible to utilize film support programs provided by relevant countries.

Support programs provided by the Korean Film Council include planning and development support, international co-production incentives, and foreign video location incentives. Incentives have been in place since 2012 in order to support a certain percentage of global co-produced films. It supports up to 100 million ~ 400 million won (25 % of domestic execution costs) per episode for co-produced films that received more than 20 % investment from foreign countries and execute more than 200 million ~ 1 billion won out of 1 billion won in Korea. Location incentives for foreign films have been in place since 2011. It provides cash support for 20-25 % of total execution fee of foreign films shot in Korea. The International Co Production Incentive Project provides part of the project's domestic execution costs. As a result, co films with advanced countries like United States, Japan, China, and France, which can be filmed in Korea, have mainly received the support. The support was mostly given to Japan, United States, and France, Korea's traditional partners. Among the co-produced films with Europe, 42 films received support for planning and development. A total of three films have been supported by incentives for international co-production and foreign film location incentives. However, in some cases, the work could not be completed due to investment failure during the production process. In fact, there were only 15 French and 2 Belgian works that have been completed.

Nevertheless, it is noteworthy that the number of co-production increased more than 10 times compared to the 2006~2012. Main reason for such increase in the number of co-production support is due to the segmentation of the co-production method. Korea's co-production method has diversified into IP exports and remakes, overseas expansion of Korean film producers, and domestic production of foreign films in the final stage. There are also IP-based remakes of Korean films based on existing scenarios. As a result, the number of Korean production workers entering foreign markets is increasing. There is also growing number of cases where domestic film production staffs participate in overseas film production or produce their own local films with foreign entity.

On the other hand, there are criticisms that the international co-production-related provisions by the current film law as well as support projects by the Film Council do not keep up with the current trend. In the overseas market, Korea ranks among the world's top five in terms of production and audience. But at the same time, there is a widespread sentiment that Korea is a difficult place to co-produce international films despite having a strong film industry. Therefore, the internationalization of filmmaking requires a comprehensive review and strategy of overseas expansion to a wider extent.

The international co-production agreement involves national governments to promote co production, exchange the culture and contribute to the development of films with the synergy created from mutual support programs. In particular, international co-production agreements have started within European countries, led by France, and expanded to non-European countries with the base for film industry. In Korea, co-production with Europe began with low-budget international co-production in the field of art films. This trend has been maintained to this day: while co-production with China and the United States is active on commercial films, works with Europe are mainly film d'auteur aimed at entering European film festivals.

2) Current status of performing arts exchange between Korea and the EU

In the field of performing arts, for the past 20 years, there has been substantial investment at home and abroad to support modern performing arts as well as traditional performing arts.

Tab. 2: Status of co-production support projects by the Korean Film Council

Country	Support Programme	Year	No. of Support	Movie Title
France		2009	4	Volcanic fields, the flower of evil, Hanaan, the maid
		2010	5	Dance with Shadow, Cafe Rivoli, Way to Santiago, Somalia, green grape candy
	KO-PRODUCTION in Paris	2011	4	On the way home, I love Paris, Meet Rogi Wan, Illegal immigrant
		2012	5	The Belt of Möbius, Blackstones, Promises, Monsters, Bluebeard Castle, Where are you from
		2015	5	Essay in Paris, Make the Princess Laugh, the Body in Nantes, the Immigrants, the Duck's laugh
		2016	6	Veronique, the Silent Woman, Room 7, Zero Sum, Blind-12 Episodes, Woman from Northern Europe
		2017	5	Greyhacker: The Stolen Generation, Baby box, Jikji Mom: Woman of the Blue Book, Tour: The best 49 days of my life, Country Dog MARU
	International Co-production Biz-matching Support	2014	1	Coreé
	KO-PRODUCTION in Busan	2016	1	Baby box
		2017	1	Ocean

(*continued on next page*)

Tab. 2: Continued

Country	Support Programme	Year	No. of Support	Movie Title
	International Co-production Incentive	2017	1	Beautiful days
	Incentives for Foreign Film Location	2017	1	Tank Season 2
		2018	1	#French Lover
		2020	1	Quiet Morning
Italy	International Co-production Biz-matching Support	2013	1	Second Twenty
Germany		2015	1	Gluckauwulf
Belgium		2015	1	The beginning of the attack on the Bamsom Pirates
Spain	KO-PRODUCTION in Busan	2017	1	Zombie Dumb
Belgium		2017	1	Sound of Seoul
Total			46	

Source: Authos's own arrangement of data obtained from the Korean Film Council.

The Korea Arts Management Services (KAMS) was established in 2006 as a key organization to support the promotion of cultural and artistic distribution in Korea. The Korea Foundation is the official public diplomacy agency in Korea and operates programs to promote cultural and artistic exchanges in terms of culture and diplomacy.

Major projects of KAMS include the Performing Arts Market Seoul (PAMS), which was established in 2005. And it also keeps expanding the field of cultural and artistic exchanges with Europe. PAMS, as a performing arts market, focuses on events by selecting strategic regions and countries every year.

Europe and the EU have been selected as key regions three times (2007, 2012 and 2018) and received spotlights. In 2007, the International Network for Contemporary Performing Arts) was selected. In 2012, Eastern European countries were selected for the Focus Session. In 2018, there was a seminar about <Building Bridges Between EU and Korean Performing Arts> through a Focus session focusing on the EU.

KF (Korea Foundation) is working with KAMS to support overseas expansion of "PAMS Choice". Through such support, performing arts such as theater, music, and dance were given the opportunities to perform in France, Germany, England, Spain, as well as in areas where relatively few Korean works have been introduced.

Tab. 3: Other co-produced works by Korea and the Europe

Country	Number of Co-Production	Year	Name of Film
Netherlands	1	2006	Daisy
Germany	1	2013	Berlin
Belgium	1	2012	Couleur de peau: Miel*
France	7	2012	Couleur de peau: Miel*
		2018	Beautiful days
		2016	Black stone
		2011	La rivière Tumen
		2009	Une vie toute neuve
		2009	Nuit et jour
		2007	Hyazgar, desert dream
Austria	1	2011	Winter smells
Czech Republic	1	2013	Snowpiercer
Total	11		

Source: Authors own arrangement of data obtained from Korean Film Council.

In addition, KF is implementing a cultural and artistic exchange partnership project that strategically supports the overseas expansion of Korean culture and arts. Its main goal is to maximize ripple effects and strengthen its network with the local area. Through such projects, performing arts organizations, including Korean creative operas, participated in festivals in European countries and had opportunities to tour around. Tab. 4 is a European cultural and artistic event supported by KF in 2019.

In addition, they are creating a co fund for international arts with Europe and other leading foreign cultural and artistic support institutions. Through this, it will promote two-year cooperation projects with cultural and artistic powerhouses. It is expanding and since 2016, cooperation projects have been carried out with the UK (British Arts Council), Germany (German Cultural Center in Korea), and Denmark (Art Council).

As such, cultural exchange support projects with Europe are being carried out simultaneously at the level of individual European countries and the European Union. In addition, we expect cooperative projects with major cultural powerhouses in various fields, including cultural heritage, cultural cities, and audio-visual co-production.

Tab. 4: List of KF's support for cultural and artistic events in Europe in 2019

Country	Contents
UK	Inviting Korean artists to the UK Young Artists International Biennale
	Inviting of Korean Writers to the Belfast Photography Festival
Italy	Inviting of Korean Writers to the Venice Biennale
Switzerland	Zurich University Symposium on Korean Art
Germany	Karlsruhe ZKM Media Artist Exhibition and Training Program

Source: Go Joohyun(2022: 58).

Tab. 5: Collaboration with major European cultural and artistic support organizations

Year	Collaboration with	Description
2016–2017	UK (British Arts Council)	21 Korea-UK collaboration projects
2017–2018	Germany (German Cultural Center)	Heidelberg Festival Korea Week ('18 April)
2018–2019	Denmark (Art Council)	Promotion of "Korea-Denmark Mutual Culture Year"

Source: Go Joohyun(2022: 58).

4. Prospects and suggestions for cultural exchange between Korea and the EU

The First International Cultural Exchange Promotion Plan (2018–2022) was revised and reported by the Ministry of Culture, Sports and Tourism in 2020. It laid out three major policy goals: Strategic Systematic International Cultural Exchange, Response to New Standards for International Cultural Exchange and Creating an International Cultural Exchange Ecosystem.

Above all, with the spread of COVID-19, cultural exchanges using new technologies in the era of the fourth industrial revolution are gradually increasing. It leads new trends in the cultural field through experimental international co-production in the cultural and artistic contents field. In particular, it was escaped from cultural exchanges centered on one-off events, along with the need for a different approach based on the acceptance of Korean culture by region and country, current status of exchanges, and interest. The need to establish strategies for international cultural exchanges as a whole and to systematize the implementation of the project was also emphasized.

As part of this, a basic survey was conducted to establish an international cultural exchange strategy for each region from December 2020 to April 2021.

Tab. 6: Examples of strategies for promoting international cultural exchanges (2020.12 ~ 2021.04)

	Key partner countries	Other partner countries
High levels of understanding for Korean Culture	•Introducing and supporting "Korean Season" •Expansion of international co-production support	•Outstanding cultural program exchange project •Support for activities of local governments and private organizations
Low levels of understanding for Korean Culture	Non-face-to-face exchange using online platforms •Expanding human exchanges in the cultural field	•Supporting the promotion of exchanges between private organizations

Source: Ministry Culture, Sports and Tourism 2020: 20.

As shown in the table below, they set different strategies for cultural exchanges in different regions depending on the level of awareness of Korean culture and whether it is a key partner country.

In particular, Europe needs to expand support for international co-production as Korea's key partner. In fact, since the adoption of the Cultural Cooperation Protocol in 2011, the current status of co-production until 2020 increased compared to 2013. Nevertheless, as we saw earlier, some limiting factors were found in co-production of films.

First of all, movies that met the requirements for co-production in Korea and in Europe did not actually get opportunities for co-production. Above all, from 2009 to 2020, a total of 46 co-production films were supported by the Film Support Committee with Europe, but only 17 films were actually made. This is due to many causes, including non-payment of investment at the final film production stage.

In that regard, I would like to make the following suggestions. First, we need to provide clear information about the opportunity factors for Korea and Europe. In particular, co-production support with Europe shows a high proportion of low-budget art films and independent films. Therefore, it is necessary to strengthen internationalization for films in this field. In fact, the interview materials provided by the Film Council showed the following. Most Korean directors who participate in co-production with Europe had academic or production experience in Europe in the past. Either that or they often continued to have relationships with European film industry staff through participating in European film festivals. The fact that many co-production stage takes place through such a private network confirms that it is difficult to get a chance to connect with Europe, especially with a small budget. Therefore, it is necessary to relax and implement the regulations for co-production support so that low-budget, high-quality Korean films can get more co-production opportunities with Europe. We also need to come up with legislative improvements on co-production. To this end, Korean film recognition standards should be eased. Then, European film officials can recognize and pursue collaboration with Korea as a bridgehead for entering the Asian market. In addition, we should work with European film festivals and markets to expand promotional opportunities for our works so that co-produced films can receive stable investment.

Lastly, there should be improvements based on two structural factors. First of all, due to the recent growth of the Chinese film market, Western-centered global film industry sees an opportunity to enter Asia. In addition, another turning point has come in the global film industry with the rise of service platforms such as Netflix, Hulu, and Amazon Studios. In this environment, Korean film officials have formed a close partnership with China over the past few years. In that process, Korea's digital film production and distribution technology played an integral role. Therefore, this could be considered as an opportunity for European producers who want to cooperate with Korea.

In other words, co-production with Korea, which leads Asian co-production, should be seen as an opportunity. To achieve that goal, a cooperative co-production system between pan-Asian countries should be established. Only then can European countries that have signed a co-production agreement with South Korea recognize it as an opportunity to participate in the entire Asian market.

Furthermore, we also need governance-level improvements on co-production systems. There is a limit to the government's ability to come up with measures to expand exchanges in the cultural sector. Therefore, it is necessary to establish a consultation platform that allows officials from the public, private and related organizations to freely exchange opinions.

This way, by expanding the scale of film co-production between Korea and Europe, we will be able to increase mutual cultural understanding and contribute to revitalizing economic exchanges between the regions.

References

Cull, Nicholas J. (2008): Public diplomacy: Taxonomies and histories. Vol. 616, Issue 1.

Feigenbaum, Harvey B. (2001): Globalization and cultural diplomacy. Art, Culture & the National Agenda Issue Paper. Center for Arts and Culture.

Go Joohyun. (2022): "Korea-EU Intellectual and Cultural Exchange" in The Routledge Handbook of Europe-Korea Relations edited by Nicola Casarini et al. (Forthcoming).

Han Sun-Hee et al. (2019): A Study on the Status and Policy of Internationalization of Korean Film Production. Korean Film Council International Film Co-production, Korean Film Council.

Jeong Jung-Sook (2012): Measures for promoting international cultural exchanges. Korea Culture and Tourism Institute.

Khademi, Mona (1999): The Importance of International Cultural Exchanges: Some Normative Considerations, The Journal of Arts Management, Law, and Society, Vol. 29, No. 1.

Kim Hye-In (2015): A Study on the mid to long-term planning international cultural exchange policy. Korea Culture and Tourism Institute.

Marie Le Sourd, et al. (2013): EU-South Korea: Current Trends of Cultural Exchange and Future Perspectives. EENC Report.

Ministry Culture, Sports and Tourism (2017): A Basic Study on the Development of International Cultural Exchange Indicators.

Ministry Culture, Sports and Tourism (2020): Revised edition of the 1st Comprehensive Plan for the Promotion of International Cultural Exchange (2018–2022).

Mulcahy, Kevin V. (1982): Ideology and public culture. The Journal of Aesthetic Education. Vol. 16, No. 2.

Nye, Joseph S. (2008): Public diplomacy and soft power. The ANNALS of the American Academy of Political and Social Science. Vol. 616, Issue 1.

Alexander Heß and Christoph M. Hindermann

Trade effects on happiness in Asia

1. Introduction

The Belt and Road Initiative (BRI) – a gigantic endeavor – that has first been publicly announced by Xi Jinping on the 7th of September 2013 at Kazakhstan's Nazarbayev University under the title "Promote People-to-People Friendship and Create a Better Future" but has been worked on already quite some time before. For instance, the railway from China to Germany has already been operating since the 31st of August 2012.

Since its launch, the Belt and Road Initiative (BRI) project has already led to a significant increase in cross-border trade volumes across participating countries in Asia. For example, in a study from Yu et al. (2020) found according to their index that bilateral trade "[b]etween China and the Belt-Road countries has grown approximately 8 % faster than has that with the non-Belt-Road countries" (page 1). Thus, the initiative has been affecting trade – a trend that is only expected to intensify in the coming years and decades. According to Zhai (2018, p. 85) by 2030 global trade is to "[b]e boosted by the BRI, with an expansion of 5.6 % in 2030 in comparison" to a scenario without BRI investments. His (2018, p. 85) findings further suggest that the initiative likely leads to welfare gains for BRI countries that account for an annual raise of GDP by 2.9 %.

Most studies about trade focused largely on the monetary effects. Similarly, discussions and forecasts about country-specific potential outcomes of the participation and engagement in the BRI project have also mostly focused on them. Accessing research from the field of positive psychology or economics of happiness makes it possible to look into effects that go beyond these monetary ones. This study investigates the impact of trade on the subjective well-being (SWB) of citizens living in Asian countries. Thereby it aims to assess potential non-monetary effects of the BRI project that go beyond classical macro-economic outcomes. As such, it holds the fundamental premise that a good performance on these indicators is not the end goal, but merely ways and means to promote people's well-being and happiness.

In the second section of this paper, we introduce basic concepts, dimensions and measurement methods of SWB, discuss theoretical considerations on the relationship between trade and SWB, review the empirical findings on this nexus, and formulate our main hypothesis. Section three discloses in detail the data and method specifications we used for our analysis. In section four we present our results that we then discuss in section five. At the end, in section six, we make some concluding remarks and briefly give some avenues for further research.

2. Theoretical foundations

2.1. Research on subjective well-being

Research on subjective well-being (SWB) has gained massive interest amongst scholars from various scientific disciplines and publications on that subject matter have skyrocketed over the last decades. According to Diener et al. (2018a), SWB is defined as a "[g]eneral term referring to the various types of subjective evaluations of one's life, including both cognitive evaluations and affective feelings" (p. 3). Nowadays, SWB tends to be divided into three subdimensions: 1) cognitive or evaluative well-being, 2) experienced well-being, and 3) eudaemonic well-being (Stone & Mackie, 2013). Although these dimensions are intertwined and tend to correlate with each other, they still tap into different domains of psychological functioning (Fredrickson et al., 2013; Stone & Mackie, 2013). Together they form the SWB continuum.

Various measuring methods exist that aim to capture these SWB dimensions, such as large national surveys featuring different scales, informant reports, big data analyses, neuroimaging as well as experienced sampling, day reconstruction, cognitive organization, and reaction time methods (Diener et al., 2018a; Frey, 2018; Scollon, 2018). Out of these, the large-scale survey method is to date the most established method that provides one with sufficient high-quality data appropriate for both, cross-sectional and time series analysis. It is thus the most commonly practiced way to measure SWB. The scales and questions featured differ slightly from survey to survey, but they usually include both, global assessments and domain-specific SWB questions (Heß, 2020).

Despite its establishment, the survey method does not come without any doubts. Over the years a couple of issues and concerns have been raised regarding its validity and reliability. Among them, some issues refer to the context, specifically the questions' order and wording (Deaton & Stone, 2016; Diener et al., 2018a). Others address circumstances, such as the weather prevailing on the date of the interview (Schwarz & Clore, 1983). However, several studies suggest the effects are rather small (Diener et al. (2018b) reviews a couple of those) and despite these and other issues, these self-reported measures of SWB are generally considered reliable and valid. In this regard, reliability is usually assessed in terms of stability via a test-retest procedure. In a meta-analysis Schimmack and

Oishi (2005) find self-reported measures of life satisfaction to be fairly stable. Multiple studies address the validity of self-reported SWB in various ways. For instance, Seder and Oishi (2012) find them to correlate with behavioral characteristics, such as smiling and laughing, and similarly, Schneider and Schimmack (2009) find them to correlate with well-being ratings as captured through informant reports – assessments produced by individuals in the participants' inner social circle. Other studies address further biases and problems that might occur during the participants' reporting, such as social desirability bias (Veenhoven, 1996) and linguistic or semantic issues (Inglehart, 1990; Veenhoven, 1996), and find no evidence for their existence. In sum, a large proportion of the SWB research is dedicated to the quality of its measures so that one can apply them confidently.

2.2. Trade and subjective well-being

Effects of trade or more precisely of international trade have quite extensively been studied in theory and empirics. One of the focal points of research is related to its interplay with economic growth (Singh, 2010; Zestos & Tao, 2002). Economic growth in terms of GDP per capita is often viewed as an indicator for the objective well-being dimension. As mentioned in the introduction, this paper assesses the effects of international trade that go beyond this materialistic sphere of well-being (Spruk & Kešeljević, 2016) by focusing on the subjective evaluations of one's life. Since these non-monetary effects may occur through various pathways, we ask whether trade directly affects SWB by an increase of freedom as the freedom of choice theory would suggest. Veenhoven (2000) defines freedom in broad terms "[a]s the possibility to choose" (p. 3). Since scholars have grappled with the conceptualization of freedom for decades and even centuries, we will not comment on whether or not Veenhoven's definition is exhaustive. The least one can say is that his broad definition does not exclude the two basic types of negative and positive freedom. In any way, Veenhoven goes on to explain that the possibility to choose requires two things: the opportunity and the capability to choose. The former refers to the environment and involves that a) there actually is something to choose from and b) that the choice is unrestricted by others. The latter means that the individual is a) internally aware of the options to choose from and b) brave enough to make a choice (Veenhoven, 2000).

This theory is often called "freedom of choice theory" which involves a specific set of alternatives an individual can choose from Verme (2009). The larger the set, the more the freedom of choice, and the smaller the set, the less freedom of choice. Thus, an increase in international trade should translate to a larger set of products and services to choose from.

In theory, the utility or satisfaction that one draws from a particular set of alternatives to choose from may vary across individuals. Verme (2009) discusses four potential perspectives that an individual may have on such an opportunity set:

1. The number of available choices is irrelevant as long as the alternative that provides one with the most satisfaction is included.
2. A larger number of choices is always better for anyone and the degree of satisfaction should be equal for everyone.
3. The degree of satisfaction that one draws from a larger number of choices might differ but is always positive.
4. The amount of satisfaction that one draws from a larger number of choices can be both, negative or positive.

We test the hypothesis that an increase in international trade and the associated increase in freedom of choice should eventually lead to an increase in SWB in terms of life satisfaction.

However, there exist a couple of theories that contradict our hypothesis. For instance, comparison theory suggests that individuals compare their lives to the standard. Consequently, a general increase of freedom of choice should leave SWB levels about the same since the standard should increase accordingly (Veenhoven & Ehrhardt, 1995). Moreover, adaptation theory combined with set-point theory suggests that given a change in living conditions or the occurrence of a bad or good event, an individual's SWB will fluctuate only temporarily before adapting to these changes and returning to an innate set-point. Hence SWB would not permanently change if freedom of choice increases (Lucas, 2007).

Initial findings regarding our nexus are not as clear-cut as one might have expected. Bjørnskov et al. (2008) find that market openness, measured by the sum of imports and exports over GDP, is slightly positively correlated with SWB in terms of self-reported life satisfaction. On the other hand, using a disaggregated approach, Di Tella and MacCulloch (2008) found that market openness in terms of trade is negatively correlated with self-reported life satisfaction and "happiness." They speculate that this effect may be due to concerns about potential risks of being exposed to external market forces that could make the domestic labor market more vulnerable. Dluhosch and Horgos (2013) find somewhat more nuanced results, as they test for both trade volume and trade freedom. In a cross-sectional setting, they examined 32 countries included in the fourth wave of the World Value Survey (WVS). They found that trade volume in low-income countries was slightly negatively correlated with self-reported "happiness" as measured on a 4-point scale. High-income countries showed no significant correlations in terms of trade volume. Trade freedom, on the other hand, was positively correlated with "happiness" in both low- and high-income countries, although the positive effect of trade freedom was significant only for low-income countries. However, the scale may be considered a bit insensitive since it only provides four response options. A too narrow scale "can cause meaningful variations in scores to be lost" (OECD, 2013, p. 77). In addition, the "happiness" item is believed to ask for a rather affective response than a reflective one (Pacek & Radcliff, 2008). In this study, we use the life satisfaction item in the WVS, which a) has a 10-point response scale and b) asks about the evaluative well-being dimension. Similar to Dluhosch and Horgos (2013), we use both indicators of trade (trade volume and trade freedom) to investigate their effect on life satisfaction. In contrast to them, we apply a panel setting instead of a cross-sectional one and focus on Asian countries.

3. Method

This section serves the purpose of empirically investigating trade effects on SWB (as measured in terms of life satisfaction) in Asia and is thus structured in the following fashion. First, we will present our data sources for the dependent variable as well as for both the independent variables and all three control variables. We then present the model specification, outline the procedure we went through to perform a time series analysis on the data, and discuss limitations and hurdles which we faced.

3.1. Sample and data

Dependent variable: Life satisfaction as a proxy of SWB

As a proxy for SWB, we use data on life satisfaction from the WVS. First conducted in 1981, the WVS is an international research project structured in seven waves (W1: 1981–1984, W2: 1990–1994, W3: 1995–1998, W4: 1999–2004, W5: 2005–2009, W6: 2010–2014, W7: 2017–2020; Inglehart et al., 2020). We utilize data on the latest six of them since in the first wave no Asian countries are featured. In the WVS, global life satisfaction is assessed on a 10-point scale through the following question: "All in all, how satisfied are you with your life as a whole nowadays? Using this card, where 1 means you are "completely dissatisfied" and

10 means you are "completely satisfied," where would you rank your satisfaction with your life as a whole?" (WVS-7 Official Questionnaire, 2017). It is applied in the identical format throughout each wave. The number of Asian countries featured in each wave ranges from 6 (second wave) to 22 (sixth wave).[1] Each wave covers different countries in different years.

Independent variables

a) Variables of Interest: Trade Volume and Trade Freedom

To determine whether and to what extent international trade affects subjective well-being in Asian countries, we use two explanatory variables: trade volume and trade freedom. As for the former, we access data on international trade flows (exports + imports) as a percentage of GDP provided by the World Bank, and for the latter, we draw on data from the Economic Freedom of the World Index (EFW) of the Fraser Institute. The EFW consists of five areas: size of government, legal system and property rights, sound money, freedom to trade internationally, and regulation. There, freedom to trade internationally or in short trade freedom is assessed in four categories, which are a) tariffs, b) regulatory trade barriers, c) black-market exchange rates, and d) controls of the movement of capital and people (Gwartney et al., 2020).

b) Control Variables: GDP per Capita, Unemployment Rate, HDI

We use three control variables that are found to impact life satisfaction. The first two are GDP per capita and the unemployment rate, all provided by the World Bank (2021a, b). The third variable, the Human Development Index (HDI; UNDP, 2020) serves as a substitute for GDP since both are considered as measures of wealth (Costanza et al., 2009). The HDI is composed of three main components: 1) standard of living in terms of gross national income per capita, 2) education in terms of expected and mean years of schooling, and 3) health in terms of life expectancy at birth.

1 The following 22 countries are covered in the sixth wave of the WVS: Armenia, Azerbaijan, China, Georgia, Hong Kong, India, Japan, Jordan, Kazakhstan, Kuwait, Kyrgyzstan, Lebanon, Malaysia, Pakistan, Philippines, Qatar, Russia, Singapore, South Korea, Thailand, Turkey, and Yemen (Inglehart et al., 2018).

3.2. Procedure and model specification

Since the aim is to conduct a country-level analysis and the WVS only provides data on individual's life satisfaction, we first calculated the mean life satisfaction of all respondents of a country for each country per wave. Although the WVS provides data on life satisfaction throughout all seven waves, we are restricted to use only the last six since only these cover Asian countries. Additionally, the number of Asian countries covered in each wave differs which is why we have to deal with an unbalanced panel consisting of 20 countries for two to six points in time making up a total of 73 (74) observations. Since each wave covers different countries in different years, we treat the data in our analysis in such a way that each WVS wave represents a uniform point in time.

Regarding the control variables, we collect the data corresponding to the year of the interview. If that is not possible due to missing data, we select either the values of the nearest year or the mean value accordingly. We apply this procedure to all our independent variables. In case we find no adequate data, we drop the observation (see Appendix for more details).

To extract the statistical effect of our variables of interest (trade volume and trade freedom), we apply a fixed-effects panel model (within estimator) since the Hausman Test suggests the application of a fixed-effects panel model ($\chi^2 = 7.38$, $p = .02$).

$$LS_{it} - \overline{LS}_i = \left(T_{it} - \bar{T}_i\right)\beta_1 + \left(W_{it} - \bar{W}_i\right)\beta_2 + \left(U_{it} - \bar{U}_i\right)\beta_3 + \int_{it}$$

with "LS" denoting life satisfaction and thus representing the SWB dimension of evaluative WB. The independent variables to our main interest (trade volume and trade freedom) are represented by "T". Depending on the specification we add the discussed control variables to the model: "W" (for wealth) denoting GDP per capita or the Human Development Index, and "U" denoting the unemployment rate. The subscript "t" denotes a particular WVS wave.

4. Results

Tab. 1 shows the results of our initial correlational analysis, where we simply correlate each of our independent variables with life satisfaction.

As can be seen, the interpretation of these results is difficult since, except for the unemployment rate, the variables do not show a consistent pattern. In addition, most correlations are insignificant. However, this may be a consequence of

Tab. 1: Bivariate Correlations with Life Satisfaction

Dependent Variable: Life Satisfaction	*Wave of WVS*					
	2	**3**	**4**	**5**	**6**	**7**
Trade Freedom	–.67	–.21	.62	–.11	–.25	.08
Trade (in % of GDP) (log)	–.31	–.26	**.52***	.10	.02	–.07
GDP per capita (log)	–.50	–.02	.48	.15	.30	**–.51****
HDI	–.48	–.38	**.59****	–.03	.10	–.31
Unemployment Rate	–.48	–.24	–.03	**–.48***	**–.82*****	**–45****
N	6	7	14	14	22	21

* $p < .10$ ** $p < .05$ *** $p < .01$ (two-tailed)

the small number of observations (N) since a larger N would translate to a larger test statistic (lower p-value). The results of our main analyses presented in Tab. 2 provide a clearer picture.

Each number in parentheses on the top row represents a specification of the model presented in Section 3.2 where we stepwise added explanatory and control variables. All significant values are highlighted in bold. We find no evidence that changes in trade volume or trade freedom significantly affect life satisfaction. We also find no evidence for a significant effect of our trade variables on life satisfaction when running the fixed-effects panel model without any control variables (not stated in the table). In all model specifications, we find both indicators of wealth GDP per capita and the HDI to be positively correlated with life satisfaction. In at least two model specifications the unemployment rate is significantly negatively correlated with life satisfaction in Asia. The coefficient of determination (R^2) illustrates that only 15–19 % of the variation of our dependent variable can be explained by our independent variables.

Tab. 2: Panel Analyses

Dependent Variable: Life Satisfaction	(1)		(2)		(3)		(4)		(5)		(6)	
	Coef.	**t-value**	**Coef.**	**t-value**	**Coef.**	**t-value**	**Coef.**	**t-value**	**Coef.**	**t-value**	**Coef.**	**t-value**
+ GDP per capita (log)	**1.21*****	**2.78**	**1.61*****	**3.03**	**1.35*****	**2.70**						
+ HDI							**3.33*****	**2.72**	**3.80*****	**2.69**	**4.18*****	**2.77**
+ Unemployment Rate	**−0.05***	**−1.75**	**−0.06***	**−1.87**	−0.05	−1.58	−0.05	−1.48	−0.05	−1.47	−0.04	−1.16
+ Trade Freedom			−0.14	−1.26					−0.08	−0.77		
+ Trade (in % of GDP) (log)					−0.44	−0.58					−0.79	−0.96
N	74		73		74		74		73		74	
R^2	0.15		0.19		0.16		0.15		0.16		0.16	

* $p < .10$ ** $p < .05$ *** $p < .01$ (two-tailed)
Unbalanced Panel n = 20, T = 2–6, N = 73 (74)

5. Discussion

In this study trade in terms of volume and freedom was found to have no significant direct effect on SWB in terms of life satisfaction in Asia. However, it does not mean that such an effect does not exist since our study faces several limitations. First, one issue is the limited availability of life satisfaction data. The WVS covers only a small number of Asian countries, especially in its first five waves. To add to this, each wave not only covers a different number but also a partly different set of countries which further distorts our analysis. Second, we only assess country means of life satisfaction which do not reflect possible variations within specific subgroups of a country's population. Further studies shall supplement our investigation by applying an individual or multi-level analysis. Third, life satisfaction might have risen but that increase might have lasted only for a short amount of time. As mentioned in Section 2.2. adaptation theory in combination with set-point theory suggests that individuals adapt rather quickly to changes in living conditions and SWB levels only oscillate around an innate set point before they eventually return back to it. Fourth, the contrary is also possible. Trade could have a long-term effect on SWB, but this effect could occur with a time delay, as these non-monetary effects take a while before they reach the general population. Fifth, an increase in international trade may not necessarily translate to an increase of the opportunity set since it may not have affected the variety of goods and services. Further research should not only consider trade volumes but also the variety of goods and services traded.

Apart from trade, we find that wealth as captured by GDP per capita or the HDI is positively, and the unemployment rate is negatively correlated with life satisfaction. It is thus imaginable that international trade affects SWB indirectly. Singh (2010) reviews studies that find that "[m]acroeconomic evidence provides dominant support for the positive and significant effects of trade on output and growth" (p. 1554).

Our findings slightly deviate from the ones of Dluhosch and Horgos' study from 2013 (see Tab. 3 for a comparison of the results). In contrast to us, they applied an ordered probit model to analyze the happiness data at the individual level. As mentioned in Section 2.2., similar to us they found an insignificant negative correlation of trade volume and SWB as captured by the "happiness" item. However, splitting up the sample, they found a significant negative correlation between trade volume and "happiness" for low-income economies. Trade freedom, on the other hand, was positively correlated with individual "happiness" on the whole sample. Splitting up the sample, while the effect was similar for low-income economies, such an effect was not found for high-income

Tab. 3: Results in Comparison

	Dluhosch & Horgos (2013)			Our study
	Whole sample	**Low-income economies**	**High-income economies**	
GDP per capita	+++	+++	0	+++
Unemployment Rate	---	0	-	-
Trade Freedom	++	+	0	0
Trade (in % of GDP)	0	---	0	0

+++ (++/+) positively correlated with happiness (or SWB); $p < .01$ ($p < .05$/$p < .10$)
--- (--/-) negatively correlated with happiness (or SWB); ($p < .05$/$p < .10$)
0 no significant correlation with happiness (or SWB)

economies. Likewise, GDP proved to be strongly positively correlated to "happiness" but after the split, this effect only remained for low-income economies. The unemployment rate turned out to be strongly negatively correlated to "happiness" but after the split, this effect only remained for high-income economies.

6. Conclusion

The Chinese endeavor to revive the spirit of the ancient Silk Road and create the largest trade route(s) the world has yet to see is met with mixed feelings and sometimes with hostility by the global audience. The differing views do not just stem from advocates and opponents of globalization per se, but rather from anyone that questions the underlying intentions of this endeavor's instigators as well as anyone concerned about the participating countries to become dependent on the benevolence of the Chinese government. In this study, we analyzed whether changes in trade volume and trade freedom are correlated with SWB in Asia. Since the different projects within the BRI can still be considered to be in their early stages these effects are expected to grow even larger in the future.

Future research should consider the following aspects. First, it may prove beneficial to conduct a similar analysis splitting trade volumes into imports and exports, or disaggregate trade volumes even further into different commodity groups. Second, one could supplement our analyses with an individual or multilevel approach to study trade effect on SWB of specific subgroups of the population. Third, running the analyses with SWB data from other large-scale surveys, such as the Gallup World Poll would allow for a comparison of the results with those produced by this study using WVS data. Fourth, the use of SWB measures collected via a multi-method approach would be ideal to further increase validity and reliability, thereby improving the informative value of the results, which in turn inform more sound policy actions. Finally, one could further imagine that trade impacts on SWB vary depending on the SWB dimension that one is assessing. The analytical decomposition and distinction of these effects are crucial since the holders of political offices will in the course be enabled to form better and more fine-tuned policy measures that will benefit the citizens and societies in multiple ways.

References

Bjørnskov, C., Dreher, A., & Fischer, J. A. V. (2008): Cross-country Determinants of Life Satisfaction: Exploring Different Determinants Across Groups in Society. *Social Choice and Welfare*, *30*, 119–173.

Costanza, R., Hart, M., Posner, S. M., & Talberth, J. (2009): Beyond GDP: The Need for New Measures of Progress. *Pardee Paper No. 4*, Pardee Center for the Study of the Longer-Range Future.

Deaton, A., & Stone, A. A. (2016): Understanding Context Effects for a Measure of Life Evaluation: How Responses Matter. *Oxford Economic Papers*, *68*, 861–870.

Di Tella, R., & MacCulloch, R. J. (2008): Gross National Happiness as an Answer to the Easterlin Paradox? *Journal of Development Economics*, *86*, 22–42.

Diener, E., Lucas, R. E., & Oishi, S. (2018a): Advances and Open Questions in the Science of Subjective Well-Being. *Collabra: Psychology*, *4*, 1–49.

Diener, E., Oishi, S., & Tay, L. (2018b): Advances in Subjective Well-being Research. *Nature Human Behaviour*, *2*, 253–260.

Dluhosch, B., & Horgos, D. (2013): Trading Up the Happiness Ladder. *Social Indicators Research*, *113*, 973–990.

Fredrickson, B. L., Grewer, K. M., Coffey, K. A., Algoe, S. B., Firestine, A. M., Arevalo, J. M. G., Ma, J., & Cole, S. W. (2013): A Functional Genomic Perspective on Human Well-Being. *Proceedings of the National Academy of Sciences of the United States of America*, *110*, 13684–13689.

Frey, B. S. (2018): *Economics of Happiness*. Cham: Springer.

Gwartney, J., Lawson, R., Hall, J., & Murphy, R. (2020): Economic Freedom of the World: 2020 Annual Report. Fraser Institute.

Heß, Alexander (2020): Happiness and the Welfare State in Times of Globalization: A Review of Empirical Findings, *Ordnungspolitische Diskurse*, No. 2020–3, OrdnungsPolitisches Portal (OPO).

Inglehart, R. (1990): *Culture Shift in Advanced Industrial Society*. Princeton: Princeton University Press.

Inglehart, R., Haerpfer, C., Moreno, A., Welzel, C., Kizilova, K., Diez-Medrano, J., Lagos, M., Norris, P., Ponarin, E., & Puranen, B., et al. (2018): *World Values Survey: Round Six – Country Pooled Datafile*. JD Systems Institute & WVSA Secretariat.

Inglehart, R., Haerpfer, C., Moreno, A., Welzel, C., Kizilova, K., Diez-Medrano J., Lagos, M., Norris, P., Ponarin, E., & Puranen, B., et al. (2020): *World Values Survey: All Rounds – Country-Pooled Datafile*. JD Systems Institute & WVSA Secretariat.

Lucas, R. E. (2007): Adaptation and the Set-Point Model of Subjective Well-Being: Does Happiness Change After Major Life Events? *Current Directions in Psychological Science*, *16*, 75–79.

OECD (2013): *OECD Guidelines on Measuring Subjective Well-being*. Paris: OECD Publishing.

Pacek, A. C., & Radcliff, B. (2008): Welfare Policy and Subjective Well-Being Across Nations: An Individual-Level Assessment. *Social Indicators Research*, *89*, 179–191.

Schimmack, U., & Oishi, S. (2005): The Influence of Chronically and Temporarily Accessible Information on Life Satisfaction Judgments. *Journal of Personality and Social Psychology*, *89*, 395–406.

Schneider, L., & Schimmack, U. (2009): Self-Informant Agreement in Well-Being Ratings: A Meta-Analysis. *Social Indicators Research*, *94*, 363–376.

Schwarz, N., & Clore, G. L. (1983): Mood, Misattribution, and Judgments of Well-Being: Informative and directive functions of affective states. *Journal of Personality and Social Psychology*, *45*, 513–523.

Scollon, C. N. (2018): Non-Traditional Measures of Subjective Well-Being and their Validity: A Review. In *Handbook of Well-Being*, edited by Diener, E., Oishi, L., & Tay, L. 69–79. Salt Lake City: DEF Publishers.

Seder, J. P., & Oishi, S. (2012): Intensity of Smiling in Facebook Photos Predicts Future Life Satisfaction. *Social Psychological and Personality Science*, *3*, 407–413.

Singh, T. (2010): Does International Trade Cause Economic Growth? A Survey. *The World Economy*, *33*, 1517–1564.

Spruk, R., & Kešeljević, A. (2016): Institutional Origins of Subjective Well-Being: Estimating the Effects of Economic Freedom on National Happiness. *Journal of Happiness Studies*, *17*, 659–712.

Stone, A. A., & Mackie, C. (2013): Subjective Well-Being: Measuring Happiness, Suffering, and Other Dimensions of Experience. National Research Council, Washington: The National Academies Press.

UNDP (2020): Human Development Report 2020. The Next Frontier: Human Development and the Anthropocene. http://hdr.undp.org/en/content/human-development-report-2020

Veenhoven, R. (1996): Developments in Satisfaction-Research. *Social Indicators Research*, *37*, 1–46.

Veenhoven, R. (2000): Freedom and happiness: A Comparative Study in Forty-Four Nations in the Early 1990s. In *Culture and Subjective Well-Being*, edited by Diener, E., & Suh, E.M., 257–288. Cambridge: MIT Press.

Veenhoven, R., & Ehrhardt, J. (1995): The Cross-National Pattern of Happiness: Test of Predictions Implied in Three Theories of Happiness. *Social Indicators Research*, *34*, 33–68.

Verme, P. (2009): Happiness, Freedom and Control. *Journal of Economic Behavior and Organization*, *71*, 146–161.

World Bank (2021a): GDP (Constant 2010 US$). https://data.worldbank.org/indicator/NY.GDP.MKTP.KD

World Bank (2021b): Unemployment, Total (% of Total Labor Force). https://data.worldbank. org/indicator/SL.UEM.TOTL.ZS

World Values Surveys (2017): WVS-7 Official Questionnaire. https://www.worldvaluessurvey.org/WVSDocumentationWV7.jsp

Yu, C., Zhang, R., An, L., & Yu, Z. (2020): Has China's Belt and Road Initiative Intensified Bilateral Trade Links between China and the Involved Countries? *Sustainability*, *12*, 6747.

Zestos, G., & Tao, X. (2002): Trade and GDP Growth: Causal Relations in the United States and Canada. *Southern Economic Journal*, *68*, 859–874.

Zhai, F. (2018): China's Belt and Road Initiative: A Preliminary Quantitative Assessment. *Journal of Asian Economics*, *55*, 84–92.

List of authors

Joachim Ahrens is Professor for International Economics at PFH Göttingen, Germany. Email: ahrens@pfh.de

Anastasia Barannikova, Ph.D., is researcher at the Center for Maritime Transport and Spatial Logististics at the ADM Nevelskoy Maritime State University, Vladivostok, Russia. E-mail: Electronicccm@yandex.ru

Joohyun Go is research professor at the Institute of East and West Studies at the Yonsei University, Seoul, South Korea. Email: joohyun.go@yonsei.ac.kr

Alexander Heß is Ph.D. student at the University of Erfurt and a lecturer at the University of Applied Sciences in Zwickau, Germany. E-Mail: alexander.hess@uni-erfurt.de

Christoph M. Hindermann, Ph.D., is working as a trainer for finance, controlling and statistics in Germany. E-Mail: hindermann@gmx.de

Duyeon Kim, Ph.D., is an Adjunct Senior Fellow with the Indo-Pacific Security Program at the Center for a New American Security (CNAS), Washington D.C., USA. Email: dkim@cnas.org

Artyom Lukin is associate professor at the Oriental Institute, School of Regional and International Studies, at the Far Eastern Federal University, in Vladivostok, Russia. Email: artlukin@mail.ru

Tereza Novotna, Ph.D., is researcher at the Department of Political and Social Sciences of the Freie Universität Berlin (Otto Suhr Institute of Political Science/Center for European Integration), Germany. Email: tereza.novotna@fu-berlin.de.

Jagannath P. Panda, Ph.D., is researcher at the Manohar Parrikar Institute for Defence Studies and Analyses, New Delhi, India. Email: jppjagannath@gmail.com

Werner Pascha is Professor Emeritus of East Asian Economic Studies/Japan and Korea at the Institute of East Asian Studies (IN-EAST) of the University of Duisburg-Essen in Germany. Email: werner.pascha@uni-due.de

Hans-Ulrich Seidt (Dr. Dr. h.c. mult.) is president of the German-Korean Innovation Center (InDeKo), Germany. He served from 2009 to 2012 as German ambassador to the Republic of Korea. Email: Seidt.Berlin@t-online.de

Bernhard Seliger is representative of the Hanns Seidel Foundation in Seoul, South Korea. Email: seliger@hss.de

Ralph M. Wrobel is professor of economics, especially economic policy, and coordinating member of the East Asia Centre at the University of Applied Sciences Zwickau, Germany. Email: ralph.wrobel@fh-zwickau.de

Emerging Markets Studies

Edited by Joachim Ahrens, Alexander Ebner, Herman W. Hoen, Bernhard Seliger and Ralph Michael Wrobel

The Peter Lang series *Emerging Markets Studies* includes works which address opportunities, problems, and challenges of socio-economic development and reform in so-called emerging markets. These comprise middle-income developing and transition economies which are relevant for the world economy due to a large market potential, a favorable or improving investment climate, or due to the availability of important natural resources. Emerging markets have realized or show the potential to generate sustained socio-economic development and growth processes over time.

The volumes in this series seek to address three key questions: What are the determinants of successful socio-economic development, What are appropriate reform strategies to overcome impediments to catching-up processes, and How do politico-institutional factors affect the performance of an emerging economy?

The scope of the series is comparative, institutionalist, and international. The overall focus of all titles is to enhance the understanding of socio-economic catching-up processes and their institutional foundations from a political-economy perspective. Due to the complexity of development processes and policy reform, various methodological tools and academic approaches may prove to be appropriate. Hence the series includes contributions from various disciplines such as economics, political science, or sociology.

Vol. 1 Dominik F. Schlossstein: Institutional Change in Upstream Innovation Governance. The Case of Korea. 2010.

Vol. 2 Manuel Stark: The Emergence of Developmental States from a New Institutionalist Perspective. A Comparative Analysis of East Asia and Central Asia. 2012.

Vol. 3 Bernhard Seliger: The Shrimp that Became a Tiger. Transformation Theory and Korea's Rise After the Asian Crisis. 2013.

Vol. 4 Dirk Johann: The Reconfiguration of a Latecomer Innovation System. Governing Pharmaceutical Biotechnology Innovation in South Korea. 2013.

Vol. 5 Roman Vakulchuk: Kazakhstan's Emerging Economy. Between State and Market. 2014.

Vol. 6 Joachim Ahrens / Herman W. Hoen (eds.): Economic Development in Central Asia. Institutional Underpinnings of Factor Markets. 2014.

Vol. 7 Axel Wölk: A Taxonomy of State Capitalism and the Developmental Phases of Russia, Kazakhstan, Singapore and South Korea. An institutional comparative Analysis. 2021.

Vol. 8 Tamar Jugheli: The Institutions of State Business Relations. The Case of Food and Agriculture Sector of Georgia. 2021.

Vol. 9 Bernhard Seliger / Ralph M. Wrobel (eds.): Korea, the Iron Silk Road and the Belt and Road Initiative. Soft Power and Hard Power Approaches. 2022.

www.peterlang.com

www.ingramcontent.com/pod-product-compliance
Ingram Content Group UK Ltd.
Pitfield, Milton Keynes, MK11 3LW, UK
UKHW021832100926
8556IPUK00004B/291

9 783631 860663